Private Matters

Private Matters

IN DEFENSE OF THE PERSONAL LIFE

Janna Malamud Smith

Addison-Wesley Publishing Company, Inc.
Reading, Massachusetts   Menlo Park, California   New York
Don Mills, Ontario   Harlow, England   Amsterdam   Bonn
Sydney   Signapore   Tokyo   Madrid   San Juan
Paris   Seoul   Milan   Mexico City   Taipei

Library of Congress Cataloging-in-Publication Data

Smith, Janna Malamud.
   Private matters : in defense of the personal life / Janna Malamud
Smith.
     p. cm.
   Includes bibliographical references and index.
   ISBN 0-201-40973-9
   1. Privacy. I. Title.
BF637.P74S55 1997
155.9′2—dc21   96-38158
                                                 CIP

Jacket design by Leslie Goldman
Text design by Janis Owens Design
Set in 12-point Garamond by Carol Woolverton Studio

1 2 3 4 5 6 7 8 9-MA-0100999897
First printing, April 1997

For David

Contents

Acknowledgments

Many people encouraged me and helped me think through and write this book. Particularly, I wish to thank Miriam Altshuler, Lois Ames, David Britton, Elzbieta Ettinger, John Finneman and the American Press Institute, Fran Givelber, Leston Havens, Sue and Warren Hovland, Deborah Judd, Nan Lee, Ann Malamud, Nina Masters, Elizabeth Maguire, Nancy Miller, Jacqueline Olds, Tim Seldes, and Myron Sharaf.

Additionally, I'd like to thank my sons, Peter and Zachary. Also my family and friends who endured this escapade; my colleagues at the Cambridge Hospital; Sydney and Silke Moss at Le Pli; and the librarians at Widener Library, the Schlesinger Library, and the Harvard Law School Library.

Most of all, I thank Doris Kearns Goodwin and David Smith.

Private Matters

Prologue

I first began thinking about privacy when my father, the writer Bernard Malamud, died in 1986, and we were left to settle his literary estate. My mother sought opinions from me as she made her decisions. She had to decide whether to encourage or discourage people who wrote asking particular details of his life; whether to publish an unpublished manuscript or place it in an archive for scholars; whether to save all letters from his friends. Should she sell manuscripts or give them to the Library of Congress? Should any writings be sequestered until some time in the future or even be destroyed?

I found the questions vexing, partly because they were objectively difficult and partly, as I now look back upon it, because I was still actively grieving my father's death. I was not eager to have my private father—the one I knew and carried with me—tampered with by someone else's appraisal. In the aftermath of his death, as he made his way from real to remembered, I wanted him left alone. Not only did I feel myself vulnerable, but I felt he was.

My mother pondered what to do when a biographer called. I experienced the idea of someone writing his life as a loss, as having what seemed at once fragile and crucial to me, stolen and transformed. Furthermore, as I wrote in an article in *The New York*

Times Book Review,[1] I felt uneasy about the kind of biography any-one could receive in a publishing climate that often favored sensa-tional books. I did not want to hide my father; I just did not want yet to share him. The undertaker could have his body, but I wanted to ward off the biographer, at the wheel of a different hearse, de-manding either his soul or the details of my family life.

Many people agreed with the sentiments in the essay: the sympathy for writers and family members who had burned letters and papers, the reflexive protectiveness, the desire for privacy. Needless to say, I realized that I came down on one side of a com-plex truth. I believe it was the physicist Niels Bohr who said that the opposite of a small truth is a lie, while the opposite of a large truth is another large truth. At their best, biographies offer a rare opportunity to look closely at people's lives, to consider and hold complexity. They offer possibilities beyond those readily at hand, and ways of calibrating our own smaller abilities. I enjoy reading them, and as I said in the *Book Review* article, so did my father.

Though he won the National Book Award in 1958 for *The Magic Barrel*, Dad did not become widely known until his novel *The Fixer* (published in 1966) won both the National Book Award and the Pulitzer Prize. I remember a family debate that year about whether to allow *Look Magazine* to spend several days in our house photographing. Dad decided against it; he wanted to protect our privacy and the primacy of his writing over his life. At the same time, the idea that a magazine even wanted to visit was delicious to him—and surprising. His father was a poor immigrant grocer, his mother and brother both suffered from schizophrenia, and he had come a long way. He enjoyed the invitation even as he refused it.

My father sought privacy because without it he could not create fiction, and our family was organized to protect this need. We hesitated before we knocked on the door of his study; we tiptoed through the late afternoons, diving at phones to prevent a second ring, so he could nap and prepare for an evening of reading; we accepted that he distanced himself from his relatives and rarely spoke about his past. (His mother died long before I was born, his father soon afterward. Once as a child of five I briefly met his stepmother and brother, Eugene, in the Brooklyn grocery. The memory is faint, and probably remains because they let me pick the Popsicle of my choice out of the store's small freezer—a novel treat.) He guarded his past so that he could use it in his fiction without feeling exposed. Yet Dad's personal reserve and wish for privacy did not mean that he was isolative or unsociable. He enjoyed society as well as solitude, and friends often dropped by in the evening, or came to dinner.

The success that attracted magazine attention was exciting to me—and troubling. My father's achievements made me proud, but they also kept making him larger at a time when I needed him to stop growing, and possibly even to shrink a little. Throughout adolescence I wondered how I could come to terms with a parent who increasingly resembled an inflated creature from the Macy's parade. Furthermore, there was the problem of his fiction. I decided not to finish *The Fixer* after reading the part where Yakov Bok, seeing a woman's menstrual blood, flees a sexual encounter. Reading a parent's fiction is a strange experience. Not only does it sometimes offer you more than you want to know, but it can feel eerie, like a dream where familiar things get jumbled and strange.

My eventual solution to Dad's fame was to seek anonymity—what I did not then name as a kind of privacy. In college I studied American history and literature, but I put it aside. After trying different jobs, traveling, and marrying my husband (who among his many virtues possessed the last name of Smith), I went to graduate school in social work and spent the next fourteen years in a hous-

ing project clinic doing long-term psychotherapy with poor people
who lived in and around the project. The work was difficult, wonderful, and deeply formative. Learning psychotherapy in any context is a large and transforming enterprise. But learning it by
working with, and coming to love, people struggling with poverty
provided a second, different, education. Additionally, it allowed
me private space away from my father's accomplishment.

Psychotherapy is much concerned with privacy. You create a
confidential place and encourage open exchange. As therapist, you
attempt to use the resulting intimacy to help people resist feelings
and circumstances that crush them. You constantly rediscover that
all is not as it appears. Emotional truth is layered and paradoxical.
Even the wish for privacy turns out to include contradictory feelings: shame, inhibition, exhibitionism, self-protection, a search for
control, shyness, guilt, a longing for others to come find you. The
desired legacy of psychotherapeutic encounters is a person made
sturdier because he has used the privacy of the relationship to increase his tolerance for his own feelings. So, too, my respect for the
psychotherapeutic process anchors my understanding of the functions of privacy.

That our society is full of contradictory currents about privacy
pays tribute to the complexity of our own psyches. We cannot fully
appreciate the legal struggles over privacy or the battles about databanks or the dilemmas of sensational journalism until we understand the *personal* purposes privacy serves. *Private Matters* explores
cultural, psychological, sexual, historical, intellectual, and emotional dimensions of privacy and private life. The book investigates
aspects of privacy in an attempt to shed light upon what it is and
why it matters and how it protects important kinds of freedom.

Many contemporary books and news stories about privacy focus on diverse ways that it is being invaded. For example, in April 1996, two marines were court-martialed for refusing to give their blood to create a DNA databank. The Marine Corps had demanded a sample of each soldier's blood so that in the event of a war, bodies and body parts could be identified after battles. The soldiers who protested felt that their superiors had not adequately weighed the benefits of stockpiling DNA samples against the serious privacy violation it sanctioned.[2] The story ran in newspapers and on television for several days. Left unaddressed in the reporting was the underlying question of why we might want to shelter people from a lifetime of almost absolute identification. However helpful and at times humanitarian such a capability could be, in a world where people are regularly slaughtered by race, ethnicity, nationality, or religion, such information might not always be used benignly.

Ellen Alderman and Caroline Kennedy's book, *The Right to Privacy*, explores legal arguments about privacy and documents many contemporary privacy invasions: strip searches for traffic tickets, hidden cameras in hotel rooms, urine testing as a part of job applications, television cameramen filming in people's houses without their permission, and more. In this book I wish to describe the context of the privacy debate, to expand our understanding of the diverse ways that privacy is violated, and to point out the complex causes and effects of such invasions.

Much that is written about privacy is premised on the idea that privacy, once plentiful, is only now endangered. While privacy *is* endangered, it was hardly a staple in the past, when most people had little. In fact, even though computer databanks and surveillance cameras capture our attention, these technologies come out of social changes that *increased* people's capacity to construct more

7

private lives—lives that were often more separate, individually chosen, and unobserved than those lived in the past.

Historically speaking, much that we associate with privacy
appears to have emerged only during the past few centuries: the increased individual expectation of and wish for privacy, the possibility of a separate "private life," dwellings with more private space,
and the greater value placed upon personal experiences like intimacy, solitude, autonomy, and certain types of individual creativity. Privacy offers emotional and psychological opportunities that,
far from having been continually present and now endangered, are
in fact quite new, an exploration just beginning.

Consider this fictive episode: Darcy comes upon Elizabeth
alone in a room reading a letter. He expected her to be with other
people, and is startled by her solitude. This scene from *Pride and
Prejudice*, published in 1813, captures what was then an historically
recent and quite unusual phenomenon: a woman alone with a letter and her thoughts.[3] Picture Elizabeth, and you will see an essential tableau of privacy. For in a private space, with opportunity to
consider her life, there may emerge a person with a richer, more
differentiated and self-conscious sensibility.

It is no coincidence that along with a heroine who enjoys
reading, writing, and solitary walks, *Pride and Prejudice* is a novel
full of intimate letters. In the new private space, people discovered
not only that they enjoyed solitude, but that often it led them to
elaborate their thoughts and feelings and to wish to express them
to another person. Whereas on first glance we might think of the
wish for privacy as only a wish for aloneness, in fact one of its most
important attributes is that it makes possible a deeper, more chosen
openness. Privacy encourages self-expression and elaborates aspects
of intimacy. It may well be that the current flowering of memoir
writing is a perfect illustration of this seeming paradox. As people

feel more separate, it may heighten their wish to recount very personal experiences.

In a recent film version of *Pride and Prejudice,* Darcy apologizes for interrupting Elizabeth's *privacy.* Not so in the book. While the scene includes an apology, nowhere is the word *privacy* mentioned. The word existed in English, and is used in the book, but lacked the common larger usage it has today; the concept was less fully established.

Not only does the meaning of the word constantly evolve, but so does the phenomenon. Privacy is subtle, complex, and continually shifting. Deciding how much exists in a place or time is like trying to count every wildflower growing in the summer fields. At any moment many are blooming, many dying, and the season moves on before they can be surveyed. One's sense of privacy is partly subjective, partly circumstantial, the sum of a complicated equation balancing expectations, context, imagination, and control. When one discusses issues of privacy, one is discussing information and to whom it is available. What do other people know about us? How does this affect our safety, well-being, or freedom? How does it affect our sense of ourselves?

A tiny example illustrating the complexity of privacy as a subject, in this case the way that privacy, technology, and one's sense of self interweave, can be seen in the use of mirrors in rural France. Alain Corbin, a French scholar, writes that in nineteenth-century villages only barbers possessed full-length mirrors, and only men used them. Women and girls could examine their faces with small mirrors, "but full-length mirrors were all but unknown in the countryside, where peasants still discovered their physical identities through the eyes of others."[4]

What happened to self-consciousness and sensibility when full-length mirrors arrived in villagers' homes? Each woman likely reacted differently to seeing herself reflected back in the polished glass. But as mirrors became commonplace and people developed the habit of standing alone and observing themselves—had the opportunity in private to consider their own looks and were thus perhaps less reliant on having other people function descriptively as mirrors—it likely altered self-awareness. Aspects of individual identity may well have been heightened by the new opportunity to stand alone and examine how one looked, to weigh the information gathered from others against what one saw with one's own eyes. (Though whose eyes we see with when we look in the mirror is also a question.)

We could list multiple changes in nineteenth-century private life that "mirror" the development of the modern individual in Western culture. Many of them came out of increased privacy as it met up with new commodities like beds, inexpensive books, photographs, condoms, mirrors, and automobiles. Increased privacy was part of a large cultural evolution from a more communal sensibility to a more differentiated, individual one. The whole proposition that people might legitimately make important life decisions for private reasons, from a self with desires and a distinct perspective, is, historically speaking, quite new.

This notion of private choice that propelled *Pride and Prejudice* almost two hundred years ago (e.g., that what matters to Elizabeth is whether *she* loves and esteems Darcy, not whether he is a rich man who chooses her) has continually been elaborated and transferred from romantic fiction into people's actual lives—often recently. The critic Irving Howe recalled how his early-twentieth-century Lower East Side immigrant neighborhood so completely recreated communal village life from Eastern Europe that when in an American high school he encountered the writings of Emerson and Thoreau, he felt puzzled by their focus on individuals.[5]

Privacy is linked with individuality because it offers a space in which a person might become more fully him- or herself. The elaboration of love, intimacy, thought, sexuality, and friendship requires some privacy, so too the development of one's own point of view. But the temporary separateness that privacy supports is often confused with isolation, and the sheltering that privacy sanctions is not the same as secrecy. So, too, the interest in promoting situations that allow people to live more fully as individuals is not the same as advocating individualism. To state it briefly: Individualism tends to minimize interdependence and shared communal obligations, while respect for individuals tries to guide institutions, laws, and communal relationships in directions that help people live fairly and with dignity. The virtue of privacy, as I have come to understand it, is not in isolating people, but in allowing them temporary space in which they may accomplish important human tasks that are otherwise thwarted.

As a nation it seems that we're responding to increases in population, mobility, anonymity, and social fragmentation by invading privacy and attempting to reassert control through surveillance. Some of what we're doing is useful and genuinely protective. But too often we go for the DNA and the urine test without giving adequate thought to how these practices may interfere with other important objectives, how they may, for instance, inhibit or curtail the growth of individuals, or how they may create a communal atmosphere that is unduly restricting and shaming.

So, too, we are seeing the proliferation of inadequately regulated databanks that buy and sell the most personal information about us without our awareness or consent. Records of our bank account balances, medical prescriptions, and credit card purchases are considered saleable commodities, while we are denied our rightful ownership of this information. Yet society can only decide how to regulate these practices if we can determine what parts of privacy and private experience we wish to protect—and why.

This having been said, perhaps the hardest dilemma of privacy is not just how much is optimal, or the ways in which it must be balanced with communal needs, but its large fragility as a human situation—how quickly it can be harmed by other, more predatory, human impulses. The sources of privacy violation are more complicated and unexpected than they might first appear. This becomes apparent when one examines people's feelings about revelation and disclosure. The person who describes himself as "private" may be suffering from undue shame and seeking secrecy. The person who reveals much personal material may in fact be creating the possibility of a more healthy privacy. Disclosures that seem to violate privacy may be efforts to repair the depredation of older, secret harm, or they may perpetrate harm of their own.

This book explores privacy from a variety of angles to probe contemporary dilemmas and their origins, to acknowledge the diverse directions from which privacy is violated, and to remind us why privacy matters.

My Daughter, My Sister

Years ago, just out of college, I worked for a while in a large Dickensian day-care center in a poor mill city. The atmosphere was harsh. The kids were mostly from welfare families; the all-woman staff was working-class and tough. The director cared little for her job, and often in the afternoons she would leave her office, climb the two flights of stairs to her attic apartment, pour a succession of drinks for herself and the staff whom she had made her half willing guests, and tell stories. She was ambivalent about me and, having determined that I had one Jewish parent and one Italian one, referred to me alternately as "the Jew" or "the wop," depending on where I stood in her esteem—though how she kept score was unclear. She sneered at my naïveté, yet at the same time it amused her that someone with a college degree could be stupid about things she understood well. Occasionally she invited me to join the others in her apartment.

Late one afternoon, after many stories, and after the alcohol, the early winter darkness, and the departure two floors below of most of the children had deepened our unlikely intimacy, she looked directly at each of the four or five of us sitting around her small room, paused, inhaled on her cigarette, and slowly said, "I know doctors in this town who go to people's houses and deliver the babies that men fathered with their own daughters. I know about an eleven-year-old who had a baby."

She was in her early fifties then, with hair dyed orange and occasionally stuffed under a blond wig. She wore fishnet stockings, short skirts, and spike heels, and claimed to be forty-two. For all that I found implausible about her, I knew she was telling the truth. And while I felt repulsed to learn that some fathers impregnated their daughters, I also felt relieved, having discovered ugly facts to be handy for creating a rudimentary map of adulthood.

What anchored these stories in my memory was not just the knowledge they offered, but the way they were wrapped like so many veils in innuendos and fabrications about the director's own life. She let us know that her conversations with doctors were privileged: Her allure made her the recipient of confidences whispered during romantic meetings in bars or bedrooms, not offices. And there was more she wouldn't say. What was she keeping private? She implied that it was the details of her conquests, and since she was our boss, we granted her that interpretation. But it was not hard to see, underneath the bravado, a fragile woman whose urgency to recount other people's hard times was an effort to keep us off the trail of her own. The distance between the person we glimpsed and the adept courtesan she would have us envy—together with the forbidden stories she offered—held my interest. I would stare into the thick smoke of her assertions and silences and wonder, Was she as accomplished as she claimed? Perhaps she had a baby with her father or had helped a doctor deliver someone else's. Perhaps she was just expert at holding our attention with half-truths when she didn't want to drink alone.

The invitation to hear her tales also meant that I was at least grudgingly accepted by a woman—in fact a group of women—from whom I had not expected acceptance. Like me, they had all been tagged: "Polack," "Canuck," "mick." But they were older and knew more. Listening to their talk, I heard about women who died from illegal abortions, and almost in the same breath about how to pick up a man in a bar, techniques lesbians used to impregnate each other, ways to remove tattoos, and how to mix sweet sticky drinks with names like Sombrero. Though the setting was uneasy and the delivery ham-handed, the conversations at the day-care center satisfied some of my hunger to hear private talk about women's experience. I had gossiped with other women in college, I had listened in on my mother and her friends, but the day-care center was different; the women had lived harder, and the exchanges often began where the other talk left off.

Of the conversations, it is the one about pregnant children that remains most vividly in my mind. In 1974, no one I knew spoke about incest. When, a year or so later, I watched the heroine in *Chinatown*—played brilliantly by Faye Dunaway—reveal that she was both mother and sister to her daughter, the scene was shocking and exotic, but also plausible in a way it would not have been without the director's stories.

Twenty years later, both the movie and the afternoons in the day-care center seem old-fashioned, even delicate. Today, anyone who turns on the television can hear talk-show hosts interview daughters who had children with their fathers, or interview their mothers, or even the fathers themselves. Companies sell transcripts of talk shows, and it is easy to purchase episodes of *Donahue, Oprah,* and *Sally Jesse Raphael* on hundreds of topics like "Soap Opera Addicts" or "When Smart People Fail," as well as the subject variously referred to as "Family Inter-breeding" or "Pregnancy from Incest." The public discussion of incest on these programs is not only striking for its contrast to our hushed talk in the day-care center, but because as narrative, it explores one of the emblematic stories of our time—the question of what is hidden within private life.

The transcripts are remarkable documents. One wonders what someone in the future will make of them, or, for that matter, what to make of them now. Each recounts an hour-long show on which the featured guests are daughters who had their fathers' or stepfathers' babies. The women sit on the stage next to their mothers (the men's wives) and sometimes their sisters. Also present are the studio audience and one or more therapists—the "experts"— who together with the audience create a contemporary chorus providing commentary on the stories and storytellers. The hosts are attractive, charismatic, and adept: They prod the guests to reveal themselves, pump up the audience, invite the opinions of experts, and break for many commercials.

Oprah begins: "Hello everybody. We are talking today about daughters who get pregnant by their fathers and have the babies. We're going to hear one story of a family where three sisters had 13 children between them. The father of all 13 of the children is *their* father"[1] [italics added].

Sally Jesse Raphael: "Two years ago, 17-year-old Ginger had a baby, and at first, her mother, Wendy, was really thrilled to be a grandmother, but months after the baby was born, Grandmother Wendy found out a shocking secret that her daughter, Ginger had kept from her."[2]

Donahue: "More and more victims of incest and rape are keeping their babies. Do you understand that? Do you think it's a good idea? Would you keep your baby if your pregnancy were the result of a violent assault? . . . Meet Mickey Booher. Your daughter gave birth to a baby that was actually fathered by your husband."

"Yes, sir," Mickey Booher answers in front of a television

audience of millions.³ Or as Oprah observes at the end of her program, "It's been a very difficult thing to talk about, especially before 20 million people."⁴

Why are these programs on television? What are the participants doing? One looks for analogies: revival meetings, gladiators in the colosseum, *Queen for a Day,* public lynchings, circus freak shows, mass baptisms, group therapy, soap operas, tabloid newspapers. Talk shows borrow from all of these but belong to none. They are new, different, and very popular. They challenge our notions about privacy: For on them, people who may never have uttered a personal word to anyone abandon reserve, restraint and discretion and bare themselves before the camera and the studio audience.

The studio audience participation is itself remarkable. Some members have come in search of entertainment, others are "survivors" (a term Oprah insists on over *victims*) of the day's affliction who recount their own stories. One woman stands up; a host places a reassuring hand on her shoulder. The camera zooms in so you can see her lip trembling, her eyes filling. "My father raped me, too, and I got pregnant." She continues for a sentence or two and sits down. The host moves on to interview another survivor or perhaps an expert.⁵

On all the programs, experts—usually counselors or psychotherapists of various kinds—are invited to comment. One says that sex with stepchildren is incest. A second explains how America is a violent and exploitive culture. A third asserts that incestuous parents rule by brainwashing. The experts are sincere people, earnest, and often well spoken. Depending on the show and the topic, they come across either as decent professionals, trying to make a difference, or co-opted ones, lending a veneer of respectability to the ogling crowd. But then, talk shows continually shimmer between two realities: one cynical and exploitive, the other more elusive yet genuine.

On some levels they are hateful. The hosts and networks make fortunes by inviting people to expose themselves. The programs feed on helplessness, voyeurism, exhibitionism, and confusion; they take advantage of loneliness and isolation, of a dearth of other more genuine communal forums. They exploit people's fear that the world will not adequately witness their suffering.

The studio audiences on some shows attack the guests. People are mocked, challenged, and humiliated. During one *Sally Jesse Raphael* hour on adultery, members of the audience stand up to yell "slut" and "whore" at the guests on stage. On a *Geraldo* episode about "men who move back to live with their mothers," the slur is "mama's boy." If an audience becomes too worked up with a particular guest, a host may move in or cut to a commercial, but this feeble gesture seems most reminiscent of people who call off their dogs with a bland, "He won't hurt you," after the animal has drawn blood.

Much of what passes for intimate revelation by the participants is in fact a sad imitation of intimacy, a faux intimacy made more insidious because no one distinguishes it from the real thing. Although the most private topics are talked about, there is little real conversation since conversation requires continuity, thoughtfulness, and a kind of quiet that television rarely tolerates. Participants expose deep feelings, sob, and shake, then sit staring at their feet while the host announces a station break. At their worst, talk shows appear to be in the process of perfecting a kind of psychologically informed, mass-media-disseminated sensationalism, a prurient, often destructive force that needlessly humiliates and debases people and cheapens intimacy and personal expression.

But what makes such programs complex is that side by side with the lode of fool's gold sits a nugget of the real thing: important revelations and people who have good reasons for making them. By doing so they attack hypocrisy, challenge social distance, and reveal the way misuses of power corrupt and abuse privacy. They are not destroying privacy; theirs has long since been destroyed. They are offering testimony about the nature of its loss and the ways that abuses within the private realm undermine the potential benefits of privacy.

The programs draw you in. Everybody tells a tale; and sometimes, gripped in spite of yourself, you applaud, call names, smile, frown, shake your head in horror, wince, and weep. It is moving to see men and women struggle to describe painful events. Participants set out to talk superficially, and sometimes find themselves describing deeply private, sad experiences. Social conventions are momentarily pushed aside, as they state the gnawing facts of their difficult lives.

Where else can an incest survivor, lonely, injured, isolated, tell her story to millions of witnesses, receive the host's sympathy, and weep with other incest survivors? "This is what happened to me. Don't let it happen to you," a woman warns the camera. When she finishes speaking, it is with a sense that she has offered hope to girls trapped in dark bedrooms and, with the host's help, has painted the tar of shame back on the perpetrator where it belongs. One assaultive father, a Baptist "reverend," speaks by phone from his jail cell (robbery, not sexual abuse, has finally incarcerated him), attempting to rationalize how his wife wanted him to father children with his children, and how his daughters enjoyed it. He is plaintive and insistent, but Oprah has the last word: "With all due respect to you, Reverend," she announces for twenty million people to hear, "you're a liar and you're a slime."[6]

Almost like a goddess, like justice embodied, Oprah, an outspoken, powerful woman, enters the fray, dispenses absolution, defends the daughters, and vindicates their honor. They are no longer alone with their suffering and their shame. The father who has tortured them and destroyed their childhood is finally openly named. Out of the flimflam and the kangaroo court comes an honest encounter, a just moment.

Oprah offers her guests more than we ever offered the women we gossiped about at the day-care center. We were glad to talk about them, but the idea of hearing from them was taboo. No one spoke in the first person about painful experiences because the fear of being shamed was insurmountable. Justice was harsh, and any horror—even rape—was your own fault. Victims were the bearers of bad news, and rather than focusing on our common bond as women, we wordlessly decided that we were better off keeping them—and the "them" in us—at bay. We enjoyed the closeness, but the entry price was a tacit promise not to blink.

But Donahue, Sally, Oprah, and Geraldo have changed the rules. Working as psychic muckrakers, they garner the details of the horror sometimes hidden behind the facade of "private life" or "family life." "So it was a douche kind of abortion?" Donahue asks a young woman who is telling how her father used baking soda and hot water to abort her baby in the family bathroom. "Yes," she confirms.[7]

One important discovery of the late twentieth century is of the terrible things—physical and emotional—people *actually do* to each other within the privacy of home. And there is no doubt that television has aided in the achievement of this sorry recognition. In too many instances, family life is not about love, but about exploitation of power. When Donahue interviews his guest, he momentarily breaks through denial and disavowal and forces viewers to confront the fact that nice guys—church deacons, movie actors, good Christians, and bank presidents—can be violent or sadistic when the shades are drawn.

Talk-show hosts have invented a new alloy by forging psychiatry and sensational journalism. They have made themselves middlemen for isolated suburbanites, offering information about the dangers of private life while sparing viewers and asking the awkward questions for them. Television talk shows make people feel connected while they are unconnected, a paradox with many consequences.

Television offers the information of intimacy without the obligations. By creating celebrity hosts who behave like our best friends, and by flooding viewers with the intimate revelations of anonymous neighbors, television has devised a crude but potent answer to contemporary life with its enormous social isolation. You no longer have to make friends with a group of women to hear good stories. What is more, if a neighbor comes and tells you that her husband is beating her, her problem becomes yours. What do you make of her story? Perhaps you should talk to her husband, or call the police. You could offer her shelter, but then you might get more involved than you care to be. If a battered woman talks on television, you get the prurient thrill, vivid detail, the horrible, forbidden story, and none of the responsibility or the real-life mess.

When I was little and lived in Oregon, a cow with a glass plate in her side was the star attraction in the agriculture department of the local college. She had been surgically altered so curious students could peer inside her and watch her digest her cud. Contemporary television offers a similar view.

Often it seems to be desperation, loneliness, exclusion that one witnesses through the glass. One woman, describing her feelings after appearing on a talk show with her gay ex-husband and his lover, said, "I now know I'm the good guy because the audience proved that." Abandoned by her husband, who fell in love with a man soon after their wedding, she had apparently been unable to find any other way to ease her anger, guilt, and sorrow. The expiation had to come from outside herself, had to have the pomp of public ritual, the burnish of a slight celebrity. And apparently the hunger for such relief was enough to make her risk public humiliation. Privately held, her feelings had become unbearable.[8]

In the era when I worked at the day-care center, the victim of incest, the woman married to a homosexual man, were expected to keep their misery to themselves. If their lives were harmed, we didn't want to know; we demanded a solid facade. We no longer demand total silence, yet our reception is ambivalent. Collectively, we are not sure we wish to face the implications of the stories.

Lacking efficacious communal forums, talk shows are one compromise. They offer a public hearing: for many, the only one possible. But because the shows set out to entertain and make money, important and trivial revelations are commingled and lose consequence. Political change and justice, two apt public ends of trading one's privacy to give testimony, are slightly addressed while commodity triumphs.

Still, there is an important take-home message in the shows: Family privacy may shelter and sanction interpersonal tyranny. While America may have outlawed slavery and attempted to regulate civic relationships, in the privacy of the home, exploitive practices sometimes continue, unobserved. The talk shows succeed in part because they have named this predicament of contemporary life, this frontier of privacy.

America is in the midst of a debate about privacy that takes many forms:

- A newspaper editor ponders whether he should print a story that reveals that a popular athlete has AIDS.
- An author publishes an account of how he masturbates, and a reviewer on the front page of *The New York Times Book Re-*

view attacks the book, suggesting there are some details of sexuality best kept in the realm of fiction.

- A psychiatrist writes an introduction to a biography about his patient, admitting he made accessible to the biographer tapes of psychotherapy sessions; his admission stirs a controversy that makes headlines.
- A woman claims she has had an extramarital sexual liaison with a presidential candidate; he chooses to respond by being interviewed with his wife on prime-time television.

How we think about privacy has been greatly influenced during the past century by two phenomena of modern life: the development of massive media capacity, and the popularizing of psychological thinking, or more precisely, the emergence of a post-Freudian culture that takes for granted the public expression of once private experiences and parts of the mind. The confluence of these trends, the way they have become particularly entwined within the society, and the power they wield in the absence of other once potent social institutions are fueling the private/public tug-of-war. Some critics have argued for the virtues of restraint and privacy. Others have celebrated the demise of prudishness and hypocrisy. Still others have bemoaned the moral erosion and the ethos of victimization that they claim underlies public accusations and confessions. There is truth in all these positions.

All the disparate issues of privacy—whether I can listen in on your telephone conversation, whether you can publish the love letters I sent you, whether I can find out your credit rating, whether you can test my urine for drugs before you hire me, whether I can prohibit your abortion, whether you can keep me alive in spite of my wish to die, whether I should write about you or talk about you on a talk show—represent battles about power, money, values, and the elusive concept of "the common good."

We need to find our way through these issues because the

qualities of humanness that make life more than a biological event—creative and artistic expression, intellectual endeavor, sacred rituals, love and intimate sexuality, friendship, and individual dignity—are qualities that must be sheltered to thrive. Privacy shelters, and thus offers sustenance to fragile virtues.

Privacy also supports freedom to make important personal choices. If you are an Irish Catholic woman and you marry a Muslim Ethiopian man whom you love, your choice may have hurt your mother and father, caused the other members of your church to curse you, and angered your neighbors. But you have made a private choice that has come out of your own feelings and wishes. Historically, what you have done is new; until recently such gestures would often have subjected you to either isolation or persecution. (Sigmund Freud wryly observed that for most of history, anyone criticizing religion could be assured of "an effective speeding-up of the opportunity for gaining a personal experience of the afterlife.")[9] Private choice is more possible now because we live in a society and an era that is considering the idea—albeit erratically and with harsh inconsistency—that a person's intimate feelings are the heart of humanness and therefore deserve protection. How far we will expand this idea remains to be seen, the struggle about legalizing gay marriages being one current battleground.

The risk of privacy is the absence of witnesses. One person's privacy can easily become another's license to hide, harm, or create bad secrets. Privacy is ready prey to exploitation, corruption, and abuse. If, in a home, an adult feels entitled to abuse a child, the act exploits and corrupts privacy. Or, conversely, if a child makes up stories about the way an adult harmed him (statistically a much rarer phenomenon), privacy is also harmed. Talk shows address misuses of privacy—even as they often misuse it themselves in the process. The important knowledge in the talk shows is the reminder that for many people, private life is not a haven.

The virtues of privacy are further obscured by the fact that a kind of corrupted, obliterating privacy is often forced upon people with less power. Henry James describes how, in nineteenth-century London, some rich people didn't want the bother of learning the names of a succession of maids, cooks, butlers, and gardeners. So they picked one name and imposed it on each person who filled a post. "Your name was Fred. Now it is Richard. Be careful transplanting the precious rose I brought from Shanghai."

Conversely, a group of people who have been oppressed or marginalized may raise their children to keep much private—even more than other families. Once, when younger, my sons were playing at the home of African-American friends. The play was good, the exchange easy and comfortable; so much so that my boys' young friend, reassuring his older sibling of the propriety of an open comment, said, "It's okay, we're all black here." Seeing suddenly, clearly, the white faces, he fell silent. He had violated his family's careful efforts to keep him safe from the effects of racism by not letting outsiders know him—by guarding the family's privacy.

Together with their particular biology and historical moment, people are ultimately made individual by those parts of experience that are difficult to communicate, the images sorted through as sleep comes, the composite of coherent memories, fragmented pictures, habits of love, powerful feelings, and perceptions that, like so many leaves raked into a pile, arrange themselves in relationships that cannot be replicated or completely described. They become the compost fertilizing creative expression. They are at once ineffable and essential. They may be profane or sacred. "What I keep," writes the poet Gary Miranda, "keeps me alive."[10] At its best, privacy shields and nurtures what is unique and authentic in people, while its absence or its violation often contributes to dehumanizing them.

Struggles about privacy are struggles about access and control. They are about conflicting interests between individuals, and between individual and community. Privacy is a complex ecology. Like that of the earth, it is delicate, and the nature of its balance determines much about the opportunity people have to experience some of the most remarkable parts of humanness. But what is involved in privacy, and why does it matter?

2

Privacy and Private States

One way of beginning to understand privacy is by looking at what happens to people in extreme situations where it is absent. Recalling his time in Auschwitz, Primo Levi observed that "solitude in a Camp is more precious and rare than bread."[1] Solitude is one state of privacy, and even amidst the overwhelming death, starvation, and horror of the camps, Levi knew he missed it.

Uprooted by the Second World War from his life as a chemistry student and beginning chemist, Levi, a twenty-four-year-old Italian Jew from Turin, was arrested and deported to the Nazi labor camp at Auschwitz in February 1944. Six hundred and fifty other men, women, and children traveled with him. When he returned home a year and a half later, he was one of twenty who had survived. Levi spent much of his life finding words for his camp experience. How, he wonders aloud in *Survival in Auschwitz*, do you describe "the demolition of a man," an offense for which "our language lacks words."[2]

Many people carry a mental image of a Jew in a concentration camp. We see the striped jacket, the starved face with shaved head and unseeing eyes. To Levi, the picture of an emaciated man "with head dropped and shoulders curved, on whose face and in whose eyes not a trace of thought is to be seen" encloses "all the evil of our time."[3]

During the past century we have learned much about how to create an individual and how to destroy one—not that such knowledge hasn't always existed. But we have had particular opportunity to observe and explore ideas about both individual worth and mass human destruction, including the ways to destroy an individual short of outright murder. Destroying his privacy and his safety in private is one way.

A basic ingredient in such destruction is terror. I am walking with a friend in the Dordogne region of France. It is a warm midsummer day, and the blackberry bushes are flowering. During the war, my friend recounts, pointing up at an old stone house set on a small hill, a family lived there who joined the Resistance. The SS arrested the husband, tortured him, and then delivered him back to their door. The captors waited until the family, overjoyed that he was alive, ran out to hug him. Then they shot him in front of his wife and children.

Hitler's accomplices understood—as many have before and since—that if you kill an enemy, his loved ones will grieve, but if you kill him in a way that also terrorizes them, you will accomplish more effective harm. Psychologically fractured by fear, these "enemies" will find it harder to oppose you. Yet they remain alive and able to till fields that feed your troops. The English who fought Indians in seventeenth-century Virginia summed up this approach neatly, observing that "terrour . . . made short warres."[4]

When you set out to destroy someone psychologically, destroying his privacy turns out to be one effective and common tactic. When Primo Levi talks about solitude in the camp being more precious and rare than bread, he helps us understand its place in life. One function of privacy is to provide a safe space away from terror or other assaultive experiences. When you remove a person's ability to sequester herself, or intimate information about herself, you make her extremely vulnerable.

Consider Vera Wollenberger, a woman who spent much of her young adulthood protesting East German communism. For her dissent she was harassed, fired from her job, and imprisoned. After communism collapsed, Wollenberger, elected to Parliament, helped enact a law allowing people to read the secret files kept on them by the East German government. Reading her own, she realized with horror that the intimate and damaging information that filled it could only have been offered by her husband. No one else knew the particular details.[5] Violating the privacy she expected to hold in common with him, her husband took advantage of her trust in their intimacy (a private state) to betray and exploit her, probably in the hope of increasing his own power. What must it have been like to recognize that her spouse was responsible for her imprisonment? After such a betrayal, what would happen to her ability to love?

The totalitarian state watches everyone, but keeps its own plans secret. Privacy is seen as dangerous because it enhances resistance. Constantly spying and then confronting people with what are often petty transgressions is a way of maintaining social control and unnerving and disempowering opposition. While spying efforts sometimes backfire and increase the loyalty of friends and intimates, too often they succeed. And even when one shakes real pursuers, it is often hard to rid oneself of the feeling of being watched—which is why surveillance is an extremely powerful way to control people. The mind's tendency to still feel observed when alone (a phenomenon related to Freud's idea of the superego) is probably biologically and culturally indispensable, but it can also be inhibiting. Used malevolently, surveillance badly harms individuals in part by really endangering them, in part by overstimulating their vigilance. Feeling watched, but not knowing for sure, nor knowing if, when, or how the hostile surveyor may strike, people often become fearful, constricted, and distracted.

Nadezhda Mandelstam was married to the Russian poet Osip Mandelstam who was arrested and imprisoned by Stalin and eventually died in a labor camp. In her memoir, *Hope Against Hope,* Mandelstam relates the terrible havoc wreaked by Stalinism, and she details the insidious psychological harm of surveillance. She describes how the dictatorship destroyed trust—often by destroying the sanctuary within privacy—and "atomized" the society. Anything a person said in private could be reported to government spies, and used against him to demonstrate his disloyalty, for which he was then imprisoned and often killed. Spies were everywhere, and when unable to find damaging material, they made it up. Since the conversations they reported had theoretically occurred in private, no one could disprove the accusations. Mandelstam observes how, when such practices destroy people's safety, everyone becomes a little mad:

> An existence like this leaves its mark. We all became slightly unbalanced mentally—not exactly ill, but not normal either: suspicious, mendacious, confused and inhibited in our speech, at the same time putting on a show of adolescent optimism. What value can such people have as witnesses? The elimination of witnesses was, indeed, part of the whole program.[6]

Constrained and frightened, harassed people often lose their efficacy. Their privacy has been destroyed by surveillance and fear. (It is this same phenomenon as it sometimes occurs in family life that serious discussions on talk shows attempt to witness and describe and that psychotherapists treat.)

It is of course not just communist or fascist governments that use such tactics. The United States has often spied on and persecuted dissidents: Emma Goldman, the Wobblies, and Malcolm X are a few who come to mind. Surveillance and harassment have grown in America along with the rest of government. Curt Gentry's eight-hundred-page biography of J. Edgar Hoover offers an endless catalogue of the FBI chief's appalling misuse of spying sometimes for political, sometimes for more self-serving, purposes. Here is a small example:

> On learning that one magazine publisher was considering an expose of the FBI and its long-tenured director, Hoover struck first, viciously. Favored newspaper contacts all over the country received a plain brown envelope with no return address. Inside was a packet of photographs showing the publisher's wife engaged in fellatio with her black chauffeur.[7]

Such surveillance betrays intimacy—and all privacy—by observing people while they are enjoying the freedom of being unobserved. The FBI's attempt to make Martin Luther King commit suicide by sending him and his wife tapes of his sexual infidelities is another example of this approach. Along with the videos, King received an anonymous letter. Knowing that he had attempted suicide as a twelve-year-old child, the writer, an FBI agent, encouraged King to end his life.[8] As we learn more about J. Edgar Hoover, his morbid shame about his own sexuality, his secrecy, and decadence, the way he persecuted others in the name of patriotism seems not only awful, but obviously self-defensive. But such insight is cold comfort to the people whose lives he destroyed or harmed.

Safe privacy is an important component of autonomy, freedom, and love, and thus psychological well-being, in any society that values individuals. In fact, by reversing to the smallest detail all that was perpetrated against Levi, Mandelstam, Wollenberger, and King, we can extract a standard. Summed up briefly, a statement of "how not to dehumanize people" might read: Don't replace names with numbers. Don't beat or torture. Don't terrorize or humiliate. Don't starve, freeze, exhaust. Don't demean or impose degrading submission. Don't force separation from loved ones. Don't make demands in an incomprehensible language. Don't refuse to listen closely. Don't destroy privacy. Terrorists of all sorts destroy privacy both by corrupting it into secrecy and by using hostile surveillance to undo its useful sanctuary.

But if we describe a standard for treating people humanely, why does stripping privacy violate it? And what is privacy? In his land-mark book, *Privacy and Freedom,* Alan Westin names four states of privacy: solitude, anonymity, reserve, and intimacy.[9] The reasons for valuing privacy become more apparent as we explore these states.

Solitude is the most complete state of privacy. A person seek-ing solitude separates from others so that she cannot be seen or heard, and so that she is not easily intruded upon. In solitude, as opposed to the other states of privacy, she is most free to relax her body.

What is considered physically private varies in different cul-tures and different families. Anthropologists suggest that most peo-ple, no matter where or when they live, seek privacy for sex and defecation.[10] But other habits are more local and temporary. In pri-vate today, a person might remove undergarments, use the toilet, sleep, pick his nose, masturbate, examine and cleanse parts of his body, or sniff his own odors. The heroine in Marie Cardinal's memoir/novel *The Words to Say It* describes her adeptness at discretely reaching her hand down under her clothing to check her menstrual flow. And when alone, she privately examines her blood. "I remember taking out the tampon that stopped the blood, which I began to watch gently flowing, drop by drop. . . . It was an activity to watch the blood work its way out of me; it had a life of its own now, it could discover the physics of earth-bound things, weight, density, speed, duration. It kept me company and at the same time was delivered over to the indifferent and incomprehensible laws of life."[11]

Similarly, in his memoir *Self-consciousness,* John Updike describes the close attention he paid to his body because of his psoriasis. Years later he remembers the smell of the medicine, the "insinuating odor deeply involved with my embarrassment. Yet, as with our own private odors, those of sweat and earwax and even of excrement, there was something satisfying about this scent, an intimate rankness that told me who I was."[12]

Alone with our bodies, we allow ourselves to know them thoroughly—the shape of an arm, the bend of a toenail, the pattern of freckles or scars. In private we learn and continually update our knowledge of the small details that make up our physical being. It is a vast and fundamental entry in the lexicon of our identity. Freud believed that the primary ego is a body ego—that the first and most basic knowledge we have of ourselves is through the feelings in our body, our physical gratification, pain, hungers, and needs. The body is the plowed field in which the self grows. As the body changes, it alters and recreates the self. Souls and private scents are inextricably commingled.

It is not only when we are alone that we come to know our bodies. The touch of others is critical for comfort because it allows us to learn where we begin and end. It can offer pleasure or pain. A baby deprived of human touch is a baby unlikely to survive infancy. But in the presence of others, once out of earliest childhood, the intimate and thorough explorations of the body are limited and inhibited by demands for propriety and conformity.

In some Catholic orders, a nun was forbidden to examine her own body. Even when she bathed, she was covered with sheets. While the repression of sexuality is obvious (though it's easy to imagine such an effort backfiring by creating a tabooed eroticism), more subtle is the impact such strictures must have had on the woman's sense of self and individuality. Did she collect knowledge with her fingertips instead of her eyes? Or was her mind so completely on God that she just didn't care? Diminishing individual identity heightens receptivity to authority—something military leaders have understood for centuries. Discouraging people from private knowledge of their bodies probably eases that process. An opposite approach is that of feminist doctors who hand women mirrors and encourage them to examine their own vulvas.

Solitude frequently gets represented by a man alone in nature—something that television commercials play upon endlessly. Often the image replaces the experience: Urban highways are crowded with Land Rovers and Jeeps theoretically designed to allow people to go alone into the wilderness—to drive beyond the roads or to ford streams. Gas guzzlers, short on comfort, awkward on crowded streets, these cars have little practical purpose in city life except, I suspect, the profound one of maintaining the fantasy of solitude in nature against the besieging reality.

Americans have long loved the idea of the man alone in nature. Whether of Thoreau, Natty Bumpo, a Native American, or a cowboy, the image is deeply held. Entering nature we identify with him, like children with superheroes. The solitude he inhabits is a child's fantasy of life without dependency, of sublime confidence, of conflict without ambiguity or compromise. The nature that frames him is a stage set, a passive backdrop for human assertion constructed to flatter him as separate, free, and strong.

Real accounts of nature describe the difficulty of physical toil and the constant danger of dying—men in their fishing boats lost at sea, women frozen in storms, children eaten by wolves. The perception of beauty and freedom is set against the deep fear, even terror, of harm and death. The natural world that the Pilgrims encountered was, according to William Bradford, "a hideous and desolate wilderness, full of wild beasts and wild men." New England fishermen understand this feeling. Only when summer people started visiting the coast did houses get fitted with decks and picture windows. People who daily worked and died at sea had no urgency to contemplate the water from their kitchen tables.

In the suburban world, wilderness dangers are overshadowed by civilization's; we fear stalkers more than bears. People generally possess a more distant and split image of nature. On the one hand, it is a weakened and perhaps dying leviathan harpooned by overpopulation, technology, toxic waste, and the pollution of contemporary life—not a place to seek solitude. On the other hand, the contemporary sense of nature is still the wide open spaces, pristine—or at least pastoral—beauty, a spiritual haven, the site of personal liberty, freedom, and autonomy. The nature in which one seeks solitude has often already been subdued. Nineteenth-century transcendentalists and romantic poets, facing the encroachments of industrial society, wrote about solitude in this nature and tried to define why it mattered.

"I went to the woods," Thoreau asserts in a famous passage from *Walden*, "because I wished to live deliberately." Or, as he states earlier, because he wished to be awakened by the "undulations of celestial music instead of factory bells."[13] Solitude allows people to regulate their rhythms and behaviors away from the influence of others. No one controls what you do or when. No one else's alarm clock wakes you. No one's questions or needs interrupt your train of thought or feeling, or your solitary pursuits. Solitude does not have to be in nature, but when set there, frees people most completely from the regulation, control, and constraint of society. Even more than the factory bells, it is the direct influence of other people, particularly in their more oppressive and intrusive dimensions, that one temporarily eludes in solitude.

/Why is it that I am drawn to sit alone on a small beach watching the ocean, the circling gulls and ospreys, the piles of smooth stones surrounded by wild indigo, morning glory, and hawkweed? My answer is common. I love the peace of not having to take account of others. I am amazed by the beauty. I am reminded that my concerns are small and that what good or damage I do is small. The large wild domain indifferent to my existence is both soothing and thrilling. Alone in nature, one confronts its grandeur. Sensing its scope, it is the rare person who feels no awe. Solitude in nature places a person directly in contact with a vivid, original force.

One may, like Wordsworth, experience nature as a moral force that reinforces and enhances one's virtues. Nature, he asserts, is "the anchor of my purest thoughts, the nurse, the guide, the guardian of my heart, and soul of all my moral being." By closely watching nature, he believes, one uncovers the divine and feels its resonance within the self. A related use of solitude occurs in some kinds of meditation, when people sit alone in order to examine and reflect more rigorously. When this ancient practice is undertaken as part of a religious pursuit, people seek to become closer to a god or to holiness. Otherwise, it is to calm oneself, or use contemplation as a route to knowledge.

Seeking solitude, but not nature, people wish for time alone to "center" or to "get back in touch" with themselves. But what does this mean? Since I have had children, commuting to work forty minutes in traffic has changed from onerous to almost pleasant. It is privacy I can count on having. As the traffic inches along, my thoughts drift freely to situations at work, exchanges at home or with friends, problems I need to solve, plans, feelings, and fantasies. If a story on the radio is sad and my eyes tear, no child looks at me with worry. If an old song reminds me of a good time and I sing along, no adolescent passenger complains that it's a bad song and I'm off-key. A car in traffic is not completely private, yet it suffices.

We seek solitude because our psyches are permeable membranes. When we come in contact with others, we tend to absorb feelings, thoughts, moods, and opinions. A child says you're unfair for making her start her book report today. Are you? A client asks to change his appointment from Tuesday to Monday. Can you? A spouse gives you a look that suggests it's your turn to fold the laundry. Is it? A friend describes events that have made her sad. Is that why you now feel sad? We separate from others to sort through all we have taken in, to replay pieces of exchanges, to evaluate them, to rework them—and ultimately for the peace in which to listen attentively until we can hear our own notes amidst the jangle.

The essence of solitude, and all privacy, is a sense of choice and control. You control who watches or learns about you. You choose to leave and return. Even Thoreau left his cabin to seek companionship. Often we are all our own worst company, and nothing can relieve us except the comfort of others. Unchosen solitude quickly becomes painful isolation. Frederick the Great, wishing to hear the original language he believed had been spoken before the Tower of Babel, reportedly isolated a group of infants in hopes that when they talked, they would speak the ancient lost language. Though fed and clothed, they died.

People in solitary confinement have to fight constantly against madness. In fact, the way they often preserve their sanity is by learning to dissociate, to alter their own mental state, and use fantasy to evoke images, memories, and feelings of loved ones. Yamil Kouri, a doctor jailed in solitary confinement in Cuba for allegedly conspiring to overthrow Castro, recalls that he survived the darkened two-foot-by-two-foot cell for two and a half years by meditating continually.[14] Paradoxically, one can defy isolation by evoking memories of intimacy.

Enforced or protracted solitude is unbearable to most people. But solitude in moderation, held in check by its being a sought and limited departure from the company of others, allows freedom. Alone, we create stories about ourselves as we would wish to be. We can feel our own feelings free from the direct influence of others, think our thoughts uninterrupted, spin out fantasies, and follow the images of the imagination. In his book *Solitude,* the psychoanalyst Anthony Storr argues that its value has been hidden in this century because of psychology's obsession with intimacy. Storr suggests that many highly creative people, like Beethoven and Kipling, were extremely solitary and that solitude is often a prerequisite for creativity. Some people want to be left alone to imagine.[15]

People need privacy from others so that they can rest from the strain of being what others desire—responsive, civil, engaged, conventional. "We pray to be conventional," writes Ralph Waldo Emerson, "but the wary Heaven takes care you shall not be, if there is anything good in you."[16] To think and create, people often need solitude because its privacy allows not only mental continuity, quiet, and relief from feeling noticed, but latitude to experiment with half-formed ideas and ridiculous solutions.

Still, that image neglects the full cycle. Solitude is half a heartbeat. Artists seek solitude so that they can create what they then must take before the public. Without an eventual audience, no matter how small, solitude can become, in Emerson's words, "the safeguard of mediocrity."[17]

Most images of solitude are male: men alone, men in nature, men making art. Almost the only time women traditionally were allowed solitude was in prayer—as they conversed with a saint or a god. Emerson's mother, who bore eight children of whom five survived, sought solitude to pray. "She led a deeply religious life. Every day after breakfast she retired to her room for reading and contemplation. She was not to be disturbed."[18] At the hearth, surrounded by children and family, in the imagination, we place women in the presence of others. A woman alone is usually perceived not as seeking solitude, but as abandoned, unattractive, isolated, and lonely, or conversely as dangerous, unattached, destabilizing. A woman without a man is a woman after your man—ask any country western singer.

When women venture out alone—whether into wilderness or empty alleys—they often feel apprehensiveness about their own vulnerability. It is not wolves or snakes that raise contemporary fears, but the violence of men. In a chilling *New York Times* "Hers" column, Susan Brison describes setting out alone for a country walk on a beautiful summer day in southern Europe:

> I sang to myself as I set out, stopping to pet a goat and pick some wild strawberries along the way. An hour later, I was lying near death, pleading for my life with a brutal assailant who had jumped me from behind. I hadn't heard or seen him coming. He dragged me off the road and into a deep ravine, beat me with his fist and with a rock, sexually assaulted me, choked me repeatedly and, after I had passed out four times, left me for dead.[19]

A woman alone is a woman easily overpowered and hurt. And while all the ramifications of such violence are terrible, one of the worst is the way it harms women's freedom to relish solitude. The story includes a cautionary tale about solitude: It can be dangerous. It may be that we associate the glory of solitude with men, and its liabilities with women. Underlying that unfortunate polarization is the recognition that the aloneness people seek can be risky; it can undermine communal life, or make individuals too vulnerable.

A second state of privacy is *anonymity*. To be anonymous is to be unidentified, unnamed, unnoticed: a walker in a city, a member of a crowd. With the absence of recognition can come a liberating privacy. People often seek anonymity when the conventions of their surroundings, when the burden of being known, threatens to obliterate vital dimensions of their being. It seems no coincidence, for example, that the nineteenth-century feminist Margaret Fuller fell passionately in love and had a child while living in Italy, not in New England. Being surrounded by people at home with narrow ideas about women hindered her wish to have both passion and a mind. In Rome, she found freedom in not knowing or being known. (To find equal freedom, an Italian woman of her era might have expatriated herself elsewhere.) So, too, in *My Own Country*, Abraham Verghese, a doctor in Tennessee treating people with HIV, describes how frequently gay men left their small hometowns and moved to the city to find a place where they could possess their sexuality and their lives.

Anonymity in an urban setting is in some ways equivalent to solitude in nature. Like solitude, anonymity offers space. But because we are surrounded by other people, our aloneness is less complete and more easily disrupted. In an anonymous state, we are alone because we don't stand out or invite identification. No one interrupts us, we believe that no one notices us—though that is not certain. We may notice others and create their meaning without having to entertain their subjectivity. Anonymity, you might say, is privacy for people who don't want to be really alone.

Ernest Hemingway liked to write in places where he could be in the private world of his work, but still among people. In *A Moveable Feast,* he describes sitting and writing in a café when a pretty girl comes in. He would like to approach her, but he realizes she is waiting for someone—he assumes another man. Nevertheless, she becomes "his" because he can fantasize and write about her. He writes, "I've seen you, beauty, and you belong to me now, whoever you are waiting for and if I never see you again, I thought. You belong to me and all Paris belongs to me and I belong to this notebook and this pencil."[20]

Anonymity allows people to express thoughts or feelings they might suppress in a relationship where they feel ashamed, vulnerable, or frightened. Writing about the way anonymity permitted intimacy in the letters women wrote to the birth control crusader Margaret Sanger, her biographer Ellen Chesler recounts: "They wrote of strict and falsely modest mothers who had told them nothing of sex or birth control, of callous physicians who claimed ignorance of reliable methods, of husbands who abandoned them when they chose continence over the risk of another pregnancy, of illegal abortionists who cost them their fertility. They wrote with a sisterly affection and intimacy made possible by distance and anonymity."[21] When not worried about being identified, people will say what they are otherwise ashamed to say.

Anonymity is a tentative and unsteady state of privacy. In a hurry to get somewhere, a neighbor, stuck behind a car dawdling at a stoplight, honked her horn angrily. A few seconds later she became embarrassed when the driver, an elderly man, turned around and recognized her. She had expressed her dismay rudely because she felt anonymous. She assumed that her behavior would not be identified with her. This response and the embarrassment it sometimes occasions, familiar to all of us, is the stuff of contemporary urban life.

Honk a horn, deface a sign, state an unacceptable wish—anonymity supports the mischievous, the petty vandalisms against each other and authorities that give us room to mock perceived hegemonies and to release "incorrect" but genuine feelings. Unfortunately, crime and serious assaults are also based in anonymity. The terrorist, bank robber, housebreaker, and rapist cover their faces to hide their identities and to avoid social sanctions. They may know their victim, but hope not to be recognized by him.

The proliferation of certain kinds of crime testifies to the overabundance of anonymity in contemporary life. Like solitude, anonymity offers the most when it is temporary—and freely chosen. When undesired, anonymity leads to dehumanization and isolation. Many people, though they have friends, feel alienated and reduced because they participate in fragmented communities too large and impersonal to recognize or value them. Their anonymity becomes burdensome.

Sitting before computers linked by modems, some users of the Internet make up names, identities, true or untrue stories about themselves, and exchange unverifiable messages with other people. Good things come of it: vital exchanges, useful information, psychological adventure, creativity, and recreation. Yet the Internet reflects the culture's dilemma of too much anonymity. No one on it has to answer for himself. People make contact with each other, start to build relationships, exchange information, and cannot verify what is fantasy and what is fact. While this is an age-old problem, usually embodied in a story of a deceiving stranger who arrives in a village—like Wickham in *Pride and Prejudice*—it reaches almost absurd heights in computer relationships where no observing community is present to contradict an individual's deceptions.

Reserve, the third state of privacy is forbearance, tact, restraint. In a state of reserve, unlike solitude, we are together with people, and unlike anonymity, we are usually known to them. We may be intimate. Our state is private simply because we do not choose to reveal the full extent of what we feel, observe, think, or experience. We set aside our immediate perceptions, sometimes our frankest opinions—preserving them (and often us) for the future. Reserve is a house with glass walls, but no one mentions it.

Highly variable among cultures, reserve tends to be a type of privacy available in the absence of most others. The Utku Eskimos, who during the long arctic winters share close quarters with a number of family members, signal their wish for privacy by withdrawing into their own sleeping space, not speaking or responding to people around them. They are awake, but no one approaches them.[22] Kids on subways often use headphones to the same end, or family members, television. In situations where other privacy is denied or undesirable, reserve offers an opportunity to move away. The state is most easily sustained when surrounding people agree not to intrude.

Levels of reserve vary from person to person, family to family, neighborhood to neighborhood. Standards continually shift. At the end of *The Age of Innocence,* Edith Wharton's novel set in late-nineteenth-century New York society, Dallas Archer talks openly with his father, Newland Archer, about his parents' relationship. Contrasting Dallas to his parents, Wharton observes, "it had never been possible to inculcate in him even the rudiments of reserve."

On this occasion, Dallas brings up the passionate love for another woman that his father once felt and then renounced. He startles his father with the news that his mother knew about her husband's feelings. She told Dallas that Newland had given this love up at her request. Wharton writes:

> Archer received this strange communication in silence. His eyes remained unseeingly fixed on the thronged, sunlit square below the window. At length he said in a low voice: "She never asked me."
>
> "No. I forgot. You never did ask each other anything, did you? And you never told each other anything, you just sat and watched each other, and guessed at what was going on underneath. A deaf-and-dumb asylum, in fact! Well, I back your generation for knowing more about each other's private thoughts than we ever have time to find out about our own."[23]

Wharton suggests that in a state of reserve people do not necessarily know less about each other's private experience; they just learn by watching rather than speaking, and they preserve privacy by not speaking about what they believe they know. While Wharton—through Dallas—gently ridicules the idea, she also romanticizes it, implying that reserve does not obscure understanding, that perhaps it enhances it. In this sense, the privacy of reserve is the privacy of not being forced to openly acknowledge what it is known that you know.

Words can be indelicate, and can tear the fragile gauze of lifelong intimacy. In their inexactness or awkwardness, they may cause unnecessary pain by making something too explicit. Over a long marriage, each partner's love has vicissitudes. Does it do more harm or more good to document them aloud? When people live at close quarters, small irritations are frequent. Some are better unnamed. Some feelings can be universally understood to be present, and thus do not warrant expression.

Various types of reserve dominate most exchanges. Sometimes we lower our eyes or look away. Frequently adults admonish children, "Don't stare." We offer privacy by not letting our interest be noticed, by pretending not to hear something that is said, by deflecting with silence or platitude a remark that threatens to intrude into private space or to reveal "too much." Reserve is a cornerstone of civility. Its premise is that most exchanges are better off partial, most days improved by not telling much to many.

The disadvantages of reserve, and particularly the price to a person's life of being overly reserved, are explored in Kazuo Ishiguro's novel *The Remains of the Day*. The story is narrated by a butler who has devoted his life so entirely to serving a rich Englishman in a large mansion that he has forgotten himself. He has not married or had children. Stevens prides himself on being a superb butler, for whom reserve is an essential professional quality. One evening, in the middle of looking after his lordship's guests, Stevens is called to the attic bedside of his father who has just suffered a stroke and is dying. Though others gathered around the bed are visibly distraught, Stevens shows no emotion, saying dryly, "This is most distressing. Nevertheless, I must now return downstairs."[24]

For Stevens, it is a point of honor neither to show emotion nor to acknowledge feelings or behaviors in others that might reveal their personal state. The lack of acknowledgment preserves privacy. Reserve is the essence of the butler's art because a butler must be extremely intimate with the people he serves without developing the habits or expectations of intimacy. Normally, if you help or watch someone change from nightclothes to street clothes, you share a close relationship. You are good friends or lovers or a parent with a young child. But a butler often must view his employer intimately without taking it as an invitation to closeness. Unfortunately, Ishiguro implies, the demands of the job are ultimately so dehumanizing that anyone expert at it is rendered useless for more intimate human relationships.

Too much reserve leaves people isolated, misunderstood, and guessing. Do you like me or hate me? Are you angry or sad? Am I helping or hurting? People get edgy when they cannot figure out where they stand. Yet almost all exchanges require some holding back of what is thought or felt because our most private thoughts and feelings are too idiosyncratic, vacillating, boring, unsocialized, and bald to be more than occasionally tolerable to other people. The capacity for reserve is as important to sustaining intimacy as disclosure is. It offers a basic form of emotional safety.

"There are people," the psychoanalyst Leston Havens has observed, "to whom we would say nothing. Even when the hot iron comes toward us and the manacles are clamped tight, we will say nothing."[25] Havens is referring to the way in which we instinctively and at times powerfully recognize that revealing something about ourselves—no matter how trivial—to someone we judge as untrustworthy will harm us. Without the capacity and the freedom to stay silent, to guard one's psychic privacy, there is no possibility for authentic relationships. Sometimes reserve is the only way to resist people who have more power. It allows us to choose to whom we speak.

One evening after a large Los Angeles earthquake, I turn on the television news. The story begins innocuously enough with footage of a twisted freeway filmed from a circling helicopter. We see rubble, destroyed buildings, fires, broken water mains, and listen to residents recount ordeals. The scene shifts. We are at the site of an attempted rescue. An apartment has collapsed, and men and bulldozers are digging in the rubble. They have just found the body of a woman's only child, her daughter. The woman is out of sight, and then she comes into the camera frame, screaming.

I expect the camera to offer us one look at her and then cut away. But it does not. She is wearing a gray pantsuit and sunglasses, and she cannot stop running and screaming. Her husband tries to grab her and pull her into his arms, but her grief is so intense, her body cannot allow itself to be held still. A man at the scene stands looking away from her, his reserve intuitively granting her the privacy that the camera refuses to offer. I look away and back, in my mind telling them to stop, and finally when she settles for a moment in her husband's arms, the screen cuts back to the somber faces of our local news anchors.

As I go to bed, I cannot shake the profound trauma of a woman I have never met. Does the television news editor feel I must see her to understand that earthquake? Her grief is vivid and somehow timeless. She looks like a mother would look. Parents digging children out of the ash around Pompeii two thousand years ago would know just how she felt. The horror of the event is vividly transmitted. But there is something wrong with witnessing the intimate traumas of people we don't hold close. Violating her privacy by allowing the camera to defy reserve, we violate a collective standard of honoring life and death by shielding people when their suffering is extreme.

Intimacy is the fourth state of privacy.

I am standing with a friend on a long, crowded beach. It is a hot day, and we have rolled our slacks so that foam from the waves hits our ankles and splatters our legs. My children swim in the glare and green water, and we both watch them, vigilantly tracking their movements among those of other swimmers. People walk by us. We talk, but with eyes fixed on the water, we do not often look at each other. Standing with arms almost touching but eyes rarely meeting is conducive to good talk. This beach reminds my friend of one she used to visit as a child. She describes it, and then speaks of her life growing up. I am content, caught up in her story, and the large umbrella of intimacy with which it shelters us. In "Midrash on Happiness," Grace Paley writes about how much her happiness depends upon such moments. "To walk in the city arm in arm with a woman friend (as her mother had with aunts and cousins so many years ago) was just plain essential. Oh! those long walks and intimate talks, better than standing alone on the most admirable mountain or in the handsomest forest or hay-blown field."[26]

Intimacy is a private state because in it people relax their public front either physically or emotionally or, occasionally, both. They tell personal stories, exchange looks, or touch privately. They may ignore each other without offending. They may have sex. They may speak frankly using words they would not use in front of others, expressing ideas and feelings—positive or negative—that are unacceptable in public. (I don't think I ever got over his death. She seems unable to stop lying to her mother. He looks flabby in those running shorts. I feel horny. In spite of everything, I still long to see them. I am so angry at you I could scream. That joke is disgusting, but it's really funny.) Shielded from forced exposure, a person often feels more able to expose himself.

At moments, questions of intimacy become euphemistic questions of sex. "Are they intimate?" often means "Have they had sexual intercourse?" An intimate relationship may sometimes be observed in the way couples touch, kiss, or stand close in public, but many expressions of physical intimacy are private. Deep kissing, the touching with hands, mouths, or genitals or breasts, buttocks, and genitals tend to be private expressions of physical intimacy. Not all physical touching, even when it occurs in private, is intimate. One characteristic of violence is that it is contact—often to intimate areas of the body—without consent.

Sometimes out of lust, joy, lack of privacy, or the wish to shock, private touching occurs in public. Sometimes people get a kick (or an orgasm) out of being seen, of having others witness their pleasure. But often, making it public diminishes intimacy.

The heart of intimacy, its essence, is that in it one comes as close as one is capable of, or as close as one feels permitted, to revealing oneself to another person. One attempts to express frankly to another one's inner experiences, desires, feelings, and perceptions—though the expression is inevitably limited and incomplete. Intimacy requires trust and confidentiality. Intimacy may grow simply through experiencing events together, but often it grows through the sharing of private thoughts and feelings. The warp and woof of its development are the alternating cycles of revelation, bearable response, and gradually heightened trust. In the course of falling in love, each lover tells his beloved a story of his life. Othello recounts the effect of telling Desdemona about himself. "She thank'd me and bade me, if I had a friend that lov'd her, I should but teach him how to tell my story, and that would woo her. Upon this heat I spoke. She lov'd me for the dangers I had pass'd, and I lov'd her that she did pity them."[27]

Desdemona is wooed by Othello's story. She feels awe and tenderness, feelings that deepen love. He offers her a man she can admire, a person worthy of her affection. So, too, her sympathy wins him. He has revealed himself without feeling shame.

In *War and Peace,* Princess Natasha and Princess Marya, originally enemies, become intimate friends while sitting together at the deathbed of Prince Andrei—Marya's brother and Natasha's onetime fiancé. After Andrei dies, Natasha risks telling Marya of her love:

"Masha," she said, timidly drawing Princess Marya's hand toward her. "Masha, you don't think I'm wicked, do you? Masha, darling, how I love you! Let us be real, bosom friends!" . . .

From that day there sprang up between them one of those tender, passionate friendships that exist only between women. They were continually kissing and saying tender things to each other and spent most of their time together. If one went out, the other became restless and hastened to join her. Together they felt more in harmony than when apart. A tie stronger than friendship was established between them: that special feeling of life being possible only in each other's company.[28]

Love and intimacy are often wound together—though not always. We may preserve a habit of intimacy with people we no longer love. Loving someone, we desire increased intimacy. Put in a situation with another person where intimacy grows, we often come to feel love. And ultimately, love is private. Displayed too long before an audience, it becomes performance.

Intimate expressions occur in private because revelation makes people feel vulnerable. Imagine an intimate moment, then imagine it observed, and it changes. The sensibility jumps back, like an animal startled by a loud noise. Privacy not only sanctions intimacy, but appears to be a precondition of its most complete expression.

When people are not held, thrown, or forced together by geography, tradition, enslavement, simple dominance, economics, or kinship, then intimacy, chosen closeness based in love or tenderness, becomes a desirable alternative. Even were it not intrinsic to creativity, autonomy, and dignity, privacy would be invaluable simply for its role in supporting the possibility of rich and pleasurable intimacy.

A compelling image of Franklin Roosevelt is of him on his yacht relaxing by fishing, sleeping, and spending time with close friends. While president, Roosevelt drew enormous sustenance from the laughter, gossip, sexual intrigue, and warm friendships that privacy permitted. In the face of impossible political situations, he appreciated that creative public solutions often first came to mind when one was enjoying privacy. While Eleanor Roosevelt rarely relaxed, she too used private relationships for emotional sustenance. Whenever she wished to muster courage for a task that frightened or overwhelmed her, she would create intense, intimate friendships. The love emboldened her. Doris Kearns Goodwin's biography *No Ordinary Time* describes how much the courage and political force of both Roosevelts rested on their personal relationships.

Why is intimacy so sustaining? This question is key to understanding the importance of privacy. If aloneness is our predicament, then everything rests on finding ways to bear it. Love and friendship fulfill this mission. Love because it suggests we are acceptable and thus deserve to give and get respite. Friendship because it puts a person near us proffering this possibility. When, as Grace Paley suggests, we metaphorically or actually walk "arm in arm" with a lover or a friend, we have company with whom we can comment freely upon the passing scene, and each of us is allowed to be. As we will see in the next chapter, choosing the company we keep is both quite modern, and an important function of privacy.

Stevenson at the Inn

In September 1878, the twenty-seven-year-old Robert Louis Stevenson—not yet a successful writer—left Le Monastier, a tiny village in France, and began a strenuous twelve-day country hike. Arriving at night at the village of Bouchet St. Nicholas, Stevenson took a room at an inn, sharing it, he noted in his journal, with a family he had never met. Though a common rural practice, it stirred the young writer:

> The sleeping room was furnished with two beds. I had one; and I will own I was a little abashed to find a young man and his wife and child in the act of mounting into the other. This was my first experience of the sort; and if I am always to feel equally silly and extraneous, I pray God it be my last as well. I kept my eyes to myself, and know nothing of the young woman except that she had beautiful arms, and seemed no whit abashed by my appearance. As a matter of fact the situation was more trying to me than to the pair. A pair keep each other in countenance; it is the single gentleman who has to blush.[1]

The tiny *auberge,* a two-story cottage with a dirt floor and one guest room, had its kitchen adjoining the stable so that Stevenson and his donkey "could hear each other dining." "In the kitchen cooking and eating go forward side by side, and the family sleep at night. Any one who has a fancy to wash must do so in public at the common table."

I first learned about the night at the inn from Richard Holmes's book *Footsteps*. Holmes, a biographer, recounts how as a young man he decided to follow Stevenson's route through the French villages and replicate his walk. When I started thinking about privacy, I kept seeing Stevenson in the inn. Who was this man, and what was he doing there sharing a bedroom?

Robert Louis Stevenson, according to recent biographer Ian Bell, was "a deliberate exile, a man of no country but that of his own imagination."[2] When, in the mid-eighties, I encountered Stevenson through Holmes, he was mostly forgotten. Since then, he has surged back with multiple biographies appearing. The renewed interest arises partly because 1994 was the one-hundredth anniversary of his death, but also because his status as exile and world citizen so predicts contemporary life.

Robert Louis Stevenson thought of himself as a person apart, a bohemian. He endlessly displeased his long-suffering father by rejecting Calvinism, bourgeois propriety (he fell for his wife when she was married to someone else), and the family desire that he become a respectable engineer or lawyer. Raised in a conventional Scottish home, oppressed by the expectations he felt in Edinburgh and by his own lifelong bad health, Stevenson wanted out. Nowadays we barely notice such impulses; in fact, we are more surprised by the person who wants "in." Someone, for instance, who goes to live in a cult or a monastery makes us nervous. We worry about how membership swallows individual identity, how submission precludes choice. We bemoan a collective consciousness of a sort that has arguably dominated large portions of human history. Someone who lets a parent choose his career or spouse strikes us as weak. We worry about his sense of self, and forget how new are our expectations.

During Stevenson's lifetime, assertions of separateness still had some novelty. Not, as one might expect, because Stevenson's father was truly rigid and harsh, but because he was conflicted. Full of love for his son, the elder Stevenson wanted both to indulge him and to make him conform to propriety and tradition. The father's ambivalence made room for his son's rebellion. Thus Robert Louis would write—with true adolescent passion—a verse attacking "fine, religious, decent folk," which ends, "Give me the publican and harlot."[3]

The hike in France was one of many gestures he made to break away, explore the larger world, and write. This continued throughout Stevenson's life; when he died at age forty-four in Samoa, Tusitala, as they called him, was carried to his remote island grave by native chiefs.

You might say that Stevenson spent that night in the inn on the cusp of two sensibilities. The bedroom was not shared just by unrelated people, but by two worldviews—one rural and traditional, communal, the other quickly becoming urban, modern, and separate. Stevenson compares himself with the peasant couple. They are not self-conscious about the lack of privacy, but he is. The young woman looks at him unabashed. He keeps his eyes to himself. He blushes. She is used to such proximity, he assumes. He is not.

Imagine. The small bedroom is crowded by two beds. The one shuttered window is open; there is cool air and waning evening light. Stevenson tries not to look at the family in the other bed, particularly not at the young woman. But his glance falls on her arm. In spite of his discomfort and his fatigue from hiking all day, he thinks about her under the covers. He turns his back and un-buttons his pants, hampered by the embarrassment of removing boots and pants in front of strangers. He wonders if she can smell him. He coughs quietly and feels relieved that he brings up no blood. What if he has to use the chamber pot? He blushes at the thought. In bed, he props himself up on one elbow and writes in his journal, seeking distance from his awkwardness. He observes and records his own reaction. Awaiting sleep, his mind drifts be-tween images from his day's walk and of the family in the bed. Their presence accentuates his aloneness, and he misses Fanny Os-bourne, the married American woman with whom he is in love.

Imagining Stevenson's experience highlights what he did not write about: undressing, dreaming, longing, fantasizing, being ill, urinating, defecating, or loving. In his mind, these were private matters—certainly not for a journal he intended to publish. (*Ulys-ses* is still forty years in the future. Freud is only starting out.) In a letter Stevenson wrote a few years later, he bridled at the idea of telling his readers about his sickness, "the blood on [his] handker-chief." "I should think myself a trifler and in bad taste if I intro-duced the world to these unimportant privacies."[4]

But though we might find him reserved by the most open contemporary standards, his writing and his struggle contain a self-consciousness that we recognize. The creature may not be com-pletely hatched, but the shell rattles and cracks, the beak chips through. Stevenson observes himself. He records his reaction to the absence of privacy. By writing in a journal, he says his experience is important, his trip is important. His wish for more privacy for sleep is not just spoiled fussiness (a state he knew), but something intrinsic to the creation of a strong individual sensibility and the wish to live a life of one's own making.

Philippe Aries writes that "until the end of the seventeenth century, nobody was ever left alone. The density of social life made isolation virtually impossible, and people who managed to shut themselves up in a room for some time were regarded as exceptional characters."[5] In our dismay over narcissism and anomie, we forget how recent and basically untried is the idea of a more separate person.

If we were to reduce Stevenson's blush, his wish for privacy to its most basic level, we might call it an eye problem. He felt other people's eyes on him, and it made him uncomfortable. People have always been watched: by God, priests, and ministers, by sentries and soldiers, by their patriarchs, by their mothers, nurses, and neighbors. Watching people is the way we make them feel alive and safe, it is also—as we noted when describing surveillance—how we make sure they do what pleases.

We know from infant research that babies are hard-wired to engage with eyes. When my sons were tiny, I occasionally cut aluminum pie plates to resemble round faces with big eyes and smiling mouths. When I hung "pieman" from a chair so that he dangled over a baby lying on a blanket on the floor, the content infant would babble away, discussing the universe with his inanimate but attentive friend, hooked by the oversized fake eyes.

Watching is a crucial and central human experience, and one way we encourage a self in children. Watch me, a child demands. She demonstrates what she has learned, and if we approve, we applaud. We reinforce her mastery. We direct her self-esteem by encouraging her to aim at mastering what we admire. (We learn to admire what she masters.) We also inculcate an awareness of our watching as a way of monitoring behavior. In the past we often said, "God is watching you." Many still do, but in contemporary America the watching gods tend to represent diverse social perspectives.

What matters is not just the inevitable fact of eyes, but the moral and intentional frame we assign to them—the quality of their gaze. How they hold us or judge us matters. So, too, whether they belong to a collectively held authority, to a particular other person, or almost randomly to a billboard—as in *The Great Gatsby.* Whether and when they are loving or contemptuous is extremely important.

Stevenson, a sickly only child, was closely watched by his mother and father and by his nursemaid. Alison Cunningham, the nurse who helped to raise him, often spent nights as well as days with her charge. When, not infrequently, he was too sick to sleep, she stayed awake with him. She was intensely religious, and terrorized him with stories of an angry Calvinist God. For much of his childhood, he had awful nightmares about messing up and going to hell.

Stevenson's parents were both inclined to hypochondria. Made more anxious by parenting a single sickly child, they scanned everywhere for sickness. They scrutinized themselves and him in a hopeless contest against bacteria. They loved their son, and feared he'd die at any moment.[6] (In Western Europe and America, as the nineteenth century progressed, it seems that middle-class parents gave birth to fewer children but attached to each one more intensely.) As a child, unable sometimes to leave his bed for days, he escaped the intrusive adults, preserved his privacy, by voyaging within his mind. Stevenson made up stories and fantasies; he began his travels through fancy.

The result of such a childhood was a paradox. Those many anxiously watching eyes made Robert Lewis Stevenson feel important, but exposed. In all likelihood, they followed him to the inn in France and popped up on the other side of the bedroom. They probably accompanied him to Samoa. (His mother did.) My hunch is that he could sometimes make them look away, or close, but that internal associations and the reactions of others jostled them back wide open, watching him with their mix of praise, damnation, and overanxious concern. The paradox is that he could tolerate his separateness because they kept him company wherever he went.

In its most basic sense, having privacy is having control over our bodies, our possession, our intimate environment, and the information—whether by watching, listening, touching, or reading—other people can gather about us. The wish for privacy is the wish to control what is known or revealed about ourselves and our intimate world. I like Sissela Bok's succinct definition. Privacy is "the condition of being protected from unwanted access by others—either physical access, personal information, or attention."[7]

It turns out that the human mind plays privacy like a three-dimensional game of checkers. The added axis is the psyche, the subjective self that carries around feelings about eyes it has known, even when they are no longer there. Should I ever approach a musical instrument, I am stopped dead by the frown of a particularly sour clarinet teacher under whom I once squeaked. Long gone from my actual world, in the psyche she stands timeless, scowling, guarding the mind's gate against errant musical impulses.

Conversely, when we can create a sympathetic audience in our mind, it may increase our sense of privacy vis-à-vis internal and external critics, and it may allow us freedom. Stevenson wrote *Travels with a Donkey in the Cevenne* to Fanny. He was alone but in love; doubtless, she was on his mind as he hiked. Perhaps he addressed his journal to her. Likely as not, the idealization of new and intense romantic love allowed him to see himself—and his writing—with fresh and enthusiastic eyes. If his mother and father, and others in Edinburgh who disapproved of his wandering life devoid of typical ambition, watched him with disappointed eyes, what a relief it must have been to have them grow dim beside the brilliant beam of a new and approving gaze.

By suggesting that Stevenson was perched between worldviews when he shared a bedroom in the inn, I meant that the more separate urban man was encountering the more collective rural past. Urban life changed privacy, offering the possibility of more autonomy and personal freedom. This change dictated, for better and worse, that the eyes we think most about would go from outside—in our real communal surroundings—to inside our heads. There each of us would have to integrate and make peace with them. Communal eyes would be replaced, on the one hand, by the intensity of the small family, which, like Stevenson's parents and nurse, leans close over the cradle, and on the other, by less immediate authorities often internalized through our imaginations: media images, public opinion, and electronic surveillance by businesses and bureaucracies.

To understand both Stevenson and our present experience, it helps to start in the past when travelers sharing bedrooms was commonplace. They might have shared a bed. Consider Sarah Kemble Knight, traveling in 1704 on horseback from Boston to New York, who woke in her bed in an inn to find two strange men sharing a second bed in her room! Or Fanny Kemble, an Englishwoman traveling in the United States in 1839, who bristled when an innkeeper offered to put her in a bed with another woman. She protested and he apologized—but only because he had failed to realize that the women were unacquainted.[8]

Nor was tight space just for travelers. In colonial New England family members, friends, and strangers all shared beds. Furthermore, even when houses had more than one room, the wooden walls were full of knotholes not infrequently used—according to records of colonial court testimony—by the curious to watch other people's illicit encounters. People lived at close quarters. Rooms were often small and cramped. Separate space was frowned upon: In more than one colony during the seventeenth century, living alone was forbidden or heavily fined. It was taken for granted that people would watch each other. Obedience to God, family, and society demanded it. Common property—like shared grazing land—supported it, as did the limited daily mobility and the limited opportunities for other kinds of recreation. What else could you watch?[9]

Although these patterns changed—sometimes long ago—we remember them in fragments that survive today. For instance, an African-American woman who grew up thirty years ago in a small southern town described to me how closely her behavior was watched: One Sunday afternoon she sat on her boyfriend's lap out on his front porch. Someone who knew her family saw her, and word of her impropriety reached her parents before she had walked home. "I never," she exclaimed, "did that again!" The writer Annie Ernaux, recalls in her memoir, *La Place*, how, growing up in France after the Second World War, all the women in the village knew each other's menstrual cycles because they could see the pads hanging to dry on the laundry lines.

"The neighborhood," writes Antoine Prost, "is a public stage on which everyone is required to present his or her private life."[10] While some suburbs are heterogeneous and many people no longer see themselves as guardians of the block, some still do. In the early eighties, a woman living in a predominantly Irish neighborhood in a Boston suburb threw a party for the staff at the inner-city public school where she worked. Two African-American teachers came.

The next day, neighbors visited the woman and asked her why she had invited nonwhite guests. If outsiders see how nice the neighborhood is, the neighbors reasoned, they will want to buy houses.

In many places, well into this century, the community, not the family or the individual, defined the circle of privacy. In *Cider with Rosie,* a memoir of growing up in a village in the Cotswalds in England in the early part of this century, Laurie Lee recounts how the young men in his village murdered someone they disliked. Every villager knew exactly what had occurred, but no one revealed anything to the police inspector from London who came to solve the crime.[11] In *Colored People,* Henry Louis Gates describes growing up in a small African-American community in West Virginia. Everybody knew everything about everybody else's business. But white people, even those who lived nearby, were told nothing. In both memoirs, one witnesses a group life preserved by the wall of silence it builds around itself.

But what about the individual who thinks differently? In the past, in a village or small town, if you defied common values, where could you turn? Unless you left, there was much loneliness and little sanctuary. Perhaps the most moving moment in *The Scarlet Letter* occurs when Hester, ostracized by the community for her adultery, meets with her lover, Dimmesdale, in the forest. In the freedom of the woods, she unpins the letter from her chest, tossing it into a pile of leaves: "The stigma gone, Hester heaved a long, deep sigh, in which the burden of shame and anguish departed from her spirit. O exquisite relief! She had not known the weight until she felt the freedom."[12]

In the forest, away from the village, unobserved and in private, the moral disapproval of the community falls away from the outcast lovers, and they feel momentarily freed and enlivened. The dilemma of the village, the small town, the tight neighborhood, the dilemma of being known and observed, is that the pleasure of feeling known and related is accompanied by the demand to conform to the practices of the community. The margins for nonconforming private behavior and private choice is narrowed to protect the common life.

What individual privacy did exist in the past? It is hard to say. The quotient is complex, varied by moment, place, and individual mind. Suppose two sisters shared a bed and sometimes held each other as they fell asleep, watched each other pull dresses over undergarments, or listened to each other pray, but never told what they witnessed or said much about what they were feeling. Was their individual experience more or less private than if they slept in separate bedrooms but sometimes exchanged confidences?

Some comparisons about privacy can be made. First, however much one person in the past could observe another, he had to be nearby to manage it. In the days before the camera, telephone, tape recorder, car, and computer, information had to be obtained by watching, by speaking with a witness, or by speaking with someone to whom a story had been told. Information relied heavily upon human carriers.

Second, in many communal situations some privacy was supported by long-standing habits of modesty and reserve. Emilie Carles, a woman who grew up at the turn of the century in a small village in the French mountains and whose mother was killed by lightning when she was four, observed that although she followed her father everywhere and often shared a bed or a bedroom with him, she never recalled seeing him with less on than his long underwear. [13]

For people settling remote parts of America, there was wilderness to provide privacy. It was often easy for a person in search of solitude to walk to a private spot outside. America rarely managed the settled, established communal surveillance that Europe knew. People kept moving; land was abundant. Even when people were piled together, the greater proximity may have been counterweighted by a focus on common tasks.

Some people might have been expected to tell their sins to their priests or ministers, and many people may have told a lot to their god in their prayers or to each other in the form of stories or folktales, but fewer offered self-conscious descriptions of inner states to, for instance, a spouse. People who believed in an observing god lived in a subjective state where they assumed that a deity knew their thoughts and feelings, and their family and neighbors knew their actions. Most people were used to an intimate surveillance that, while not unlimited, tended to set the boundaries of privacy around families or whole communities rather than individuals.

As Americans left frontier farms and rural villages, they first moved into cities, then back out to suburbs. Suburbs were sometimes newly built; sometimes villages gradually changed beyond recognition by the increased population density and the altered living habits of their urban settlers. Starting just before the turn of the century, the arrival of the streetcar, the automobile, the telephone, the radio (and, later, television and the computer) began to make possible the suburban life that now dominates America.

Population statistics vividly document the enormous change in the size of community in which most people live. In 1790, the population of the United States was 3.9 million people, of whom about 5 percent were considered urban dwellers—a total of about 190,000 people. But in the 1790 census, anyone who lived in a town of more than 2,500 was counted as an urban dweller! The largest of the twenty-four urban centers had a population of 50,000 people; most had between 5,000 and 10,000. And 95 percent of the population lived in smaller places.

One hundred years later, in 1890, the United States had 63 million people with about 33 percent living in the cities. And the cities had grown enormously: 1,318 places had more than 2,500 inhabitants, three had 1 million or more.

Today the population of the United States is over 255 million people, of whom *75 percent live either in cities or in suburbs.* In the most recent census, thirty-five cities had populations exceeding 1 million people. In fact, there were 126 "large metropolitan areas" with populations greater than 150,000 people. A total of 960 places in 1988 had populations greater than 25,000 people.[14]

The "typical" American, according to census data, is now a married woman who lives in the suburbs in a three-bedroom house, works as a clerk for a private company or corporation, commutes to work alone in her car, and has two telephones and two television sets, which she watches for more than twenty-eight hours a week. She is Protestant and does not attend church weekly.[15] She and her husband have their own bedroom, possibly with a lock on the door, often with its own bathroom and television. The children are likely to have their own bedrooms, certainly their own beds, and maybe their own television. Even though the "typical" adult is married, an historically unparalleled percentage of adults live alone.

People not only have much more physical privacy than they once had, but as wealth has increased and suburbs have grown, people have consistently decreased their community involvement so that they have more social privacy. Control over private behavior, previously in the hands of the family, the community or neighborhood, and the church, is now redistributed, with more power granted on the one hand to individuals, and on the other, at a greater distance, to the bureaucracies and institutions that attempt to keep track of vast numbers of mobile people. This change, its scope and rapidity, is so dramatic that we have not really begun to comprehend it.

Remarkably, a contemporary adult living in a suburb is unlikely to have more than a few people in her life who have known her across time and in varied settings. Chances are her family and her childhood friends no longer live in the same neighborhood nor work for the same company. She is likely to live in a suburb where she wasn't born, and where her family history is not known, where she, in fact, is not well known. Her church attendance is erratic, and she belongs to few local organizations. Unless she is in her car, her house, or at work, it is hard for her to go somewhere where she will not encounter strangers. Her life is more private because the whole scope of her experience is not coherently observed by people who know her.

In contemporary urban America, people are continually surrounded by strangers. At the large suburban supermarket fifteen minutes from our house, where I shop, I can remember only one or two occasions when I encountered someone I knew. Though I now recognize several employees' faces, I know no one there well enough to greet. Shopping, for suburbanites, is often not a social experience. At its worst, it has become an indifferent, impersonal, anonymous hour in a vast warehouse that makes one long for the village market or the neighborhood grocery store. But such nostalgia finesses ambivalence. People have continually sought to increase their privacy and enlarge their private life—the portion of their life relatively unmonitored and uncontrolled by others. "My favorite thing to do when I leave a long draining day of work," a colleague who works with hospitalized children muses, "is to drive to a mall where I know no one, and just wander around. It's so relaxing to be anonymous." A neighbor comments, "Don't wax nostalgic with me about the joys of communal life and extended families. I grew up in one that was awful and unsupportive. I couldn't wait to get out."

The amount of privacy possible in suburbia is historically remarkable. As I sit here writing, my husband is at work, and my children are at school. No boarders, relatives, servants, or slaves are present, and I am alone in my house. No one observes me or knows how I spend my time. It is a rare occasion when someone knocks at the door. Should I decide not to answer, there are no necessary consequences. The answering machine filters telephone calls, and I can choose not to speak. Only if I announce my destination does a neighbor know where I'm going when I set out by car or on foot. No one censures me on whom I invite to dinner, what I wear, how I raise my children, whether I worship, when I menstruate, whom I vote for, what I believe, the kind of birth control I use, the organizations I belong to, or most other dimensions of my daily life outside of work. Even at my work, as a clinical social worker in an urban hospital and a psychotherapist in private practice, little of what I do is observed, and certainly not by neighbor, employer, or minister.

I am one type of typical American. At the beginning of the century my Italian Catholic grandmother, then a six-year-old child, crossed the ocean with her family from Naples to New York. The man she married immigrated from Naples some years later. Around 1905, my Russian Jewish grandfather left a small village outside of Kiev and eventually landed in Brooklyn. The woman he would marry arrived about the same time from another similar Russian village. My parents met in New York City, married against both their fathers' wishes, and moved to Oregon. I grew up in Oregon, Vermont, and Massachusetts. I married a man whose forebears were Dutch and English, Protestant, and who lived variously in New York, Texas, and Pennsylvania, where he was born. Eventually, he too moved to Massachusetts. In twenty years, we've lived in three different Boston suburbs.

What group do we belong to? What land do we inhabit? Like birds blown out of flocks by a fierce hurricane, we—and so many of our peers—find ourselves in unfamiliar territory. Imagine such a place after a storm, an acre turned aviary, crowded with unmatched birds, where the arctic tern circles above the flamingo, and the kestrel perches beside the parrot. Baffled by dislocation and difference, but grateful for dry ground and invigorated by novelty and possibility, each goes about its business.

The enormous amount of everyday privacy is not the whole story. Ironically, because of developments in technology and the growth of data-collecting bureaucracies, increased privacy in one realm is forfeited in others. The simultaneous trends are so at odds that the result is bizarre. I might commit adultery without being pinned with a scarlet *A*. I could declare atheism and not, like Robert Louis Stevenson, enrage my father. (Or like Americans in the early nineteenth century, face criminal proceedings.) Yet if I drive alone in my car, stop at a random gas station, and pay with a credit card, I am easily traced. The technology exists for a satellite to photograph my license plate, a computer to run the plate number by its master list of registered cars and transmit the data to a police car. Though I may feel anonymous, a police officer can identify mine amidst thousands of other cars on a superhighway.[16]

If I work for an employer that chooses to do so, my telephone calls may be monitored or recorded, my presence in the bathroom filmed, any computer messages I send to other employees read, my urine screened for alcohol or drugs.

At a doctor's office, I am assured of no more privacy. Once the doctor files an insurance claim, the private details of my medical condition are sent to an insurance company, stored in databanks, and may be given or sold to other interested parties, including potential employers. From the time I walk into a grocery store, public building, or bank, a video camera may film me continually.

We have replaced watching each other at firsthand with keeping track of each other at a distance. Federal record keeping is a twentieth-century development. It was not until after 1930 that even 90 percent of births and deaths in the United States were recorded. There was no such thing as a passport before 1914, and in fact, it was not regularly required during peacetime until the fifties. Only in the mid-forties did the government start using Social Security numbers as identification numbers on government files.[17] The FBI was founded in 1908, but functioned as a part of the Justice Department until 1935.

The word *bureaucracy* entered the English language in the mid-nineteenth century, and the phrases *databank* and *credit bureau* have appeared within the past quarter century. Starting in the sixties and seventies, writers like Alan Westin and Vance Packard warned of the loss of privacy inherent in the growth of federal bureaucracy and new types of technology; for the past twenty years, the phenomenon has intensified. In 1962, there were 1,030 computers in the whole federal government; by 1989, there were 100,000 micro computers, 27,000 mainframe computers, and more than 170,000 mainframe computer terminals.[18]

Beyond its significant marketing function, contemporary data gathering replaces accountability based on personal relationships and community norms with mass society "crime" prevention. Unfortunately, the technology of surveillance is so sophisticated that the little protection individuals have depends on the discretion of data managers and on laws protecting privacy. Government agents or private agencies can easily spy on and monitor anyone they choose. Published transcripts of the Prince of Wales' liaison with his mistress were less interesting for their revelation of the prince's stated wish to become a tampon than for the insight they offered into the surveillance capacity of the British government, which was said to be able to monitor any phone conversation or fax transmission *anywhere* in the world.[19]

While life-saving, helpful, and at times supportive of necessary communal functions, such technology has an equal potential for violating privacy and facilitating repressive social control. In the wrong hands—probably each of our hands at the right moment, and some people's hands all the time—it is dangerous and easy to abuse. The difference between the social control of the traditional community and the modern state is the potential for dehumanization through technology and large-scale bureaucracy versus the more personal cruelty and repressiveness of village violence. Personal contact and shared purpose were the compensation communities offered—a sense of belonging, of recognizing passing faces, of feeling known and sometimes valued.

Data collection provides information outside of the mitigating context of relationships. If two people have lived next door to each other all their lives, attended the same school and church, and had children who play together, they will hold what they know about each other differently than the way a bureaucrat employed by a credit bureau holds either of them. People today live with a greater feeling of daily privacy, but in many ways, it an illusion—a kind of virtual privacy. No one knows you very well, but many strangers hold pieces of your life. On the other hand, there are times when it is very relieving not to deal with people who know you. The indifferent bureaucrat has his place.

Furthermore, technological surveillance makes life convenient. I may, for instance, use my credit card all over the world. Surveillance also sometimes makes life safer. I like the little camera above my head if I bank by machine in isolated places. The fact that terrorists are often quickly arrested testifies to the usefulness of the capacity to trace purchases and telephone calls. While not convincing to the jury in the O.J. Simpson trial, DNA evidence will doubtless help solve some serious crimes. But the liability of this greater capacity to track people is that we are increasingly reliant on government restraint and on effective laws. There is no doubt that would-be dictators armed with all the powers of contemporary surveillance technology can become more successfully repressive. So, too, company bosses acting in the name of "efficient" management. Companies increasingly feel entitled to monitor telephone conversations or e-mail.

The enormous domain of daily contemporary life has far outdistanced the range of traditional village life where the boundaries of information usually followed the paths of personal contact. On the most basic level, this dislocation underlies the way in which privacy is now so different. The AT&T suggestion that we use a telephone to "reach out and touch someone" provides the perfect paradox. The telephone extends the *reach* of all who wish to exchange private information, far beyond the *range* of touch.

The solitude of the wilderness, the community of villages and neighborhoods, has gradually given way to the contemporary suburb, which holds vestigial pieces of each of these places, but belongs to none of them. Today the descendant of Robert Louis Stevenson traveling alone could sleep alone, whether in the smallest village inn or, more likely, in a hotel so large and impersonal that one guest is unlikely to greet another in the lobby, much less share a bedroom. Locked in his room, he could watch Oprah on television and witness strangers disclose intimate details of their lives. Alone in his bathtub, bathroom door locked, clutching his portable phone, he could telephone anywhere in the world and speak as intimately as he cared to. If some bored detective or government employee chose to listen in, chances are Stevenson's great-grandchild would never know. How bored, lonely, or content this contemporary traveler felt would—more than in the past—depend on how much company he sought, how much contact he chose to make.

4

Reverend Beecher and the Press

It is no coincidence that during the same decade Robert Louis Stevenson was sharing a bedroom in an inn and struggling to become a citizen of a larger world, the American newspaper industry was coming into its own. This juxtaposition might sound odd, but, in fact, newspapers expanded in nineteenth-century America to fill voids created by the greater anonymity of urban life and the increased privacy—and anxiety about privacy—of citizens.

In the last quarter of the nineteenth century, newspaper publishers massively raised circulation in part by convincing the public that they would guard citizens against corruption within the new, urban institutions. Since a city dweller could not know firsthand what his elected officials were doing or how tax-supported public services were running, the press would watch on his behalf. In their investigative function, newspapers attempted to compensate for the loss of personal surveillance once possible in small towns.

But less widely recognized is how newspapers also offered what we might call mass psychological surveillance. As individuals moved into communities where they were more anonymous, printed gossip and celebrity stories became more important. The stories offered characters and dramas for citizens to share. They also let people know that someone was still watching—if not them, then at least their celebrity proxies.

Though he is mostly forgotten today, the story of Rev. Henry Ward Beecher powerfully illustrates the important emergent dilemmas of privacy and private life, and its ties to the development of newspapers and celebrity culture. Reverend Beecher was the most famous and successful minister in post–Civil War America, some said "the greatest man of this half century." An affable, charismatic, smart, warm, and lonely man who knew how to write popular sermons (carried in many newspapers) that caught the spirit of the time, Beecher became a huge celebrity.

In 1875, Henry Ward Beecher was put on trial for adultery, and the case was covered in the newspapers with an intensity unprecedented in American journalism. Never before had any single story received such sustained attention. When, one cold January Sunday, Mrs. Henry Ward Beecher strolled from Brooklyn to Manhattan across the frozen East River, a *New York Herald* reporter followed her and reported that Mrs. Beecher "experienced no fear of the fragile nature of the bridge," implying that the white-haired and dour Eunice Beecher was used to life on "thin ice."[1] Her loss of privacy occasioned by the reporter's presence—a new development—escaped comment.

The Beecher story is the late-nineteenth-century equivalent of the contemporary coverage of the trials of O.J. Simpson and Susan Smith. It is a mistake to think of these recent media cases as a new phenomenon. The television camera and the very "intimate" interview are new, but the style originated well over a hundred years ago. As in the present, legal battles that caught the public eye were about more than a defendant on trial.

When, in late October 1872, *Woodhull and Claflin's Weekly* published the first accusations against Beecher, one hundred thousand copies of the little paper sold out. The publishers, Victoria Wood-hull and here sister Tennessee Claflin, were jailed, accused of sending obscene materials through the mail. They had made, raged a U.S. Attorney, "a most abominable and unjust charge against one of the purest and best citizens . . . of the United States."[2] Abominable or not, the story of adultery quickly found its way into the daily newspapers.

By the summer of 1874, charges were flying back and forth, and so much gossip had been printed that Beecher's church, the congregationalist Plymouth Church of Brooklyn, felt forced to launch its own inquiry. It was to be confidential, but testimony and private letters written by Beecher, his lover Elizabeth Tilton, and her husband, Beecher's former close friend Theodore Tilton, made their way into the press and were reprinted or summarized in newspapers all over the country. In July, when Beecher addressed the church commission, the Associated Press *alone* sent thirty reporters to take down his words.[3]

At the beginning of the trial in January 1875, a jaded *New York Daily Tribune* reporter yawned that it was likely to be a boring event as every detail "had already appeared in print." He could hardly have been more wrong. In fact, the courtroom, meant to hold three hundred, was daily crammed with twice that number, and thousands of others were turned away by the police. Six hundred people dressed in wet wool (soaked by the bad January weather) and crowded together soon created such a stench that perfume machines were installed, and perfume was regularly sprayed into the air.[4]

New York newspapers hired stenographers and published each day's testimony verbatim. Telegraph wires, some strung directly into the court, sent summaries to newspapers all over the country. According to Robert Shaplen in *Free Love and Heavenly*

Sinners (originally a 1954 *New Yorker* piece), one enterprising reporter climbed a tree across from a witness's home so that he could peer into a window. Fearful of missing something should he decamp, he stayed put and sucked food through a hose.[5]

Reporters in the courtroom used opera glasses to study Mrs. Beecher while she sat stoically—day in and day out for the six months of the trial—beside her sixty-two-year-old husband listening (until the following July, when he was acquitted) to testimony about his improprieties. "Half a dozen times yesterday there looked to be an incredulous smile upon her face, but when closely inspected the smile seemed to have retreated into the strange, cold countenance," observed the *New York Herald* at the start of the trial.[6]

In 1875, no newspaper could reproduce photographs, and few dailies printed illustrations. Many Americans weren't quite sure even what their president looked like. In the absence of images, reporters wrote long descriptions with frequent references from literature to capture their subject: "If you will take the popular picture of Longfellow's Evangeline, the small headed wistful girl looking out to sea, and whiten the hair and increase the pain on the face, you will very nearly arrive at an idea of Mrs. Beecher."[7]

Though the first newspaper interview—of Rosina Townsend, the madam of a house of prostitution where a grisly and sensational murder had occurred—had been printed in 1836, no newspaperman would have felt it proper to put prying questions to Mrs. Beecher. (This prohibition also ensured that she would not offer a separate point of view about her situation.) If what she thought and felt could be gleaned from her face, fine, but beyond that, she was a married "lady," and her feelings were private. A polite question to her about a Sunday outing may well have been pushing the limits of etiquette. Reading the discrete remarks about

Mrs. Beecher's walk on the ice in the context of contemporary television, one has the sense of having followed a huge river to a tiny,
burbling source.

In 1855, when Theodore Tilton married Elizabeth Richards,
Henry Ward Beecher performed the service. Although Elizabeth
was the original member of the congregation, Beecher and Theodore became fast friends, attracted to each other in part by their
shared interest in abolition and women's rights. The men got along
so well that Tilton, a journalist, sometimes wrote newspaper articles in Beecher's name to help the minister keep up with the overwhelming public demand. Tilton's career prospered, and by the
1860s he was the editor of the country's most popular religious
weekly, *The Independent,* the owner of a large house in Brooklyn,
and a sought-after lecturer. Eager to be in the company of other accomplished people, he made his home a gathering place for intellectuals and political activists.

Henry Ward Beecher was even more of a phenomenon. One
of thirteen children of a twice-married rural Connecticut minister,
Lyman Beecher, and brother to the writer Harriet Beecher Stowe,
Henry moved to Brooklyn in 1848, where he preached and wrote
so successfully that he became a national idol. Tourists put him on
their itineraries, and as many as three thousand people came on
Sundays to hear him, often crowding onto ferries from Manhattan
dubbed "Beecher boats."

How popular people embody (and create) their era is always
telling. Audiences loved Beecher's sermons partly because he was
an exuberant performer who acted out his ideas and wept openly
when moved. But the sermons also offered his parishioners a more
relaxed religious philosophy compatible with their new urban and
increasingly commodity-oriented life. In the course of the nineteenth century, Americans began to move to cities. Forced by de-

pleted farmland to abandon rural towns, looking for work and good times, they often left behind the families, churches, and community structures that had dictated and monitored behavior. The city offered them not only a chance to make money, but a hitherto unimaginable degree of liberty and anonymity. Beecher's sermons sanctioned this new life with its greater privacy.

What made Beecher's "gospel of love" so popular, the historian Altina Waller has argued, was that it adapted ideas from transcendentalism to justify the new—more private—life. Again and again, Beecher admonished his listeners to value the ties of the heart—of affection and "affinity"—above the ties of duty to kin and community. Waller writes, "Beecher's genius was that he articulated for the uprooted individuals of his congregation a set of values that might replace contractual bonds with affinity—a mysterious, psychological attraction that most closely resembled the intuitive emotions of women."[8]

Rather than duty, Beecher felt that this love "should be a model for all types of human relationships; husband-wife, parent-child, male as well as female friendships." The love would guide a person toward virtue, so he would no longer need "the external coercion of government, doctrine or family in order to lead an honest, moral, successful life."[9]

The cities, Beecher argued—and stenographers who sat through his sermons made sure that his words were recorded verbatim for newspapers all over the United States—offered a new universe that could be successfully and morally navigated by those who took their bearings from their hearts. Beecher suggested that private feeling could become a source of morality, one that might replace external coercion. In 1858, one of his parishioners published a book of his comments she had transcribed. His intimate approach shows in the text:

I NEVER knew my mother. She died when I was three years old that she might be an angel to me all my life. But one day, in after years, turning over a pile of old letters in my father's study, I found a packet of her letters to him, beginning with her first acquaintance with him, and coming down into her married life; and as I read those pages, at last I knew my mother. . . . I remember that there was one letter in which she first spoke freely and frankly of her love. That, to me, is the Gospel of John. It is God's love letter to the world.[10]

Striking about this passage is the recognition of letters as a repository of intimacy, the revelation of his parents' private feelings, and insight into how the early loss of his mother helped create his later emphasis on love.

Beecher's own family relationships had not been happy. After his mother died, he spent a lonely childhood frightened of his demanding, authoritarian father and the terrible visions of hell he preached. Nor was his marriage happy; he found his wife cold and felt poorly understood. Soon after their wedding, the Beechers had moved away from her family in Massachusetts to Indiana, where she was lonely and unhappy. It is hard to tell if she was a miserable person or merely miserable in the marriage. In mid-nineteenth-century America, divorce was rare and stigmatizing. Whatever the cause of their unhappiness, Beecher complained about her to various friends, and later, when they had moved to Brooklyn, sought refuge in the Tilton household and the company of his close younger friend, Theodore. At Tilton's urging, Beecher also befriended Elizabeth and the Tilton children.

Beecher's unhappiness might not have led to an affair with Elizabeth had she not also been lonely. By the mid-1860s, Elizabeth and Theodore's marriage was rocky. As Theodore became more successful, he became contemptuous of his wife. He criticized her lack of sophistication, despised her family, hectored her about her failings, made fun of the way she spoke, and on at least one occasion told her, "Don't keep near me. I do not wish comparisons to be made."[11] He was ambitious, moody, and full of himself, and felt that her imperfections reflected badly on him. To maintain a large house in style, Tilton lived beyond his means, and he could lessen his debt only by lecturing. Consequently, by the mid-1860s, he was frequently on the road. On at least one occasion, Tilton slept with a woman he met—and told his wife.[12]

During this same time, Henry Ward Beecher was trying to write a novel, and although the book was due at the publishers, he had writer's block. He needed an admiring muse and found one in Elizabeth. She praised his writing, and he praised her. The book progressed. (Unfortunately for posterity, the result was many hundreds of unreadable pages, called *Norwood.*) Although Beecher was famous for *not* making pastoral calls, from 1866 on he made many to the Tilton household, especially when Theodore was away.

During the summer of 1868, the Tiltons' new baby died of cholera; in the fall, Tilton departed on another speaking tour, and Elizabeth turned to Beecher for solace. In October 1868, they became lovers, and continued a sexual relationship for the next year and a half. They justified their passion in the language of religion and affinity, and kept it secret until 1870, when Elizabeth confessed to Theodore, who was beside himself.

The Tiltons' unhappiness might have remained private had they not had so many well-connected friends. Unfortunately, in their rage and confusion, the people in whom they separately confided—the suffragists Victoria Woodhull, Elizabeth Cady Stanton, and Susan B. Anthony, and Tilton's boss, Henry Bowen, a successful newspaper publisher—were public people with power who had their own axes to grind. On her deathbed, Bowen's first wife, Lucy, had confessed a liaison with Beecher, and the memory festered.

It was the women's rights advocate Victoria Woodhull who blew apart the elaborate cover-up constructed by Tilton and Beecher—the two having become reluctant co-conspirators when they realized that bad publicity could destroy them both. Woodhull, who had learned of the affair early and may well have slept with both Beecher and Tilton, had alienated the public by her outspoken politics. Beecher's sisters were among many people who publicly mocked and criticized her for her advocacy of free love. Why not enjoy a little revenge by telling on their famous brother? The Beecher sisters, she opined in her newspaper, had no business snubbing her, since a gentleman informant has assured her that Henry Ward Beecher "preaches to at least twenty of his mistresses every Sunday."[13]

Such a mess. And at the same time, such a lively story, of intrigue, fame, double standards, human frailty, and Victorian manners. What makes the tale worth retelling more than a century later is not just its good gossip. The Beecher scandal is one of the first great American media/privacy stories. It is the template for contemporary stories, having helped define the way that the press, celebrities, and the public play off each other about private matters. Furthermore, it suggests how easily a philosophy that encourages private love as moral creed can break its banks and spill over into public scandal.

When Victoria Woodhull denounced—or perhaps we should say when she "outed"—Henry Ward Beecher, it was not because she disapproved of his sexual practices. Just the opposite, she argued that he was a great man, that great men tended to have great sexual appetites, and that these appetites needed to be indulged. What she found insufferable—as radicals typically do with liberals—was his hypocrisy: "Speaking from my feelings, I am prone to denounce him as a poltroon, a coward and a sneak . . . for failing to stand shoulder to shoulder with me and others who are endeavoring to hasten social regeneration which he believes in."[14] She was furious because, like her, he believed that relationships should be private, but when push came to shove, he left her alone on the barricade:

> I believe in the law of peace, in *the right of privacy*, in the sanctity of individual relations. It is nobody's business but their own, in the absolute view, what MR BEECHER and MRS TILTON have done or may choose at any time to do, as between themselves. And the world needs, too, to be taught just that lesson. I am the champion of that very right of privacy and of individual sovereignty. But, that is just one side of the case. I need, and the world needs MR BEECHER's powerful championship of this very right.[15]

Victoria Woodhull's assertion of a right to privacy may be the *first* American public cry for such a right. But it was more likely her championing of free love that kept her off many people's dinner list. (According to biographer Lois Beachy Underhill, it was Woodhull's sudden espousal of communism that really galled. A rather dramatic departure since Woodhull, a famous Vanderbilt protégé, had opened the first woman-run brokerage on Wall Street.) Eventually Woodhull grew weary, reversed her views on marriage, moved to England, married an aristocrat, and scrambled to keep her upper-class British relatives from uncovering too much of her flamboyant past.[16]

Why, Victoria Woodhull wondered, should she catch all the criticism and Beecher all the glory, while she was merely openly advocating the practices that he was privately consummating? He, in turn, felt that she was a loose cannon rolling his way. Her invitation that he join her was an invitation to commit public suicide.

Yet, though they may have wished to strangle each other,

Beecher and Woodhull were both social reformers who shared the premise that increasing some types of privacy—protecting intimacy, shielding relationships from public surveillance, leaving people alone—was a good idea, even the basis for a better world. Beecher seemed to have viewed his own adulterous affairs as the occasional by-product of his efforts to explore spirituality and morality in friendship and love. It is easy to see Beecher's philosophy merely as a smoke screen for his lust or as a rationale for his narcissism, but doing so misses half the story. However hypocritical and destructive some of his actions, he was grappling with a real problem. As was Victoria Woodhull.

In both their experience, traditional, authoritarian family life had been painful. Woodhull's father and alcoholic first husband had both abused her. Beecher, it seems, sorely felt his lack of maternal love. They were trying to define a way of living that would allow freer, fuller, and richer private relationships. This would include the freedom for a woman to control her sexuality or leave an abusive husband, for a child to renounce destructive parents, for a man to seek from a second the love a first wife didn't provide—the freedom to make private choices in search of intimacy and love that were not exclusively controlled by external codes. Much of what they sought has in fact become law or common practice.

A similar complex web of intimate friendships that thrived among the transcendentalists thirty years earlier is described by Joan Von Mehren in her biography of Margaret Fuller, *Minerva and the Muse*. Their experiments, though less overtly sexual and more cerebral, prefigure Beecher and Woodhull. Fascinated by the possibility of intimacy, by passionate friendships, by the development of their own ideas and psyches, men and women like Ralph Waldo Emerson, Bronson Alcott, Sarah Ripley, and Elizabeth Palmer Peabody held long conversations and wrote many letters to each other. Recounting a similar phenomenon even earlier (in a seventeenth-century London salon), Theodore Zeldin writes, "As the yearning for more intimate conversation grew, and the obsession with sincerity became more absolute, only letters seemed an adequate refuge for the pondered exchange of private thought."[17] One thinks of Vermeer's seventeenth-century woman, alone at the window, letter in hand.

Von Mehren describes how the transcendentalists read each other's diaries or circulated packets of their letters. For example, Margaret Fuller lent Ralph Waldo Emerson portfolios of letters she had exchanged with Sam Ward and Anna Barker.[18] Deeply interested in the individual, both Fuller and Emerson understood that people could use privacy in the form of intimate friendship to explore and expand each other and themselves. In a sense, they anticipated something that later would become codified within psychotherapy.

Emerson was drawn to Margaret Fuller. He loved her, at times intensely, but she made him nervous. When she drowned, shipwrecked tragically within sight of Fire Island returning from Italy with her husband and son, Emerson was grief stricken. He sent his friend Thoreau to look for traces of her or her manuscript that might have floated ashore. On July 19, 1850, Emerson wrote in his journal, "I have lost in her my audience." Emerson's comment is poignant, his loss devastating. Anne Sexton wrote, "You don't write for an *audience,* you write for some *one* who'll understand." Margaret understood.

A few paragraphs later, Emerson continues:

> She poured a stream of amber over the endless store of private anecdotes, of bosom histories which her wonderful persuasion drew out of all to her. When I heard that a trunk of her correspondence had

been found and opened, I felt what a panic would strike all her friends, for it was as if a clever reporter had got underneath a confessional and agreed to report all that transpired there in Wall Street.[19]

No doubt Emerson felt his share of panic remembering the private thoughts and feelings he had confessed to her. The translation of his fears into an image of a reporter under the confessional is vivid and prescient. It captures perfectly the dilemma of privacy that encourages intimacy and self-disclosure: Feeling more alone, I feel more urge to confide. By confiding in you, I am freed to become more myself because your love and interest confirms and emboldens me. But I also worry how you will hold what I have told you, how you will feel toward me, what you will say to others. What will happen to me if my private words are broadcast abroad, turned into headlines? How will I bear the shame of being seen and known in ways I did not intend? What is said in one moment, in one context, might be repeated and misconstrued in another.

Emerson's journal entry suggests that the turn inward toward the more private self made the development of the image of a nosy press (the reporter under the confessional) psychologically predictable. The press became the collective projection of the anxiety, guilt, and shame people felt not only about revealing their thoughts and feelings, but probably also about an upsurge of illicit wishes. Tempted by increased privacy to confessions or actions that could publicly shame them, people handled their anxiety in part by worrying that newspaper reporters were spying on them. For famous people like Emerson, this could have been true; for most, it had little basis in fact. But because people tend to read celebrity stories feeling unconsciously, "I wish this had been me" or "I fear this could have been me," there was a psychological identification that gave basis to their fears.

In the late nineteenth century, newspapers offered the diverse city dwellers stories they could hold in common. Collective stories create a shared culture, and their task was partly to replace the informal gossip of village life; it was impossible to whisper fast enough to pass important gossip to a whole city, and few were inclined to whisper to strangers.

During the era of the American Revolution, when newspapers first proliferated, it was not because they sent reporters to write up precise and evenhanded political stories. There were no reporters. Newspapers were produced by printers, and they made a place for themselves by printing gossip. They collected hearsay—often allegations against British soldiers—circulating on the street. In the years leading up to the Revolution, writes the newspaper historian Thomas Leonard, "printers were modest about claiming their news was true."[20]

Truth was secondary. What mattered was spreading a story that spoke to people. Since their earliest days, newspapers have had two main purposes. One has been to provide information—the departure schedules of boats, a merchant's list of wares, the time and place of public meetings, bits of domestic and foreign news. Their other function has been to address the collective psyche. In its barest outline, the psychological struggle of the revolutionary era was over the question of whether or not you owed obedience to your father, Great Britain. Was his authority legitimate, and therefore were you bad for defying him? Or was he corrupt, and therefore were you entitled to rebel? Stories were gathered and published, debating the psychological point. When the colonial newspapers spread stories about a grandfather who found a British soldier in bed with his granddaughter, they were declaring "father" corrupt.

The media serves a similar psychological function today. An astute friend observed during the 1991 Clarence Thomas/Anita Hill hearings that the debate captured the attention of the American public because it spoke to deep collective psychological fears in contemporary Americans. Every woman fears that she will be harmed by a man—in private, without witnesses—and no one will believe her accusation. At the same time, every man fears he will be accused of harming a woman in private, without witnesses, and that he will be unable to prove his innocence.[21] The Thomas/Hill fight perfectly captures the dilemma of a culture anxiously exploring the idea of gender or racial equality, particularly a culture where life is so private that much can occur without witnesses.

Saying that people tune into private stories because they are prurient, titillating, and gossipy and that the media plays the stories to make money is true, but it misses the psychological draw—why money can be made. The stories that really catch hold are the ones that embody pressing psychological themes—collective conscious and unconscious struggles that are seeking resolution.

The reason I followed the Woody Allen/Mia Farrow battle, and avidly read the testimony in the daily paper, is that I had for years harbored a quiet hope that the couple would somehow manage an independent, adult marriage. Was their image plausible: Could two adults remain uncorrupted by success and wealth, live in two separate apartments, enjoy enormous autonomy and freedom, and still parent their children and love each other in a responsible and loyal way?

The answer, in this case, was a resounding no. But as a voyeur, I could not lose. The evidence was disappointing, but also reassuring. While it quashed a fantasy wish, it offered self-righteous satisfaction, validating and reinforcing my own more modest and conventional life choices.

If I press my nose to someone else's window, it isn't to see everything inside his house. There is much that would not satisfy my curiosity enough to repay the effort. The privacy I want to invade is that which allows me to learn the denouement of some story about which I have my own psychological urgency and for which I lack an ending. While in an earlier era, I might have sought the answer by watching my neighbors, or foresworn the question by following inherited traditions, today I become interested in celebrities whose images are particularly calculated to evoke such feelings. I then read the newspaper stories that bore into their privacy to display the "realities" underlying the image.

Beecher was a celebrity in an era that was just inventing the form. Toward the end of the Civil War, when Abraham Lincoln raised the U.S. flag at Fort Sumter, Beecher stood by his side and delivered an address to celebrate the occasion. Beecher had become, in his contemporaries' eyes, a man on whom they could pin their sense of virtue. For people demoralized by the horror of the fratricidal war, he embodied the goodness they wished to see in themselves, the moral high ground they wished to claim. A man so "beautiful and grand in his simplicity—thinking only of love to all men, giving himself anew to the service of Christ and the good of the race" could not have committed adultery, insisted Francis Williamson in his four-hundred-page contemporary account of the scandal. "It is simply incredible that the man who thus wrote and lived, with the eyes of the world upon him, should be a liar, a sneak, a perjurer, a debauchee, and a confirmed, persistent hypocrite. The millions who during this long period have been cheered and strengthened by his words cannot believe it."[22]

In part, the public support for Beecher expressed a wish for a simpler world. These supporters wanted him to be innocent to confirm that their ideas of virtue and purity were possible. Confronted with strangers, they wanted to be able to trust their own perceptions and to distinguish easily and intuitively between a good man and a bad one.

The public support also expressed some acceptance of Beecher's behavior as private and the feeling that, while they wanted to know every detail, they didn't want to convict him for it. In order to save his career, Beecher told countless lies, many of them at once convoluted and transparent. Most of the people around him, especially his congregants, didn't seem to care—they liked him.

Furthermore, the closer the public looked, the more it seemed that Theodore Tilton was not the innocent wounded party he made himself out to be. His wife, estranged from him, denied the affair. Nor did it help Tilton's cause when one of her servants, a former slave named James Woodley, testified that he had seen Victoria Woodhull and Tilton "sitting together with their arms around each other."[23] Others testified that they had seen Beecher and Elizabeth in equally compromising positions, but it did not seem to matter. After all, they were not the ones making accusations.

Newspaper audiences could not get enough of the story. Not only did New York newspapers transcribe the testimony, but by March 1875, three months into the trial, the *Daily Tribune* advertised for sale the whole "verbatim report"—if anyone had missed a day. The press continually fired and then fed the audience's hunger, expanding the limits of its own capabilities in the process. Perhaps the single most amazing fact of Beecher's acquittal is that *fourteen minutes* after the jury entered the Brooklyn courtroom on July 2, 1875, and reported their split vote to the judge, the first newspaper was out on the street announcing the verdict![24]

Why did everyone pay so much attention? Beecher was a big celebrity, but there were other reasons. Sex scandals about clergy have always sold well. As early as 1731, a small colonial newspaper called the *Weekly Rehearsal* devoted five issues to recounting a story from France about a Jesuit's affair with his spiritual charges.[25] Any culture that is overtly repressive of sexuality—as white America has usually been—ends up sensationalizing sex. Since it is forbidden, people find it doubly gratifying—almost irresistibly so. The descriptions of the sex are themselves titillating and pleasurable. The reader can enjoy imagining Beecher's or Woody Allen's tabooed seduction, and then righteously condemn them for behaving badly.

Such stories also explore collective values. Woody Allen's affair with Mia Farrow's adopted daughter would not necessarily have offended another generation in just the way it offended today. During most of the nineteenth century, the age of consent in New York City was ten. Allen's behavior offends now because of our heightened awareness of how children's psychological growth is enhanced by emotional safety, and our recognition of the destructiveness of incestuous relationships.

Americans also watched Allen and Farrow slug it out as part of an ongoing exploration of whether men or women are more powerful. The findings—a messy, almost pathetic draw, slightly tilted toward Farrow—are different from Beecher's day when, in the crunch, his audience confirmed the power of men and ministerial virtue. Eunice Beecher kept mum. And although Elizabeth Tilton, still tormented by her guilt, in 1878 wrote a widely published letter confessing the adultery with Beecher, it was of little consequence.

Even though the Beecher case broke barriers for the press, and demonstrated that stories about celebrities could sell prolific copy, the public felt ambivalent, especially when the subjects involved were *not* celebrities. When, in 1884, Joseph Pulitzer's newspaper *The World* published seventeen woodcuts showing the faces of "pretty girls" in Brooklyn, he stirred up a hornet's nest of outrage. Even other newspapers accused him of invading privacy. These girls, the critics complained, were not public figures. The newspaper had no business exposing their faces for strangers to contemplate.[26]

The first great argument for privacy was written by Samuel Warren and Louis Brandeis in direct response to this kind of newspaper controversy. Published in 1890 in the *Harvard Law Review,* the seminal piece declared that people had a right to privacy and that newspapers were dangerously invading that right. "Instantaneous photographs and newspaper enterprise have invaded the sacred precincts of private and domestic life," the authors complained, "and numerous mechanical devices threaten to make good the prediction that 'what is whispered in the closet shall be proclaimed from the house-tops.'"[27]

Trying to say just why privacy is so important, Warren and Brandeis argued for a right to privacy to protect the notion of an "inviolate personality." *Inviolate,* according to *Webster,* means not only "not violated," but "pure and unprofaned." Warren and Brandeis's language sounds a little stiff one hundred years later, and their idea of a person as even potentially pure and unprofaned has certainly not thrived in the twentieth century. But their deeper assertion is that privacy is a critical ingredient for human dignity. "I take the principle of 'inviolate personality,'" lawyer and privacy scholar Edward Bloustein observed, "to posit the individual's independence, dignity and integrity; it defines man's essence as a unique and self-determining being."[28]

Gossip, complain Warren and Brandeis, "belittles and perverts. It belittles by inverting the relative importance of things, thus dwarfing the thoughts and aspirations of a people."[29] While they spoke generically of gossip, they referred specifically to newspaper gossip, and the distinction is important. Gossip between acquaintances is fundamentally different from newspaper gossip for two reasons. First, whispered gossip is meant to offer a balancing private counterpoint to a public story. For example, at work a boss misses a lot of days, but does not say why. Company employees whisper that the boss is temporarily crazy from stress because her child is gravely ill. The gossip binds the workers' anxiety by offering them a way of understanding their unpredictable environment, while giving the boss time to negotiate the crisis without creating public scandal. Even though whispered gossip invades privacy, it also preserves it by specifically avoiding public declamation.

Second, gossip between people who know each other is different from newspaper gossip because it is constantly shaded by the nuances of a more complex relationship. If I whisper with one colleague about another, whatever story I tell is affected by my colleague's view of me, as well as her independent relationship with the subject of our talk. In media gossip, the reader has no personal relationship that might temper knowledge and provide context. "The whispered word over a back fence had a kind of human touch and softness while newsprint is cold and impersonal."[30]

Learning something unpleasant about someone one knows well is a very different experience from reading about the failings of a celebrity. It is more upsetting, and thus it is harder to have a simple reaction. Your own feelings are too complex. If a close friend you love lets you know that somehow he has acted badly, sorrow, anger, puzzlement, worry, and anguish are more typical responses than easy condemnation or outrage. Stories written about celebrities don't have anywhere near the depth, emotional richness, and resonances of stories told among people with common connections. Elaborating such stories to balance our increased separateness, we end up possessing a mass culture that is blunted and without nuance.

Many forces are at work in the media coverage of a celebrity trial. Perhaps first and foremost, newspapers—and now television companies—compete for money. But beyond that (if there is a beyond), the nation uses these events for addressing psychological and social agendas on a large scale. People combed newspaper accounts to determine for themselves if Beecher *was* a good guy. Was he a representative American? They were also making up their minds about whether anyone should be tried for adultery. They wanted to know if more privacy, and the accompanying shift from more contractual to more feeling-based bonds, was a good thing. Could people be pure without coercion?

Some years earlier, the transcendentalist Bronson Alcott wrote, "Individuals are sacred. The world, the state, the church, the school, all are felons whenever they violate the sanctity of the private heart."[31] Beecher echoed this idea. He was invigorated by the possibility of focusing on "the private heart" as a basis for guidance and self-definition. Not surprisingly, the heart proved a complex guide. Altina Waller notes that although Beecher survived his trial, he did not survive the press: His reputation was damaged, and he and his congregation abandoned the "gospel of love."

But Beecher's own retreat did not close the question; rather, it underlined it and posed it for the future to answer. His was one of many voices describing an increased sense of individual possibility based in private experience. When Warren and Brandeis spoke about "inviolate personality," or Victoria Woodhull about "individual sovereignty," they were asserting the importance of the individual and the necessity of honoring privacy as a means of protecting the possibility of a more fully realized individual.

Beecher's story suggests that the increase in privacy, the invention of celebrity, and the large-scale media interest in the celebrity's private life grew up simultaneously; the nation developed a new public ritual to expiate the sins of this new privacy. But the press was but one response to the new urban life. In an odd transformation, Emerson's anxious scenario of a nosy reporter under a confessional was about to metamorphose into a psychotherapist and patient conversing in a consulting room.

5

Dr. Jekyll and Mr. Freud

I f newspaper stories and celebrity gossip were one approach nineteenth-century America used to offset the new anonymity and increased privacy of urban life, psychotherapy would gradually develop as another one. Although not commonplace until well into this century, modern psychotherapy can be said to begin with Sigmund Freud's and Josef Breuer's observations about hysteria, first written up in the decade following Beecher's trial. Freud's early work was contemporary also with Robert Louis Stevenson's emergence as a popular writer, ambivalent about his status as public figure. Stevenson's literary success and courtship by the American press intersect in most interesting ways with Freud and the development of psychoanalysis, and with our discussion of privacy.

In 1887, Robert Lewis Stevenson, visiting in America, agreed to write regular articles for Pulitzer's *World* and for *Scribner's* magazine—two of the most popular American publications of the decade. That both would turn to Stevenson is hardly surprising since his recent novel, *The Strange Case of Dr. Jekyll and Mr. Hyde,* about the corruption that hides beneath respectability, was music to their ears. "There is not a crime," Joseph Pulitzer had said, "there is not a dodge, there is not a trick, there is not a swindle, there is not a vice which does not live by secrecy."[1]

After years of depending on his father to supplement his small earnings as a writer, Stevenson was pleased by his new financial independence. But his status as darling of the media both pleased and troubled him. In 1886, he had written to a friend, "Let us tell each other sad stories of the bestiality of the beast whom we feed. What he likes is the newspaper; and to me the press is the mouth of a sewer, where lying is professed as from an university chair, and everything prurient, and ignoble, and essentially dull, finds its abode and pulpit. . . . There must be something wrong with me, or I would not be popular."[2]

Although few now read the once very popular *Dr. Jekyll and Mr. Hyde,* people refer to it, saying about someone whose civility covers a deeper nastiness, "He's a real Jekyll and Hyde." He changes unexpectedly from nice guy to frightening monster; he is "schizo." Stevenson's best-seller is a treatise on split personality; exploring the dark side of people that hides behind their careful respectability. Set in a city, it explores themes very similar to ones the press and public explored in Beecher's trial (e.g., is a publicly respectable man privately good?) and that Freud explored when he articulated a view of human nature that focused on unconscious mental processes usually hidden from view.

What is hidden tends to be more secret than private. Though we often use the terms interchangeably, secrecy is active hiding. Sometimes people hide to preserve privacy that is under siege. For instance, a child surrounded by adults who do not respect her privacy may hide her diary. (She is forced to make it secret to keep it private.) A homosexual, to avoid losing his job or, in some instances, his life, might hide his sexual interest. (Gay activists have made their sexuality public in an effort to use political and social action to liberate the secret so it may become safely private.) Other times, as described by incest survivors and others on talk shows, hiding corrupts privacy by exploiting the cover it offers.

The private becomes hidden and secret when we or others around us—the family, the boss, the society—declare that some practice is unacceptable, shameful, or illegal; or sometimes, simply when others are intrusive. (Secrecy is also sought by some primarily as a way to gain or manipulate power.) The boundary between privacy and secrecy is often fluid, ephemeral, and subjective. Information that one moment with one person feels private, with another later the same hour feels secret. Social tolerance plus mutual respect ensure the most expansive and safest privacy; intolerance plus hostile surveillance, the narrowest and most endangered.

What society forces into hiding varies by time and place. Occasionally something happens that alters the cultural ecology, and experiences that had been hidden are allowed to venture out. For example, the slightly increased power of women in the United States during the past two decades has allowed more open discussions of rape, abortion, battering, incest, and breast cancer.

Just such an ecological change took place at the end of the nineteenth century. While there were many causes, one important participant was Sigmund Freud, who developed ideas about the unconscious mind and about a way of changing a person by creating a public/private space where he might transform secrets into privacies.

Eighteen eighty-six, the year Stevenson published *Dr. Jekyll*, was the year that Freud turned thirty. Having married, completed his medical training, and started a family, Freud was beginning his long career, which, like Stevenson's novel, would focus on exploring the hidden dimensions of human nature. Stevenson was born in 1850, Freud in 1856, and it is odd to realize that the two men were contemporaries. In fact, *Dr. Jekyll* invites Freud. It is, Stevenson notes in the full title, "The Strange *Case* of . . . " And cases call out for detectives or doctors.

Dr. Jekyll and Mr. Hyde recounts the downfall of Henry

Jekyll, a wealthy, proper doctor who wants everyone to admire him for his *public* rectitude, virtue, and kindness. But he also wants *secretly* to indulge all vice. Eager to find a freedom without consequences for his reputation, he develops a drug that allows him to mold the licentious and evil parts of himself into a second separate person. This rendering of the bad from the good is a major ordeal, provoking "a grinding in the bones, deadly nausea, and a horror of the spirit that cannot be exceeded at the hour of birth or death."

So emerges Edward Hyde, a deformed repulsive man (much smaller than Jekyll!) whose impulses run free, "drinking pleasure and bestial avidity from any degree of torture to another; relentless like a man of stone." Splitting off his dark side into Hyde, Jekyll discovers that he can indulge and disown it at the same time: "Henry Jekyll stood at times aghast before the acts of Edward Hyde; but the situation was apart from ordinary laws, and insidiously relaxed the grasp of conscience. It was Hyde after all, and Hyde alone, that was guilty."[3]

Imagine yourself as Hyde, running free in a suburban neighborhood, able to harm without consequence. You break windshields, run over dogs, torment children, rob and terrorize joggers, molest neighbors. One's impulse is to recoil from the fantasy with a renunciatory, "Not me!" Hyde is frightening. It's not that such license is without appeal. There are antisocial, perverse, even ghastly things each of us might try. The terror comes from feeling no external limits. Since no one who sees you even recognizes you, your anonymity becomes complete, your very existence becomes ambiguous, your isolation profound. You are in a free fall. No confidant helps you live with yourself. Knowing about Stevenson, it is not hard to feel his own fear in Hyde—perhaps the very fear that Beecher addressed for his constituents.

Hyde prowls the city, wreaking havoc, and finally murdering

a man. Mortified, and afraid of arrest, Dr. Jekyll reins in his other self. But addicted to sensual pursuits, he cannot bear the abstinence; Hyde has developed a will of his own, and he wants out. In fact, Jekyll finds himself transforming into Hyde without meaning to—or even swallowing medicine. Eventually, the upright Dr. Jekyll becomes stuck as the deformed and decayed Edward Hyde, and lives as a recluse cared for by puzzled servants until he commits suicide to avoid discovery.

Little wonder that Stevenson wrote this book. According to his stepson, Lloyd Osbourne, the basic idea came to him in a nightmare. It seems that no matter how far Stevenson traveled from Edinburgh, he could not escape the effects of his nurse and her terrifying, violent version of heaven and hell. Though laying his psyche at her feet is simplistic, her power to frighten must have been confused for him with the fact of her proximity during his many life-threatening illnesses. Beyond his fragile health, what likely frightened him most was his own urgency to throw off external control.

Ian Bell tells us that Stevenson wrote *Dr. Jekyll* in a white heat. The first draft took three days but did not satisfy his wife, whose criticism sent him into such a rage that he tossed the manuscript into the fireplace. He wrote a new (and she felt better) version in three more days. Fanny later recalled:

> That an invalid in my husband's condition of health should have been able to perform the manual labour alone, of putting sixty thousand words on paper in six days, seems almost incredible. He was suffering from continual haemorrhages, and was hardly allowed to speak, his conversation usually being carried on by means of slate and pencil.[4]

The frantic speed suggests one of those creative bursts where the writer becomes the psyche's scribe. The dream expresses an unconscious dilemma, and the story is energized by the personal conflict it attempts to resolve. *The Strange Case of Dr. Jekyll and Mr. Hyde* has typically been read as a commentary on Stevenson's great difficulty reconciling his sensual and rebellious impulses with his Calvinist upbringing. That it sold many copies suggests that Stevenson's anxiety was widely shared. Certainly there are many resonances with Beecher's trial. Loosed from the terror of hell and the habit of communal surveillance, will we all become monsters?

Stevenson tells his readers that Mr. Hyde is evil. He is meanness, murderousness, sexual licentiousness, bad thoughts, and ugly desires rolled into one. He is everything proper society defends against, represses, forces into the shadows—a distilled form of the vices people usually try to *hide*. Hyde is the Freudian id before Freud, loosed and rampaging; parts of the self, Stevenson seems to suggest, that gain strength in exile. Unleashed and allowed to prowl, Hyde delivers only misery.

But the alternative to Hyde is an oppressive—deadening and dehumanizing—propriety. Sometimes Stevenson mocks the extreme reserve of Jekyll's contemporaries; other times he offers it up to his audience without irony. However ambivalent his attitude, his characters' views are clear. One explains why it's best not to ask questions that threaten propriety:

> "I feel very strongly about putting questions; it partakes too much of the day of judgment. You start a question, and it's like starting a stone. You sit quietly on the top of a hill; and away the stone goes, starting others; and presently some bland old bird (the last you would have thought of) is knocked in the head on his own back garden and the family have to change their name. No, sir, I make it a rule of mine: the more it looks like Queer Street, the less I ask."[5]

Questions invade people's privacy. Don't ask them. Could any sentiment be further from Freud? (Or, more accurately, the young Freud?) Writing in 1901, the doctor not only instructs a would-be psychoanalyst to ask questions, but exhorts him that if he wishes to uncover the important concealed material, he must not "rest content with the first 'No' that crosses his path."[6] He must keep pushing his inquiries, even in the face of stubborn resistance! The evil that Jekyll hid in Hyde was on its way to becoming the neurosis that Freud would force into the light and attempt to "cure." In the consulting room, propriety could occasionally be set aside.

In 1880, five years after Beecher's trial, and six years before *Dr. Jekyll and Mr. Hyde* was published, Josef Breuer, a thirty-eight-year-old Viennese physician and mentor to Sigmund Freud, began making home visits. The patient was a twenty-one-year-old woman named Bertha Pappenheim whom he and Freud would eventually write up as "Fraulein Anna O.," the first great case history of psychoanalysis.

Miss Pappenheim, an intelligent, attractive young woman, had become emotionally ill while caring for her dying father. Her diverse symptoms included deafness, muteness, paralysis of her arm and leg, headaches, and daytime sleepwalking. She hallucinated black snakes with death heads, responded only in English to inquiries addressed to her in her native German, and often refused to eat. In a manner reminiscent of Mr. Hyde, she spent long "absences" in another personality, though unlike Jekyll, she could not later recall the other's behavior.

Dr. Breuer visited her every evening at her home. Upon his arrival, he would hypnotize her—later she learned to put herself into a trance—and then she would talk. The conversations eased her symptoms; some disappeared after she told Breuer about troubling feelings immediately preceding their onset. Miss Pappenheim referred to their meetings as her "talking cure." Writes Breuer:

> It was in the summer during a period of extreme heat, and the patient was suffering very badly from thirst; for, without being able to account for it in any way, she suddenly found it impossible to drink. She would take up the glass of water she longed for, but as soon as it touched her lips she would push it away like someone suffering from hydrophobia.[7]

Four, five, six weeks went by, and although she could slightly lessen her terrible thirst by eating fruit, she could not drink. One night while hypnotized, the patient started complaining about an English "lady-companion" who looked after her, and whom she disliked. With great disgust, she recalled watching the woman's dog drink from the woman's own water glass. After describing her disgust to Breuer, the patient "drank a large quantity of water without any difficulty and woke from her hypnosis with the glass at her lips; and thereupon the disturbance vanished, never to return."

Nursing an ill, beloved father is difficult for any young woman. Perhaps she was terrified to watch him deteriorate, or resentful of how it interfered with her own life. Maybe she felt lonely. Did she wash him? Did she empty his bedpan? Did caring for him repel her, or perhaps occasionally arouse her? Where was her mother? Perhaps it was unbearable to watch a beloved father die. Chances are that the unacceptable feelings of disgust that stopped her drinking water had diverse origins, and were displaced upon the dog. Or so Freud has suggested.

Freud did not "discover" the unconscious any more than Columbus "discovered" America. In *The Discovery of the Unconscious,* Henri Ellenberger documents a long, rich exploration of the subject before Freud. But by developing psychoanalysis, a technique for examining the unconscious and describing its domain, he radically changed our view.

Freud attempted to claim from folklore and religion, and *rename* for psychology and "science," many parts of the mind. Josef Breuer and "Anna O." helped him by discovering "the talking cure," which would become the basis for the central psychoanalytic technique of free association, a method for understanding the unconscious. But more than that, the talking cure offered a way of expressing suppressed perspectives. People often feel better, even get better after saying what they were forbidden or unable to say. There are two basic reasons. First, they are less alone because speaking sincerely to a receptive listener is relieving. Second, they have created a new perspective by structuring and organizing inchoate feelings with words. The new angle subverts existing prescriptions.

Renaming is complex. With new names come new avenues of meaning, profound yet often unobserved losses, changes of status, unforeseen possibilities and radically altered understandings. Lest we minimize or sentimentalize the potential violence of renaming, Stephen Greenblatt offers a cautionary and illustrative tale in his book *Marvelous Possessions.* When the Spaniards were exploring Mexico in the sixteenth century, they came to a land and asked its name. The Indians couldn't make out any meaning in the question. So they replied *uic athan,* which means "We don't understand you." Ah, the Spanish leader knowingly told his scribe, write down that they call this place "Yucatan."[8] The expression of incomprehension turned into a place name.

Freud's renaming of mental experience has profoundly affected how we think about people and private experience. In psychoanalysis, rather than keeping thoughts and feelings to yourself, you are encouraged to share them with your analyst. All of them. Especially the most secret and shameful. Reserve is to be tossed out

the window. "Just say whatever comes to mind" is the famous re-
frain that begins a treatment. So embedded in contemporary culture as to have become clichéd, it is hard to grasp what a fresh and
wicked invitation the suggestion must have offered in the context
of the late nineteenth century, especially in a family like the one
Robert Louis Stevenson grew up in—where rules were many, and
open transgressions poorly tolerated. Stevenson's father temporarily
disowned him when he learned that Stevenson and a group of university friends had started a club with a constitution that began,
"Disregard everything our parents have taught us."[9]

Freud offered a place where one could do just that, and father
never had to know. Imagine how embarrassing, exciting, liberating,
and strange it must have felt to walk into Dr. Freud's drawing
room, lie down on his carpet-covered couch, and give voice to the
improper feelings you had assiduously kept to yourself—and often
from yourself.

Imagine you are Dr. Jekyll entering that consulting room—
your hat in hand, your repressed desires champing, pulling to
break free, to carouse as Hyde. But at the same time, you are hoping to find some way to stop yourself and fend off disaster. (Imagine you are Henry Ward Beecher trying not to seduce another
parishioner.) During an interlude of attempting to remain as your
upright self, you are tormented by the imprisoned Hyde, who
scrawls "blasphemies" in the margins of your books. Perhaps it is
this "symptom" that you call to the doctor's attention, or the fact
that Hyde has *made you* tear up your revered father's portrait.

A worried friend begs Jekyll to tell him his secret. "Make a
clean breast of this in confidence; and I make no doubt I can get
you out of it," pleads Utterson. But Jekyll, thanking him deeply,
fends him off: "This is a private matter, and I beg of you to let it
sleep."[10]

If your story is too private to tell your best friend, why would you talk to Freud? Because he is a stranger? Because you have heard that he interests himself in queer things and so might be less shocked than some upright friend? Because he is less likely to gossip? Because he is a doctor and his approach is "scientific"? Though psychoanalysis has not yet become—often for better as well as for worse—as scientific as Freud intended, he emphasized science in the hopes of creating a space to explore human feelings and conflicts apart from the confines of social convention. But more, you might turn to Freud because, unlike your friend who is sure your predicament is something he can "get you out of," Freud appreciated that the human condition had no easy exit.

Freud (telescoping his life's work) believed that if someone like Dr. Jekyll lay on the couch and recounted his feelings, allowed them to pass uncensored from his lips, allowed their deep unconscious roots to be interpreted, his urgency to become Hyde *might* diminish. Jekyll's ego *might* expand to allow breathing space between the urgent impulses and severe repressions. Much of the brain operates outside of consciousness. Could people learn to observe some of the operations? If they did, could they bear better the tragic, difficult nature of life?

Or, to put it another way, by transforming his secrets into privacies, Jekyll might change his relationship to them. Ideally, he could come to feel his desires and, at the same time, feel a little more control and choice about whether to carry them into the realm of action. Freud wondered if (and later psychotherapists hoped that) with therapy, Jekyll might flail around less. Instead of having to fend off unconscious impulses as "not me," he could come to own them as part of himself. Once owned, their power to choose his actions without his awareness would diminish. Instead of the endless war between the id (impulses) and the superego (the strict conscience), the ego—or aware self—would be strengthened. Warded off and unknown parts of the unconscious would become familiar to the self, and the shameful and secret would become somewhat more bearable and private.

But why would a person tell his most shameful thoughts, feelings, and fantasies to a therapist? Probably out of desperation. Jekyll is emotionally dead, and Hyde is a terrorist. When people feel awful, they wish for relief. Profound comfort often comes from feeling that someone else wants to understand. No matter how mortifying the process of revealing private or secret feelings, if the person who is listening to you neither doubles over in laughter nor flees the room in disgust (and sometimes even proposes a novel interpretation of your behavior), you tend to gain relief. You are less alone. Your predicament changes, catches the light at a different angle, held now in a new understanding offered by a second person. Psychotherapy uses publicly framed (e.g., contractual, paid, dated and timed, regulated with the intent of benefiting the payee) *intimacy* to turn secrets into privacies.

But here matters become more complicated. Freud and Breuer initially thought that it was simply the revelation that brought the relief—not the relationship. Consequently, Miss Pappenheim's year-and-a-half-long therapy with Dr. Breuer ended disastrously. In the course of their daily intimate conversations— some of which took place in her bedroom, while she lay in bed and he sat beside her—Miss Pappenheim developed passionate feelings for Dr. Breuer. In fact, she announced one night that she was going to have his baby, and threw herself into what turned out to be an imaginary labor. The shocked doctor, already feeling guilty because of his wife's complaints that he was spending too much time with his compelling patient, fled her bedroom and never returned. The abandonment devastated Miss Pappenheim, who required hospitalization. Though she gradually recovered and pursued a success-ful social work career, she is said to have bristled whenever anyone mentioned psychoanalysis.[11] Who blames her? She was treated poorly, and her betrayal was published in terms that exposed her by focusing on her psychological pathology while propelling her doc-tors' careers. Yet their explorations were not insincere.

Whenever I think about "Anna O.," I wish that Verdi had learned of her and written her libretto into opera. The trio between "Anna O.," Mrs. Breuer, and Dr. Breuer would be gorgeous: the honorable doctor whose work has led him deep into passionate feelings he did not expect; the attractive, intelligent, and stymied young woman, ill, constrained by circumstance, wanting freedom, wanting a life, and in love with her doctor; the doctor's wife, watching her husband disappear into a relationship that he calls "medical duty" or "scientific discovery." Yet suddenly, he becomes aware that his scientific passion has become personal, and has al-most led him to violate his morality—his most cherished idea of himself. He is horrified. Anna, having opened herself to him so fully and lost him so suddenly, is completely bereft. The dramatic paradox is that though he is innocent, she has been betrayed. It is the last great nineteenth-century story. After Freud, the possibility disappeared for a drama based in such psychological innocence. The romantic tragedy became family drama, its more sophisticated participants became self-conscious and embarrassed.

Breuer did not understand, and only a decade later would Freud begin to reflect upon how next to impossible it was for a pa-tient to reveal her most intimate experiences without developing feelings for the listener. In the beginning, analysts concentrated on the details of the revelations and didn't realize that their patients were often powerfully reliving *with the therapist* feelings that their stories described. So, too, sometimes the therapists were drawn into the enactment, or unconsciously relived something of their own. Though Breuer did not act on his passion, other analysts did, and sometimes caused harm. Carl Jung, for instance, carried on a love affair with his patient Sabrina Spielrein.

Freud gradually perceived that the process of psychoanalysis often released intense feeling. In an effort to allow something new to happen, he decided that in the context of the consulting room, he would call the feelings "transference." By giving them a different name, he hoped to disengage them from normal exchange. Don't respond in kind, he advised therapists. Stand back and examine. Hold the patient's feelings (and your own, soon to be named "countertransference") up to the light like reels of film, and you will gather profoundly important information about the psyche. Do not act on what you feel. Use it as evidence. Talk about it. And appreciate that the positive feelings, the love, that the patient and you have for each other, if unexploited, may well allow her to risk psychic change.

Transference is a much discussed and ultimately perplexing idea. At its worst, it is devastating. For it attacks our certainty—threatens our view of the opera's drama by revealing too boldly the deeper tragedy: "You are not innocent, and your heart isn't really breaking only over me." But transference also offers the possibility for creating greater psychic freedom. Psychotherapy changes the usual terms of intimacy by redirecting them. If, as the British psychiatrist and researcher John Bowlby and others have demonstrated, attachment is the basis of human psychological survival, and attachment style dictates much of how one experiences life, transference offers a second chance by examining and altering people's ways of connecting to others.

Though psychotherapy is an extraordinarily private relationship (the patient and therapist have unusually intimate conversations in the context of high confidentiality), it is also public, or, as Robert Kegan writes in *In Over Our Heads,* "a part of one's public life."[12] The fact that it is at once public and private is its essence. The patient pays the therapist to listen; in return, the therapist abstains from turning the private space and its intimacy to his own ends. (Contemporary efforts aimed at protecting this delicate status have led to public institutions—courts, licensing boards, insurers, etc.—increasingly monitoring therapists.)

Transference is a public renaming of the private experience of feeling that creates a freeing paradox (what I feel is both for you and not for you), and allows material that is initially—sometimes—secret from the self to be turned into knowledge that is conscious but that may be kept private. (The patient knows and has spoken about things that he may choose never to speak about so intimately outside the consulting room.)

Freud makes no appearance in *The Strange Case of Dr. Jekyll and Mr. Hyde,* but imagine if he had. Imagine that the despairing Dr. Jekyll had decided to slip away from his friends, rent a room in Vienna, and seek treatment:

> After many weeks of daily visits to Freud's office, Henry Jekyll noticed one day as he walked up the street toward the doctor's house, that he had to restrain himself from impulsively kicking the analyst's son who, immersed in a sidewalk game, unwittingly blocked the door. And when the maid answered his ring, he snarled at her. He was in an ugly mood, but since he denied that a man as good as Henry Jekyll could possess such feelings, he decided that Hyde, quiescent now since treatment had begun, was waking. Before he had time to think further, Jekyll was ushered into Freud's consulting room, where he shook hands with his analyst, and lay down on the couch.
>
> "Hyde is waking," he announced and waited. The room was silent except for the faint sounds filtering in from the street. Irritated that his comment had won no response from Freud, and that

in general he could not figure out why or when his analyst chose to speak, joke, chat, or sometimes even lecture, Jekyll repeated himself, this time almost shouting—despite his rule never to lose control.

"HYDE IS BACK." As the words escaped angrily from his mouth, he began to shake in the fashion that had come to announce an impending transformation. "Noooo," he groaned, more to himself than to his analyst, but it was too late. He closed his eyes, attempting to steady himself against the tornadoes swirling around his head. His fingernails dug into the edges of the couch as, flooded with shame, he realized that he was becoming Hyde in front of Freud. Opening his eyes a moment later, he saw, still clenching the couch, Hyde's hideous and deformed little hands half covered by the white, perfectly starched cuffs of Jekyll's too large shirtsleeve. When he spoke, it was in Hyde's evil voice.

"Answer me, you loathsome Jewish idiot. I despise you, and I am sick of coming here!"

If the analyst noticed that he had been spoken to rudely, or that a different man lay on his couch, he gave little sign, only muttering an almost inaudible "Finally," then adding—with a tone of authority that under the circumstance seemed to verge on chutzpah—"Continue with your associations."

"Don't tell me what to do! You want my money! You want to control me! No, you want to destroy me! You and everyone else!" Once loosed, the invective poured forth wildly, stopping only when Freud announced the end of the hour. Had Hyde, as he scurried from the room, looked closely, he might have noticed small drops of sweat on the analyst's forehead. "We'll continue tomorrow," the psychoanalyst said.

The next day, restored to himself, Dr. Jekyll skipped his session, and for several days aimlessly wandered the Viennese streets, desolate and ashamed that his therapy with Freud, whose approval he increasingly longed for, had been destroyed by Hyde. He was surprised and deeply relieved when the morning post brought a letter from the doctor inquiring about his health and urging him to visit. That night Jekyll dreamed that he was a small boy being chased by an angry teacher who wished to cane him. But as the teacher drew close, he became Freud, the cane fell away, and the analyst patted the boy's shaking arm. Jekyll awoke confused, wiping from his eyes the first tears he remembered having cried since early childhood.

Treating Jekyll, Freud would likely have focused on uncovering the hidden, repressed feelings that—his theory suggested—compelled the patient to reinhabit, either in fact or fantasy, his counterpart, Hyde. Was Jekyll unconsciously enraged at his father for his severe, repressive, controlling behavior toward him? Or was it his father's exclusive sexual relationship with his beloved mother that troubled the patient? Perhaps Jekyll possessed a morbid shame of his homoerotic and other tender wishes? Or maybe unbeknownst to his conscious mind, he was fending off terror by behaving in terrorizing ways himself.

As their work progressed, Freud would become the target of Jekyll's rage, his tenderness, his loneliness, his longing, envy, hunger, altruism, hate, and love: all the feelings Jekyll wanted to disown, feelings he found inconvenient to propriety and unbearable—yet all the feelings that held his aliveness, that made him human.

Using the concept of transference—a paradox created by purposefully giving a new "public" name to private feelings—psychotherapy might create a fresh experience. Freud, like a dance teacher, could lead his partner through intricate emotional steps Jekyll had never tried. If experiences in his past had taught him only a rigid two-step—dictated that ambivalence was unacceptable—he was forbidden to hate as well as love the same person and had to keep the hate out of consciousness. Freud replied by spinning a polka, bearing with quick steps Jekyll's hate and love, intimately demonstrating for Jekyll a relationship in which ambivalence could be borne. Psychoanalysis imagines the possibility of creating a space so safe and seemingly private that even two uptight heterosexual men sitting in separate chairs and communicating in words, can bear the intimacy, tenderness, embarrassment, and desire of a dance lesson.

The process requires a delicate privacy—like all privacy, easily corruptible. Some analysts and therapists exploit it—either sexually, or by creating situations of one-upmanship, misusing knowledge, driving the treatment into secrecy, making the process a means of managing their own shame, or attempting to control the patient. Most therapists do some of those things occasionally. But when managed well enough, the private space becomes a sanctioning context for a paradoxical intimacy (the private intimacy held in public contract) that has the potential to change people profoundly by letting them tolerate feeling more and knowing more about themselves.

Psychoanalysis—as it has been practiced in the United States and modified across time—proposes that when treatment ends, a more humble Jekyll will look on Hyde with less horror and alienation, and with more compassion and ownership. Having become a more modern man, that is, having familiarized himself with his unconscious, better able to tolerate the paradox and complexity of a more sophisticated consciousness, Jekyll will no longer need a dissociated and separate Hyde, a devil, to embody his impulses. He can better tolerate his own ambivalence. He can feel without always acting. The "therapeutic re-education," writes Philip Rieff, "teaches the patient-student how to live with the contradictions that combine to make him into a unique personality; this it does in contrast to the old moral pedagogies, which tried to re-order the contradictions into a hierarchy of superior and inferior, good and evil, capabilities."[13]

We read Freud's cases one hundred years after they were written because they have become a critical part of modern literature. We recognize them now as banners that announced the arrival of a new century and, with it, the advent of the modern—freestanding, private, ambivalent, and uncertain—man and woman. Freud created and effectively advertised a plausible theory of a complex and contradictory human psyche.

Freud sang the new century's anthem of *uncertainty*. Nothing about human emotions, he suggested, is as it appears to be. Philip Rieff has observed that Freud's greatest intellectual contribution may prove to be his recognition of the universality of ambivalence: "Where there is love, there is the lurking eventuality of hatred. Where there is ambition, there is the ironic desire for failure. Although he wishes not to know it, a sore loser may be sore mainly because he almost won and is reacting against his wish to lose." Harold Bloom asserts that Freud borrowed his understanding of ambivalence from Shakespeare.[14] You might say Freud translated it from dramatic theater into psychological practice. What you see, Freud continually asserted, is not what you get; look more closely, probe more deeply, turn the mind inside out so that its lining becomes its surface. Important truth is hidden just out of sight.

By the late nineteenth century the old controls—patriarchy, community, religion, tradition—were quickly loosening. Freud wondered if psychoanalysis might allow man, through self-knowledge, to control himself more from within than through external authority. Freud was pessimistic. Some of his followers were less so. They hoped that the analyzed Jekyll, sadder but wiser, freed by self-knowledge of Hyde's overwhelming urgencies and Jekyll's self-righteous imperiousness, would be able to muddle along, ambivalent, a modern man, seeking the satisfaction of the quotidian, making his way through London and through life. His increased opportunity for privacy, created by a greater separateness and a diminution of authoritarian surveillance, could potentially be balanced and counterweighted by an increased awareness of the behavior of his mind and the whole scope of his private experience. He would be watched with his own eyes.

Reacting to the historical moment, Stevenson and Freud creatively "solved" the anxiety caused by modern life. A contemporary—who also wrote about cases—offered a third solution. In 1887, the year Stevenson visited New York, Arthur Conan Doyle, a doctor and aspiring writer, like Stevenson from Edinburgh, published "A Study in Scarlet." Sherlock Holmes, the great detective and conqueror of urban life, instantly became a success with readers. One central reason for his enormous popularity is that he magically solves the question of how to live surrounded by strangers.

Holmes's sidekick, Dr. Watson, embodies the problem. Poor Watson—injured in a colonial war, low on funds, alone without friends in London—makes Holmes his roommate, and for weeks does not dare ask his occupation for fear of violating his privacy. Watson is us. Like the doctor, we are all newcomers to the city, unsure whom to trust, how to pick a roommate, how to judge strangers and make our way safely. We are inhibited by our reserve, our wish for privacy, and our compliance with what we assume is the other person's wish.

Sherlock Holmes suffers no such plight. Upon meeting Watson, he comments, "You have been in Afghanistan, I perceive." Modern life with its large dose of anonymity doesn't stymie him. One look and he sees everything. Holmes is able, "by a momentary expression, a twitch of a muscle, or a glance of an eye, to fathom a man's inmost thoughts."[15] The detective is one up on the plodding psychoanalyst. However brilliant Freud's own speculative powers, he must still listen to his patients. Holmes is a Victorian superman. In the spirit of his era, he believes that knowledge solves all problems. He loves cataloging details. He uses his fantastic capacities not just to solve crimes, but to *undo* the new anxiety of urban life surrounded by strangers. Holmes can look at a man and know his social class, country of origin, work, the quality of his soul . . . whatever he wishes or needs to know. Conversely, he can look at a cigar butt, a footprint, a hat, and deduce a man.

The detective is in his element in the city, and unlike Stevenson, he accepts newspapers as a useful part of urban life. He writes for them, reads them avidly, and runs ads in them to lure out wily criminals. Watson tells us that Holmes has an immense knowledge of sensational literature. "He appears to know every detail of every horror perpetrated in the century." The better to solve crimes. And, of course, when the newspapers involve themselves in crimes he is solving, Holmes, far ahead, enjoys a laugh at their expense.

How can the psyche bear modern life, Stevenson asked? Freud and Doyle pondered. Both loved cases and clues and minuscule detail. Holmes would know you without your participation, simply through his own prowess; while Freud shared some of this stance, he also insisted that you must speak about your deepest and most personal experiences. After an evening watching Dr. Jekyll at a formal dinner, Holmes would have deduced his relationship to Hyde and arrested him. Freud would have tracked clues offered by Jekyll's unconscious that he might "arrest" Hyde by understanding him.

It is a paradox of psychoanalysis that while it began in the privacy of the consulting room, and was in the many ways we have suggested an extremely private experience, it evolved into an active part of public culture and exerted wide influence. Its effects on privacy are complex.

Early on, Freud struggled with himself about how much of his patients' experiences to reveal in his articles, and the famous case of "Dora" is prefaced by several pages of tortured efforts to come to terms with the dilemma. How do you take information that is exquisitely private, and write about it? Or do you? Describing a case, Freud notes, is bound to involve the revelations of intimacies and the betrayal of secrets. "It is certain that the patients would never have spoken if it had occurred to them that their admissions might possibly be put to scientific uses; and it is equally certain that to ask them themselves for leave to publish their cases would be quite unavailing."[16]

Describing himself as torn between "medical discretion" and the chance to offer scientific "enlightenment," Freud chooses to tell a disguised version of the story. But tell he does. Though he sternly rebukes physicians who would read the cases "for their private delectation," he, of all people, must have recognized that his own ideas exploded the possibility of a pure or "scientific" reader. Who would be able to, much less want to, read cases filled with tales of sexuality without the opportunity for private delectation? Case histories are fictions that, too frequently, have been structured to flatter the therapist and demean the patient. Yet therapy needs to offer stories to convey legitimate knowledge. There is a sincere problem behind Freud's dilemma.

While Freud rightly feared having his work sensationalized, he was himself something of a sensationalist. He wished to shock the staid members of his audience, to stir things up, to found a movement. By taking on the style of the sleuth, he joined the era's vernacular. He drove his young patient Dora nearly mad ("Fragment of an Analysis of a Case of Hysteria") by attributing to her all kinds of wishes about sex and masturbation that she strenuously disavowed, but that he insisted upon. She walked out. He wrote about her. Infatuated with his own ideas, Freud may have seen some part of the unconscious truth, but he misconstrued Dora's trauma, and lost the chance to help her by naming forthrightly the fact that no matter what she *felt,* her father had *behaved* badly when he offered her to his mistress's husband in sexual trade.

Freud violated her privacy by telling the story at her expense and in this way made it vulnerable to being sensationalized. Sensationalism deprives the lurid of a context that could offer it more subtle, complex, and ultimately humane meaning. It pulls for a reflex of disavowal, a claim of "not me," and silences the nagging, fearful, ashamed "me too." We make a mistake if we follow Freud into his moments of "not me" about Dora, and equally if we adopt the stance ourselves toward him. Freud's public/private ambivalence offers a template for the contradictory ways the revelations of the mind's more intimate ideas have entered and affected the public world.

In her book *Terrible Honesty,* Ann Douglas spells out Freud's enormous impact on early-twentieth-century American culture. The title itself suggests that the "terrible" honesty that Freud sanctioned within the privacy of the consulting room became a public value intent on toppling Victorian euphemism with straight talk. (This is one of Douglas's points about modernism in general.) But more, she details how artists like Eugene O'Neill, James Thurber, Edna St. Vincent Millay, F. Scott Fitzgerald, and many others were dramatically influenced by Freud's ideas. Writes Douglas, "The Freudian discourse, no matter how simplified or distorted, had by the mid-1920s eclipsed the Protestant pieties sovereign in America's official life until then. It had become *the* explanatory discourse, if not of America, then of New York."[17]

What did the popularization of Freud's ideas mean to privacy? It was—at first among urban artists and intellectuals, later more broadly—as if a whole population suddenly discovered snorkeling. Strapping on face masks, plunging their heads underwater to watch what was new and exotic, they found life below the surface so compelling that the old seascape paled in comparison. But the view underwater was puzzling.

Simply put, Americans were not sure what to make of this new knowledge. The Freudian perspective is essentially tragic, and American popular culture, as embodied in the newspapers and the media in general, has little use for a theory of tragedy based on individual fallibility. "Make sure you're right, then go ahead," Davy Crockett confidently advised. Freud said such sureness was deeply suspect. Or, as Jonathan Lear observed in a discussion of Freud, "Oedipus's fundamental mistake lies in his assumption that meaning is transparent to human reason. . . . Oedipus assumes he understands his situation, that the meaning of the oracle is immediately available to his conscious understanding. This is why he thinks he can respond to the oracle with a straightforward application of practical reason. Oedipus's mistake, in essence, is to ignore unconscious meaning."[18]

Freud did not replace what Douglas has called the "Protestant pieties." His ideas just crawled in beside them, and they've been uneasy bedfellows ever since. Consequently, the popularization of psychoanalytic ideas has often confused public discourse. The honest disclosure and the sensational one are confounded. The purpose of the private revelation and the public one are confused.

In a mass culture dominated by fragmented remnants of the old pieties, a culture that wants Hyde to be a weird "not me" experience, the possibility offered by Freudian insight too often gets reduced to a repetitive tableau of newly discovered corruption. We insist on being surprised by the unconscious. In the public discourse, Louis, the Vichy cop, stripped of irony, repeatedly professes shock at finding that there is indeed gambling going on in Bogart's café.

In the spring of 1886, Robert Louis Stevenson wrote to J.A.

Symonds, "*Jekyll* is a dreadful thing, I own; but the only thing I feel dreadful about is that damned old business of the war in the members. This time it came out; I hope it will stay in, in future."[19] Stevenson's poignant statement of his helplessness, "I hope it will stay in, in future," offers one approach to the human predicament. Using transference, psychoanalysis found and captured a second, particularly humane possibility within privacy and put it to public use, an alternative approach for Stevenson as well as Jekyll. Two people sitting in a room could use intimacy, private space, and private experience, to defuse the unbearable pressure of psychic life.

In the privacy of the consulting room, psychoanalysis offered a more sophisticated perspective that revealed a paradoxical relationship between public and private truth (i.e., accepted that they would always be interdependent and contradictory, that there would always be gambling in the café.) Swept into the strong current of the culture, psychoanalytic ideas both swelled and served its insistence that the important truth was somehow hidden, but often as corruption rather than complexity. Whereas the notion of the unconscious insists that we bear complexity, the notion of corruption preserves the sentimental ideal that Reverend Beecher is "pure" or that somewhere, elsewhere, Dr. Jekyll thrives—apart from Hyde.

6

Shame, Sex, and Privacy

You can't understand privacy without understanding shame. Although Freud wrote little about shame, later psychoanalysts (as well as philosophers as early as Plato), have recognized its central place in psychology and human life. Look closely at Hyde, and you see that the monster is constructed from disavowed parts of himself that Jekyll considered shameful—including disowned sexual wishes. Sex and shame are complexly connected, and exploring their relationship illuminates privacy.

In 1992, Richard Rhodes published a very explicit account of his sexual practices, entitled *Making Love: An Erotic Odyssey.*[1] It's a thin book, with a yellow-tan cover and a picture of a woman in underpants and a bra clinging to a man whose head is buried in her arms and breasts, his body mostly obscured behind hers. They are lying on a bed—or some other erotic neverland—alone together, confident that they will not be disturbed. Except, of course, that we see them. Underneath the picture a caption announces: "By the Pulitzer prize-winning author of *The Making of the Atomic Bomb,*" an unsettling assertion, though just why is ambiguous. Is it the publisher's effort to reassure us by declaiming their author's literary credentials? Don't worry, this erotic material is safe, the writer highbrow. Perhaps it is the ironic juxtaposition of making bombs and making love. They are letting us know that we are in the hands of an expert: someone who can shed light on how all things are made.

Making Love carries out Freud's suggestion that we tell our sexuality. Or does it? Psychoanalysis intended us to do so in the privacy of the consulting room, where the intimate experience of talking to someone would be as significant as the details themselves. But Rhodes tells his sexuality publicly, and also speculates on the unconscious associations and early experiences that helped to create it. He tells that he survived an abusive childhood, and that he has been a patient in psychotherapy. He tells about the women and boys he's had sex with, and exactly how he masturbates, and what his penis length is erect and dormant. He tells what, at least at first glance, seems to be absolutely *everything that comes to mind* about his sexual practices.

And in the process, he makes me wish he'd stop. I want to cover the explicit and personal nakedness, perhaps to protect myself from Rhodes, but more deeply to protect Rhodes from his wish to show everything. Yet, it is a protection he neither seeks nor desires, and he implies that the problem is mine, not his. To himself, Rhodes is like a doctor who, in heroic desperation, fed up with public ignorance and silence, takes the experimental cure, and recounts the results.

Still, like some petty museum functionary, I want to drape a fig leaf over him. Is this prudery? Undoubtedly in part, but most explicit books or movies don't raise any censoring impulse in me. I think my feeling about Rhodes comes in response to a particular quality of angry shamelessness within the book. The psychoanalyst Erik Erikson has observed that when a person has been shamed too much, the shaming does not lead to "genuine propriety," but in fact is likely to result in "defiant shamelessness."[2]

Unacknowledged by Rhodes, a defiant shamelessness drives *Making Love,* and controls and guides his disclosures. An example: "My daughter asked me once if I'd ever heard of someone coming to lovemaking already fully erect—she had a new boyfriend. I told her yes, I usually did, and though we're candid with each other about sex she blushed scarlet."[3] No doubt more parents should talk about sex with their kids. Yet Rhodes's unsolicited self-disclosure mortifies his daughter—violating both their privacies and making the reader wonder why the writer couldn't manage a more discreet response.

When, in his review of the book, Martin Amis writes, "What Mr. Rhodes gives us, in any event, is a cataract of embarrassment,"[4] it is this shamelessness to which Amis is referring. He feels embarrassed for Rhodes because Rhodes is unable or unwilling to feel embarrassed for himself. Later Amis expands his objections: "The reader girds himself for confession, or confession of a kind, because (sexily) one's sexual truth is always furtive, always obscure, by definition. That's why it's sexy."[5]

It's a paradox. You cannot declaim your sexual truth because the very quality that endows it with sexiness is that it is veiled, held away from language and public exposure—private. You can spell out your fantasies or catalog your preferences, but by doing so publicly, you tend to sever the facts from their personal meaning and full feeling. Open a camera when it contains film. You can look. But the light you let in destroys the images you prematurely seek.

Rhodes criticizes fiction as an inadequate vehicle for recounting personal sexual experience. "Fiction is fine, but using fiction as a disguise makes both the uniqueness of intimate experience and its common humanity easy to dispute."[6] Amis totally disagrees, re-ferring to Rhodes's idea as "spectacularly mistaken." He writes: "When fiction works, the individual and the universal are friction-lessly combined. In real life, sex demotes individuality, leaving us only with the usual sorry quiddity of various personal fetishes and taboos."[7] Once again, a paradox. Fiction preserves privacy, and by so doing allows us to expose our most personal experiences without harming them. It is as if in fiction we enter a darkroom where we can unroll unstable film, and develop it safely.

Most people would agree that sex is private. Men, and occa-sionally women, might announce that they "got laid." But how many, in the next breath, will add the *real* details: the feelings, memories, wishes, and fantasies that they experienced? Even when talking with a trusted confidant, people tend to speak selectively, mentioning some details, or thoroughly replaying some encoun-ters, but leaving out many. And with good reason. To tell every-thing is likely either to give information that makes one feel unduly vulnerable, or to betray the intimacy by overexposing it, and thus shifting allegiance from the event to the recounting.

For both good reasons and bad, sex and shame are often linked. People seek to find a way around the shame that sometimes accompanies their sexual fantasies, feelings, and practices. Prostitu-tion has thrived for many reasons; one of the most important is that by paying for sex with a woman who is socially ostracized and devalued, a man who is ashamed of his deepest sexual wishes may enact them without confronting his own shame. Society makes her the shamed one so that he does not have to be.

While reducing shame is usually to the good, doing away with it completely is not only impossible, but undesirable. The proximity of shame is *part* of what makes sex sexy. By this I do not mean that people feel ashamed having sex, but rather that shame is part of the tangled skein of sexuality. But what is shame? And what does it have to do with our larger discussion of privacy?

Although Freud never explored shame in depth, two of his near contemporaries, Charles Darwin and Havelock Ellis, as well as psychologists and analysts who followed—Erik Erikson, Helen Block Lewis, Heinz Kohut, among others—recognized and explicated its critical place in psychological life. Privacy cannot be understood without understanding shame. For one thing, it is shame about one's human needs, feelings, desires, and impulses that tends to make people straddle the boundary between privacy and secrecy, isolation and intimacy, inhibition and self-expression, and so forth. One of privacy's prime functions is to provide a place where one may either meet exposure without shame, or ready oneself to do so.

If we return for a moment to the split of self represented by *Dr. Jekyll and Mr. Hyde,* we might say that part of Jekyll's disowning of Hyde comes from his shame about those parts of his own experience that do not fall within his narrow and rigid definition of acceptable propriety (which includes his internalized idea of society's expectation). The secrecy with which he surrounds his activities is shame's hallmark. Unable to manage or transmute the shame, Jekyll splits himself into two parts, one stifled by shame and the other shameless.

In 1872, Charles Darwin wrote, "Blushing is the most peculiar and most human of all expressions."[8] As far as we know, bears and chimpanzees do not blush. Only people do. In fact, Carl Schneider points out in *Shame, Exposure and Privacy,* nineteenth-century "scientists" spent time trying to ascertain whether black people blushed, hoping by this measure to learn whether they were "fully" human.[9] (In retrospect, this was a shameful experiment.) People blush because they are self-aware, and their blush registers the difference between how they *wish* to see themselves and how they *fear* being seen by others.

Life is full of shame—from mild embarrassment to severe mortification. When people feel these feelings, the response is universal: They want to hide. In conversation, they avert their eyes, or cover their faces. They often blush. They feel confused. They feel exposed. They feel terrible, not as with guilt, simply about something they did, but about the *whole* of who they are.[10]

It appears shame is an early warning system we carry within that alerts us when we are in danger of cutting an important tie—of breaking an "affectionate bond."[11] Shame tells us loud and clear when we are at risk of revealing something about ourselves we fear will harm a connection with others important to us—isolate us from the group on whom our survival depends.

Infants are social from birth, their survival based on being able to get along. The infant's bottom line is that if she totally alienates her mother or father, her mother may stop nursing her, or her father may put her out for the crows to eat. To minimize this possibility, nature equips the child early on not only with a winning smile, but also, at least by the time she is a toddler—and probably in rudimentary forms much earlier—with the capacity for shame.

A researcher puts a dab of rouge on a toddler's nose, and then lets him look at himself in a mirror. It turns out this simple experiment is an elegant way of demonstrating the onset of self-awareness and its concomitant shame. Whereas a one-year-old will seem barely to notice his own red nose, a two-year-old blushes or giggles at the sight. His brain has developed to the point where he can recognize when the self-image he holds in his mind is different from the way he appears to other people. Flustered, he ducks his eyes, and may turn to a trusted adult to find out whether he should feel embarrassed, frightened, sad, happy, proud, angered, or amused by his predicament.

The moment when he seeks out the consensual expression on his caretaker's face is critical to understanding shame. To put it in perspective, this process—of seeking validation from an important caretaker—has been occurring countless times a day since his birth. Sophisticated studies of mutual gazing and gaze aversion by Edward Tronick and others now offer us frame-by-frame analysis of the emotional rhythms between caretakers (usually mothers) and even tiny infants. When you smile and look in your infant's eyes, she gradually smiles. But if you suddenly change your expression and look frightened, sad, or angry, she will avert her gaze—first puzzled, then flustered—and may well collapse into tears.

Much can be said about such sequences, but central to understanding shame is that an important piece of a child's view of herself and others originates in her gradual compilations of these encounters. From infancy on, children look to the people around them to learn how they should react to their world and themselves. When a toddler sticks his hand in his dirty diaper, or eats food he's spit up, he quickly reads the expressions of disgust on others' faces. Eventually, he accumulates a distilled sense of their responses that become an important—even critical—basis for his own feelings. "The affect of shame," Leon Wurmser has written, "replaces the fear of external punishment by humiliation, scorn and contempt."[12] You stop exploring your dirty diapers because you do not want to be told you are contemptible. Even in the absence of adults actually reacting, you do not want to feel the bad feeling you have internalized: the memories of *their* disgust that, because you love them, identify with them, realize their greater power, and want their love, have gradually become *your* disgust.

This internalized function of shame is inexact. As well as preventing people from acting in ways that may alienate others in their communal circle, it functions more idiosyncratically. Children internalize their caretakers' odd ideas of what is shameful, as well as their own fantasies and worries about what might be shameful. And when these compound, they may inhibit aspects of self-development. For example, if, as a child, Dr. Jekyll was taught that it was shameful to express sad feelings, he may have tried to stop feeling altogether as a way to ensure safety from shame. When you do not tolerate your feelings, it becomes difficult to know who you are in any but a narrow, lifeless way. Thus, once again, the need for a disowned Hyde.

In recent years, some writers in magazines and opinion columns have naively suggested that we introduce more shame into public culture. The talk radio enthusiasm for the punishment by public caning of the American boy Michael Fay in Singapore who had vandalized cars with spray paint is one example of this position.[13] In my experience, while there is an occasional public role for words that evoke shame, humiliating people in extreme ways tends only to increase their wish to humiliate others in secret. It is often not a useful method for encouraging mature and autonomous self-development. Shame functions best in small quantities, either in the context of loving relationships or when it violates self-love.

In the day-care center where I worked after college, worked a remarkable teacher. Born as this century was beginning, Bertha had grown up in a poor Irish-Catholic family, spent years as a governess, and eventually found her way into teaching developmentally impaired preschoolers. She was unmarried and childless, had no degrees, but she had a genius with children. When I knew her, she was seventy-two and still opening the center every morning at seven. Partially crippled from childhood polio—one leg was normal, the other like a stick—she limped through her day, patiently coaching her charges along, and rarely raising her voice even slightly in spite of much provocation. She told me once that she believed she walked only because when she was three years old and caught polio, her mother would not give in to the paralysis, and rubbed her legs day and night to save them. I suspect it was gratitude for this devotion that sustained her work.

The other teachers were mixed about Bertha. They admired her skill. At the same time, they were envious and irritated by her "good girl" aura. (A devout Catholic, Bertha didn't drink or smoke, and at the end of a long day would often climb the stairs to the director's apartment, and wash her dishes.) Her colleagues delighted in telling about the one time they ever saw her angry, a story that illustrates much about the useful workings of shame.

Bertha wanted a wading pool for the day-care center. She pestered everyone, and wouldn't quit. After some years, money was scraped together, and a local contractor hired to bulldoze and pour cement. Bertha supervised the construction, and delighted in the pool. She cleaned it, and trimmed the grass around it where the lawnmower couldn't reach. One got the sense that it realized some long-held wish that transcended the center. Had she once been governess to wealthy children who had such a pool? I'm not sure. Perhaps it was just a huge relief on hot days.

At the time the pool was built, one of the seven or eight children in Bertha's classroom was a little boy of five who would not be toilet trained. Originally, the child had been in a regular classroom, but his teachers found him so out of control, difficult, and resistant that they handed him over to Bertha. He settled down, and Bertha gradually helped him learn to talk, dress himself, and play. Many times she tried toilet training him, but to no avail. She waited patiently, fending off the criticisms of the other teachers.

One summer day, Bertha's charges were playing in the water.

As she sat on the grass nearby, chatting and watching the children, the little boy loosed his trunks, squatted, and dropped a large bowel movement into the pool. Her pool. Bertha was stunned. Pulling herself up as quickly as she could, she angrily walked over to the boy, took hold of his shoulders, and looked into his eyes. "Don't ever," she scolded him fiercely, "do that again. This pool is for swimming. From now on *you* are going to *use the toilet!*"

And he did. But why? Carl Schneider has written that "shame arises at a point where some discrediting fact or quality seems to run the risk of appearing particularly prominent, thus calling into question the status and esteem in which this person is held by the other."[14] In the simplest sense, shame is about the wish to remain loveable, and the fear that if truly known, one will be found lacking.

Bertha's anger catalyzed the boy to use the toilet, but I don't think it was because he felt coerced or battered. Many adults had expressed lots of anger at him, and if anything, their approach had heightened his resistance, and probably his despair. Bertha's anger "worked" because she and the boy had loved each other long enough for him to have accumulated in his psyche a feeling for a self worthy of her love, and because she let him know he was disappointing her. He could feel shame because he had felt love, and changed so that he would not endanger the love. Loveless shaming and other sadistic approaches might eventually have made the child so miserable, even terrorized, that he would have decided to use a toilet, but likely they would also have led to the kind of defiant shamelessness Erikson describes and Rhodes's book embodies.

Shame is an intense emotion. A little goes a long way, and too much quickly becomes harmful. I remember once, while homevisiting in a housing project, meeting a woman who had suffered for months with a large open sore on her leg. When I suggested she seek medical care, she told me she felt too ashamed to go to a doctor and admit she had not done as he or others before him had instructed. Diabetic, she worked selling donuts. She stood all day. Many times she had been told that she needed to rest her leg and control her diet. But how could she rest her leg? Her boss would fire her, then she'd lose her apartment. She kept working, and hard as she tried, she couldn't stop eating donuts. The leg festered, but the physical pain was nothing beside the prospect of feeling shamed.

Many people feel terrible and disproportionate shame. They hide, suffer alone, and refuse intimacy, afraid of being revealed if they are known. Take the prisoner who has committed abominable crimes. Speak with him intimately and at length, and underneath the cruelty, rage, and bravado very often you will hear not about an absence of shaming, but just the opposite, about so much early profound humiliation that to survive psychically he had to disconnect from his capacity to feel shame, and become shameless. Certainly, if I were to distill a single impression from years of working in the housing project clinic, it is of the awful and paralyzing shame that the larger culture forces upon people who live in poverty.

Leon Wurmser has written that shame is "the polarity, the tension, between how I want to be seen and how I am."[15] Shame allows us to live communally because it signals to us that we are being unloveable or unacceptable—we are violating the compiled instructions and specifications that we've been given about what constitutes an acceptable humanness. People's shame detectors buzz when they do not comply with some deeply inculcated sense of who they feel they ought to be. Sometimes the results can be surprising.

I had a schoolmate in college who was a very tall woman with long blond hair. She lived in New York City and had commuted to and from her high school on the subway. Girls on city subways were considered fair prey by some men, and she was not infrequently touched and molested as she rode the trains. One day, dressed in a skirt, crowded onto a car at rush hour, she realized that someone's fingers were working their way up her thigh toward her underpants. Violated and fed up, she reached down with both hands, grabbed his, and raised it into the air as high as she could. Waving it back and forth, she loudly called out to all in the car, "WHOSE HAND IS THIS UP MY SKIRT?" Everyone stared, and her mortified assailant fled at the next stop. Doubtless, he had counted on the girl's shame to silence her—to make her feel that if she called attention to the situation, she would reveal herself as loud or immodest, qualities that traditionally have made girls feel ashamed. But she turned the tables, exposing and mortifying him. With the *fact* of his hand trapped in hers, she publicly confronted his *wish* to be *seen* both as respectable by the other passengers and as powerful by her.

The particular incidents that make people feel ashamed vary widely. In a chapter on modesty in his 1901 classic, *Studies in the Psychology of Sex*, Havelock Ellis tells of a woman posing naked in front of a group of art students:

> A pupil of Ingres tells that a female model was once quietly posing, completely nude, at the Ecole des Beaux Arts. Suddenly she screamed, and ran to cover herself with her garments. She had seen the head of a workman on the roof gazing inquisitively at her through a sky-light.[16]

Having gathered data from many sources—history books, anthropology tracts, personal anecdotes—Ellis concludes that while the actual practices of cultures can be vastly different, the phenomenon of modesty is universal. A person in a tribe somewhere may be comfortable sitting without clothes among strangers, but is shamed by eating in front of them because eating is private. It is the violation of the conventions of the particular context that mortifies. Depending on its idiosyncratic meaning, Helen Merrell Lynd has observed, a person may feel massively shamed by a slight exposure—like being told that he has a spot on his tie, or a hole in his sock, or that everyone knows about his crush on someone who doesn't love him.[17]

However varied particular triggers, the underlying ideas that make people feel shame are common, and cluster around a limited number of themes. Leon Wurmser described six that are central: (1) I am weak; (2) I am dirty; (3) I am physically or mentally defective; (4) I have lost control over my body or my feelings; (5) I am sexually excited about suffering, degradation, and distress; (6) watching and self-exposing are dangerous activities and I may be punished.[18] Furthermore, people tend to feel ashamed of feeling ashamed, and struggle to hide it.

Shame is often characterized by surprise; a person feels exposed, unready. In a dream, the exam comes and I have not studied; I drive to work, but in night clothes. A remark I pass off as helpful is revealed as mean. Shame reveals incongruity. One person is visibly sexually excited on a first date while the other is not. Lynd points out that King Lear feels shame when he weeps because his tears are incongruent with his belief that kings don't cry.[19]

Shame and the wish for privacy are not the same, but they are often connected and frequently confused. Shame wanders in and out of the wish for privacy, sometimes revealing itself fully, other times affecting the scene from the wings. People often seek privacy precisely so they won't feel surprised by shame, and when allowed it in adequate amounts, are less likely to become overwhelmed by their embarrassed feelings. One *critical* function of privacy is to give the psyche time and space in which to manage shame—not unlike the way locks raise and lower water levels so that boats may traverse difficult places.

Shame and privacy are also linked by vulnerability. People seek privacy so that they can be safely vulnerable. In most societies, defecation is private because squatting makes people vulnerable—for instance, to an enemy attack. So too with lovemaking. One cannot make love without assuming a position that reduces the possibilities for immediate flight. But while the physical source of vulnerability is relevant, it is psychological vulnerability that is central.[20]

Aside from worry over children witnessing, people seek privacy for sex so they can be psychologically vulnerable. In private they can overcome modesty for the sake of enjoying lust and intimacy, and by so doing, gain respite from their separateness. When not immediately endangered, animals have no qualms about public sex. Stare at one dog mounting another, and it does not appear to inhibit him. But stare at a person, and it usually does. He becomes self-conscious. In the words of D.H. Lawrence:

> When Adam went and took Eve, *after* the apple, he didn't do any more than he had done many a time before, in act. But in consciousness he did something very different. So did Eve. Each of them kept an eye on what they were doing, they watched what was happening to them. They wanted to KNOW. And that was the birth of sin. Not *doing* it, but KNOWING about it. . . . Now, they peeped and pried and imagined. . . . And they felt uncomfortable after. They felt self-conscious.[21]

Once self-conscious, a man may worry that his body is imperfect; he is naked, and embarrassed that you are seeing his beer belly. He wonders if he will get an erection, or maintain it long enough to give pleasure. Perhaps you will judge him inadequate. He may worry that you see his feelings, find his tenderness ridiculous, mock his passion. What if you feel contempt for his manliness, or abhor his particular wishes? The fears keep close company to the more confident and passionate fantasies: He is potent, he is powerful, he is irresistible, he is loved. Depending on many things, he moves among these varied self-perceptions.

Self-consciousness is tricky—even fickle. It is highly susceptible to subtle cues and innuendos. As with the nude model Ellis describes, a slight inflection can completely alter self-perception. The woman felt comfortable with the students drawing her—we're not told just why, but perhaps because she saw herself in their eyes as a professional and an object of beauty. Whatever irreverent feelings they had, whatever contempt for her willingness to display herself, whatever criticism of her body, were unspoken and unacknowledged. But the workman who stared at her through the skylight had no such pretext, and no drawing pad. Seeing herself in *his* eyes, the model became a woman in public without clothes. The pleasant exhibitionism, the delicate freedom from modesty she had granted herself, collapsed. She imagined herself differently. And how we imagine ourselves at different moments—what we think we see in others' eyes—profoundly affects how we feel.

People seek privacy for lovemaking partly as a way of quieting self-consciousness so that they may play. In *Learning to Be Human,* Leston Havens writes:

> Sexuality . . . represents an exquisite balancing act between the demands of imagination and reality. Only the most self-possessed, only those able to be both free and compliant, can afford full conquest or surrender without actual diminution. The danger for the less fortunate is that what can be imaginative play comes to represent domination and actual submission.[22]

The imaginative play that creates and allows the richest sexuality requires intimacy without distraction, and thus privacy. But there is more. Shame inhibits play, and to play well and freely, one must be able to create a private arena that shame will not overwhelm.

At the same time, without at least an unconscious threat of shame, there is often less sexual tension. Part of sexual pleasure and abandon results from doing what could easily be deemed shameful, but eluding the shame. The revelation of self involved in sex carries with it the risk that one will have set aside discretion and allowed oneself to be intimately seen, only to be found somehow wanting. Conversely, the pleasure people feel in intimacy is often underpinned by the relief of having the potentially shamed and estranged self accepted by a lover. Privacy creates a space in which this can occur.

Shame and privacy are important to sex for another reason. Working together, they sustain awe and mystery. During this century, much effort has gone toward demystifying sex, which often had been so obscured that people suffered without recourse. People have sought information about sexuality, and reassurance that others either share their fantasies and desires or possess more unusual ones of their own. Havelock Ellis, the Kinsey Report, Margaret Sanger, Masters and Johnson, Alex Comfort, and Dr. Ruth are among many who have offered advice, reassurance, and information. Sex as procreation and stolen pleasure has shifted to an ideal of sex as intimacy, ecstasy, and self-expression. People's increased information and, oftentimes, increased sexual ease is much to the good.

Yet what is interesting vis-à-vis shame is how often it doesn't disappear as much as it migrates. Drive it from one locale, and it may flop down and settle itself somewhere else. In situations where conventional restraints about sexuality are publicly lampooned, and most of the crowd, feeling themselves relieved of shame, laughs with the lampooners, some people end up *ashamed* of *feeling sincerely* what is parodied or debased. The most embarrassed member of the audience in a Berlin cabaret may not have been the libertine whose sexual hobbies were displayed on stage, but the young man sitting next to her who believed in monogamy, and felt too humiliated to say so.

Furthermore, the erotic often thrives on what is hidden and unexplicit. Sexuality is heightened by illusion and awe. The pleasure of sex is created by real contact with a real person, but that pleasure is closely interwoven with fantasy and idealization. The other person sexually excites us through love and lust, but also because he does not blatantly contradict and squelch the fantasies that also arouse us. One reason that sexual tension runs so high at the outset of relationships is that experience has not yet tempered the impersonal hopefulness of the idealizations.

"Shame is close to the feeling of awe," Helen Block Lewis points out.[23] While at first puzzling, on closer examination, this assertion makes sense. Awe, *Webster's* states, has to do with "dread and terror." It is "a profound and reverent fear inspired by deity," a "reverent wonder tinged with fear inspired by the sublime."[24] The shame that the child feels when he imagines a transgression is the secular counterpart to the awe that keeps the devotee from transgressing. Neither wants to evoke the contempt of the powerful, important other. In a sense, awe is shame writ large. Lewis further observes about awe that "fascination with the 'other' and sensitivity to the 'other's' treatment of the self can ease the acute feeling of shame, while at the same time it renders the self still more vulnerable to shame. It is the feeling state from which one is very susceptible to falling in love. And when one is in love, one is very susceptible to the shame of rebuff or rejection."[25]

In other words, when we are in awe of others, we focus upon them with apprehension. We experience them as having strong power to judge us and find us defective or disgusting—to make us feel ashamed. When our worst fears are not realized, when they do not find us contemptible or shameful, we are inclined to fall in love—probably partly from the intensity of our relief, partly from gratitude, and from a wish to join with them and partake of their power.

Elizabeth Tilton probably felt considerable awe toward Henry Ward Beecher. Her husband had long held Beecher up to her as someone powerful, to be admired—someone whose judgment mattered. Beecher was famous and accomplished. Furthermore, he was Elizabeth Tilton's minister, and she was devout. Whereas her husband was ashamed of her, Beecher was not—at least for a while. Beecher may have felt ashamed of his meager fiction writing skills. Elizabeth's admiration helped him write. Once you understand shame, it is easy to understand the powerful feelings that Mrs. Tilton and Henry Ward Beecher must have experienced. So, too, in the case of Dr. Breuer and "Anna O." "Anna O." revealed her most intimate feelings to an accomplished and powerful doctor who could easily have ridiculed her, but he did not. Rather, he expressed interest in and acceptance of what she had to say. Little wonder that she was smitten, or that he felt embarrassed by the love and desire entangled with his professional interest.

Because the idealizations in sexuality evoke our earliest feelings about the power of the "other," (i.e., because the person a woman falls in love with evokes her childhood sense of a powerful adult), the other person's acceptance of the self becomes imbued with meanings larger than the immediate relationship. Thus the dimension of awe. And because awe evokes the sublime, and because sexuality cannot help but make people mindful of wonder, awe enhances sex. And a sense of shame preserves awe. As does privacy. By keeping sex mostly private, we agree to allow shame the power to preserve awe.

To the degree that language demystifies experience, to the degree that it reduces larger and more primitive feelings into more manageable named constructs, it also reduces awe and its companion, fear. In many situations, nothing is more desirable. People are often haunted for years by misunderstandings or traumas not simply because something bad happened, but because no one helped or even allowed them to speak about it.

But many people find it difficult to talk about sex. Both as a friend and a therapist, I have been struck by how, while some things about one's own sexuality are easily said, others can be surprisingly difficult. After endless internal debate, patients will awkwardly spit out a few words about their sexual feelings or fantasies, often mortified to tell me something I have surmised for months. Listening, I am struck by how the hesitancy and embarrassment far overshadow the confession, and how the reticence settles on different details for each person.

At the same time, people who wish that we could speak with complete ease miss the point. For while confessing and conversing are helpful, even at moments critical, if we constantly speak to everyone about the intimate details of our sexual feeling until we no longer feel modest or embarrassed, we diminish awe and illusion—and more. We shift our allegiance from the intimacy to the telling, and by so doing not only aggravate self-consciousness, but use language to create inordinate detachment. It is a delicate balance.

Speaking in print about the details of one's own sexuality is even more complicated. While in *Making Love,* Richard Rhodes alludes to the terrible pain that seems to underlie his wish to tell, in an earlier memoir, *A Hole in the World,* he describes it. Rhodes's mother committed suicide when he was an infant. His father, a railroad worker, raised him and his brother for a while with the help of different women in rooming houses, and then remarried. His stepmother, a sadistic woman, not only tortured the boys by beating, starving, and humiliating them, but helped to create a dynamic in the family that left their father humiliated and powerless to protect them.

Rhodes remembers waking one morning after an argument between his father and stepmother, shocked to see his father naked in the kitchen frying eggs. His stepmother appears, and the fight continues:

> "Aren't you ashamed to be walking around naked in front of your children?" she challenged Dad contemptuously.
> "Why should I be ashamed?" he threw back. "You tell me I'm not a man. Let them see for themselves."

Quickly the ugliness escalates:

> She grabbed the boiling teakettle off the stove and brandished it. "You son of a bitch," she shouted at him, "you think you can push me around? You go get some clothes on or I'll scald your ugly prick!"
> Dad stared at her. He believed her. He hung his head and walked out. She took over at the stove.[26]

It's a horrifying scene: horrifying that adults would treat each other this way; horrifying that children should have to witness. It demonstrates concisely how readily humiliation can be used to harm. And it reveals how shame partakes of an unspoken covenant.

Like so much else, when it occurs in private, its function—to maintain behavior worthy of love—is subject to corruption.

Rhodes's stepmother corrupted shame by using it lovelessly as a means of abuse, and his father buckled under. Rhodes and his brother suffered the awful consequences until in desperation his brother ran to the police, and they were placed in a farm school. Later, Rhodes attended Yale on scholarship, and became an important scholar.

But why did Rhodes write *Making Love?* Why does he choose to show so particularly what most people would shield? At the beginning of the book, he offers reasons that are thought provoking even if inadequate. He begins by pointing out that few people have published first-person accounts of sex. Equating himself with Kinsey and Masters and Johnson, he adds, "I believe that all that can be thought *must* be spoken and written, communicated and shared, that ignorance and silence are pain, that to speak (to write) is to contribute to alleviating that pain."[27]

Trying to understand how he survived his growing up, he recognizes the importance of his brother's love, the help of teachers, his own good mind. Yet the story is incomplete:

> But I also survived, in the years after my rescue and well into adulthood, by using my sexuality to structure and confine the extensive psychological damage the years of abuse had inflicted on me. . . . And however unfit for the parlor, such survival skills ought to be shared. The taboo against writing about one's personal sexual experience cuts us off from valuable knowledge. In *Making Love* I share what I learned. You may or may not find the experience comfortable.[28]

What a complicated series of assertions. His suffering created in him an equivalent of Mr. Hyde. Rather than inflict this "monstrous" part of himself upon others, Rhodes found ways to contain it within elaborate and compulsive sexual practices. Certainly, his ability to control so much rage in a world where many people feel obliged (or able) to contain little, can be seen as a real act of courage.

But the statement is provocative, I think, for being so openly indifferent to his readers' discomfort. One feels the rage boiling over. In a chapter about masturbation, Rhodes describes how for thirty years, he spent hours—often daily—masturbating in front of pornographic movies. About the imaginative world he entered while masturbating he writes, "It isn't a loving world; it's raw and demanding and crude, and when I enter into it I'm raw and demanding and crude too, a side of my personality I prefer to release in private in this way rather than visit upon the world. Touch, intimacy and love I find elsewhere, if I didn't I'd be sick."[29]

Rhodes connects his masturbating to his abuse. One way his stepmother tortured him as a boy was by refusing to allow him to urinate during the night. The pain of attempting to maintain continence was often unbearable. As an adult, when he masturbates and climaxes, he believes he repeatedly defies and triumphs over his stepmother. "I come so powerfully that I convulse and momentarily lose consciousness; my ejaculate, released like the urine I was once forced to retain, sprays as much as six feet across the room."[30]

Why does Mr. Rhodes write this? His rationale for his revelation, that by describing his practices he is sharing survival skills with fellow sufferers, does not ring true. It is possible that some people, troubled by particular sexual habits, or exhausted by their own shame-driven secrecy, might feel relieved to have him offer his testimony. But I wonder. Over the years, working as a therapist, I have heard many terrible stories of trauma. Usually they pull me in even when they are almost unbearable to hear. When they push me away I have found that it is often because the teller primarily wishes to hurt as he has been hurt. It seems that, at moments, Rhodes's rage overtakes him; he makes us into his stepmother, and takes aim at us. And while he has earned his anger, we are not his proper target, and we rightly cringe. For all the stories of sexual initiation, and hours spent in orgasm, *Making Love* is a bellow of rage. Rhodes's pain has blown the fuse of his shame, and made him write a book that alienates—however sympathetic you are to his wish to redress a horrible past.

Because Rhodes's father and stepmother, entrusted with his care when he was a child, badly violated that trust, twisted family privacy into secrecy to cover torture, they lost their right to privacy. And he owes them neither loyalty nor discretion. Too often propriety is observed at tremendous expense to real victims. But an interesting question is to what degree Rhodes owes these things to himself. A sense of privacy, often underpinned by shame, energizes and transforms self-expression into art by realizing a psychic wish both to transmute experience and to *connect* with others. Shamelessness may inhibit that process. Oddly, even if Rhodes had presented *Making Love* as a journal (Jim Carroll's *Basketball Diaries* come to mind), the convention of the form would have offered some protection. When people write about sex in fiction, or with more insight and detachment in memoirs, or anonymously in self-help books, they often manage to preserve privacy to such an extent that the reader feels safe to approach and partake of their experience. Aggressively determined to show everything, Rhodes pushes the reader away.

Sounding another note, Rhodes—rather like Henry Ward Beecher—emphasizes that privacy, in the form of intimacy, can be used to heal trauma, and that by building private, loving relationships one overcomes the past—an important point. Ironically,

Making Love also reminds us not only how love's power can be stunted, but how tenaciously the past sometimes stays with us, and with what complexity our sexuality and our sense of shame are entwined with our particular growing up. No child should suffer the cruelty Rhodes experienced. If his shamelessness embarrasses, he has earned a right to howl. And he teaches unexpected lessons. Like the people who describe awful experiences on television, Rhodes reminds us that the real violations of privacy have often occurred long before anyone takes his story public. Moreover, his experience illustrates why privacy about sex is the more common human wish, and shamelessness the legacy of badly damaged love.

7

Burnt Letters, Biography, and Privacy

"What shall you do—where shall you go?" I asked.

"Oh I don't know. I've done the great thing. I've destroyed the papers."

"Destroyed them?" I wailed.

"Yes; what was I to keep them for? I burnt them last night, one by one, in the kitchen."

"One by one?" I coldly echoed it.

"It took a long time—there were so many."[1]

So pass from the world the private papers and intimate letters of the famous early American poet, Jeffrey Aspern. No biographer will ever see them. Whatever might be written about Aspern's life, the story of his first passionate love will remain untold. If Aspern's name rings no bells, it is because he lived only in Henry James's 1888 novella, *The Aspern Papers*. In fact, when the tale begins, Aspern is dead, but the woman he adored in his youth, Juliana Bordereau—the inspiration for his early poems—is alive. Sort of. Easily ninety years old, and secluded with her niece "Miss Tina," in a decaying palazzo in Venice, Miss Bordereau rarely leaves her bedroom. She hasn't inspired a poem—or even set foot in a gondola—in decades; she lives on little but memories and her collection of

Aspern mementos. Over the years she has turned away any biographers who have approached her.

The narrator, a literary critic/biographer, is determined to invade her privacy. A passionate admirer of Aspern, he feels any means justified to unearth the details of his hero's life. He cannot understand how Juliana has managed to avoid discovery—or why she has wanted to—"in the latter half of the nineteenth century—the age of newspapers and telegrams and photographs and interviewers."[2] Her reluctance to talk is incomprehensible to him—quaint, silly, not serious—and he plots how to win her trust. He schemes, changes his name (lest she recognize him as an Aspern scholar), and moves into the Bordereau palazzo, paying a fortune to rent rooms from the cash-poor women, hoping to make his way into their confidence, and particularly into the elder Miss Bordereau's locked trunk.

But he doesn't anticipate that his ancient quarry is wily. While he strategizes how to get into Juliana's desk drawers, she looks for ways to entangle him with her lonely, aging niece, Tina Bordereau. It is a game of strategy, and each moves his pieces. Eventually, the narrator slips. Given an apparent opening, he cannot keep himself from plundering Juliana's bedroom. Of course, she catches him. "I never shall forget her strange little bent white tottering figure, with its lifted head, her attitude, her expression; neither shall I forget the tone in which as I turned, looking at her, she hissed out passionately, furiously: 'Ah you publishing scoundrel!'"[3]

But the match is not over. Though the elder Miss Bordereau soon dies, the narrator has not anticipated the niece's endgame. When he makes a play for the papers, she proposes marriage: Join the family, and the letters and papers will rightfully be yours. Horrified, he flees. ("I couldn't accept the proposal. I couldn't for a bundle of tattered papers, marry a ridiculous pathetic provincial old woman."[4]) When he returns a day later, she has burned everything.

Literary estates are full of battles, and many writers have destroyed what they did not want posterity to uncover: Charles Dickens burned papers; George Eliot requested that friends burn her letters after reading them; and W.H. Auden asked the same in his will.[5] But few have approached the matter with the determination of Henry James. Replying in early 1910 to a letter inquiring if he had preserved any correspondence from his friend, the writer Sarah Jewett, James responded that Jewett's letters had "submitted to the law that I have made tolerably absolute":

> the law of not leaving personal and private documents at the mercy of any accidents, or even of my executors! I kept almost all letters for years—till my receptacles would no longer hold them; then I made a gigantic bonfire and have been easier in mind since—save for a certain residuum which *had* to survive.[6]

Not only did he burn letters and papers himself, but James made his wishes clear to his nephew and executor. Writing in 1914, two years before his death, he admonishes, "My sole wish is to frustrate as utterly as possible the post mortem exploiter—which, I know, is but so imperfectly possible." The letter continues:

> I have long thought of launching, by a provision in my will, a curse no less explicit than Shakespeare's own on any such as try to move my bones. Your question determines me definitely to advert to the matter in my will—that is to declare my utter and absolute abhorrence of any attempted biography or the giving to the world by "the family," or by any person for whom my disapproval has any sanctity, of any part or parts of my private correspondence.[7]

Could any statement be more clear? Throughout his life, James passionately sought privacy. The pursuit took myriad forms and is a theme that appears repeatedly in his fiction. Nosy journalists, intrusive biographers, and people mistakenly looking to the life of an artist instead of his art populate his stories.[8]

James believed one guarded privacy to preserve art. After reading a biography of his friend Robert Louis Stevenson, James wrote that telling the story of Stevenson's life robbed his novels of "a certain supremacy and mystery."[9] Biographers were like Stevenson's pirates: blackguards trying to abscond with your treasure. If you couldn't shake free of them, at least you could make their chase hard. But James was better able to destroy letters he received than those he sent (one cannot help but wonder about the complexity of his unconscious motives), and his friends thought better of destroying his. At least *seven thousand* are extant today.[10] And it is no small irony that James became the subject of one of the most detailed biographies ever written: Leon Edel's five-volume study.

Thanks to Edel's massive work, it is possible to understand much about James's wish for privacy. Reading it, you learn how desperately Henry, born less than two years after William, wanted out from his older brother's gaze. William was critical of Henry and reacted negatively to much of his writing. In fact, throughout their lives, in spite of deep love, the two geniuses usually became cranky, unhappy, and sick when forced to spend time together. If Henry arrived for a visit, William often fled. Yet it was Henry who left America and moved to Europe, as much as anything to create a private space away from his family—from William, from his father whose ineptitude embarrassed him, and from his mother who favored him, but held him in a relationship he experienced as stifling, overwhelming, and controlling.

To realize his talent, James needed the privacy Europe offered.

Edel makes this clear. He needed the freedom of living as an outsider, observing more than he was observed, feeling no communal obligations save to his art. Distance allowed him to write what he pleased about America, and when it irritated his audience, he was safely away. He could write freely about Europe because he was American.

Though he despised newspapers that made it public, James enjoyed gossip. The stories his friends recounted to him were the raw materials of his art. But he was fierce about keeping his own life from view. After his sister Alice died—she had spent her last years in London—he panicked that a newspaper would find her diary. When his friend Constance Fenimore Woolson killed herself, he traveled to Venice to help sort through her papers—in part so that he could read and perhaps destroy any private letters or diary entries that mentioned him. (His effort bears an uncanny resemblance to Emerson's sending Thoreau to look for Margaret Fuller's papers after she drowned.) One senses that he felt considerable shame.

For as Edel gradually, powerfully makes clear, James also needed privacy so that he could—finally, well into his fifties—fall in love. To do so, or at least to admit even to himself the intimate feelings, he had to break through his fear, his aloofness, and his remote egotism. Woolson had loved him, but he had apparently been oblivious. Only after he fell in love with the young sculptor Henrik Anderson did James seem to recognize Woolson's feelings. And only after facing himself with his large omission did he go on to write arguably the greatest novels of his career: *The Golden Bowl, The Wings of the Dove, The Ambassadors.* We understand this important shift in James because Edel has described in great detail the private life the writer wanted to sequester. How might we think about such an irony?

The struggle about biography and privacy is old, and the dilemmas of the genre appear early on. One of the first biographies is Plutarch's first-century *Lives of the Noble Grecians and Romans.* Reading it, you watch Plutarch wrestling oral legend into written story. Like subsequent biographers, he senses that audience appeal might rest on leavening the serious with gossip, even as he claims that it is false. Searching for truth among conflicting tales of the parentage of Romulus, founder of Rome, he writes,

> "Others tell a tale of Romulus birth, nothing true nor likely. For it is sayed that there was sometime a king of Alba named Tarchetius, a very wicked and cruell man, in whose house through the permission of the goddes appeared such a like vision: that there rose up in the harthe of his chymney the forme and facion of a mans privie member, which continued there many dayes."[11]

In other words, Plutarch tells us, the rumor is not true: Romulus's genealogy does not include an ancestor having sex with a gigantic, disembodied penis that rose up in a chimney hearth.

Part of the dilemma of biography and privacy is the dilemma of the published word. You watch as Plutarch sorts among conflicting accounts. Communities have public stories and private ones. While the public ones are told openly, the private ones are told more quietly. They may ultimately spread widely, but they are characterized by the intimacy of the transmission: Voices are lowered, and undesirable listeners are excluded. Telling and listening cements relationships among participants. The stories create a second narrative—a counterpoint that fills out or contradicts the official story, even as it offers no overt challenge. It is like a statement of the group unconscious, like the message in a dream, but shared. Sotto voce, the fantasies and ambivalence are revealed.

Once oral legends and myths meet up with print, they begin

to lose their easy privilege of allowing fact and fantasy, public and private, to lie side by side and thus to transmit a more complex truth. Plutarch wrestled with this, and we do today. Often it translates into a struggle between biographer and subject.

An early example of this animus can be found in the nasty lifelong feud Ian Hamilton recounts between the eighteenth-century writer Alexander Pope and the publisher Edmund Curll. No matter how sleazy today's tabloid writers, Curll bested them. He wrote forty or fifty vile sketches of people "who had the ill-fortune to die during his life-time."[12] Curll was taken to court many times, punished and pilloried, and both ears cut off in an effort to subdue his nasty pen. But he kept writing. One of his less endearing practices was to borrow well-known authors' names to stick on his pamphlets—over text they had not written. He tried this on Alexander Pope, who fought back by pouring an emetic into Curll's drink.[13]

Still hoping to get even a decade or so later, Curll published some of Pope's private letters. They sold well, and he advertised to buy more. Pope, realizing that Curll had a good thing going, designed a scheme: He arranged to have Curll steal some of his letters and publish them, and then—using Curll's villainy as an excuse—brought out his own edition, with an eye on profit and a disingenuous story of setting the public record straight.

Ian Hamilton has devoted a book to documenting the struggles between literary estates and biographers, and his tale is filled with burnt letters, letters with paragraphs snipped out, and specialists being called in to unink inked phrases. Occasionally, someone is oblivious of his treasure, so there are also tales of rotting letters, letters used as scrap paper, and lost letters found. While scholars might be made ecstatic by the discovery of unpublished manuscripts or early drafts of famous works, there is no doubt that for biographers, the letter is the true cross. In Janet Malcolm's words, "Letters are the great fixative of experience. Time erodes feeling. Time creates indifference. Letters prove to us that we once cared. They are the fossils of feeling. This is why biographers prize them so: they are biography's only conduit to unmediated experience."[14]

Letters are valuable because they are private. Obviously, not all are. Most often the letter closing a bank account or mail ordering a shirt, or the one addressed "Dear Friends" and used for catching acquaintances up on family news at holiday time, is not terribly private. But it varies—as when the bank account being closed was shared with a child lately disowned, or the holiday letter announces a divorce. The letters of greatest interest tend to be those written to close friends or relatives to whom the writer feels able to speak freely.

Even private letters are various. There are letters that the recipient might show casually, letters that can be shared with intimates, and letters that the writer hopes will not be shared at all. But of course the receiver and the sender are not always agreed on the premise, and even when they are, the world may not oblige them. The private is vulnerable to intrusion exactly because the freshness it contains is so attractive. The pleasure of reading other people's private letters stems from the wish to see what they have not chosen to show.

Writing a letter is different from speaking. When we write, the people whom we address exist as we imagine them. We may see them as docile, receptive, critical, angry, touchy, loving, hurt. It may be more or less as they see themselves. But, while we write, they are as we make them; only later, when they read the letter, can they begin to amend our perspective. Think of a child playing with a doll named after her best friend. The friend she loves or excoriates is the friend internalized in her mind, a presence only partially informed by real life. When we write a letter, though we address a real other person, we also communicate with ourselves.

If, traveling alone, I write my husband, I actively reach out to him, and tailor my content to my sense of him. At the same time, I also undertake a psychological process with myself. Because I choose among impressions to describe some and not others, I organize a story that highlights a few of many perceptions. As I write, I try to make explicit *for myself* a series of feelings that are inchoate—and often confusing—until I form them into language. I allow what has been preconscious or unconscious to come into awareness. Or if already conscious, I offer it the further emphasis of words. So, too, when I write how I miss him, I not only speak to my husband, I comfort *myself* by summoning him—or at least summoning my loving feelings for him, and making them active within my mind. I fight loss, and its attendant mental dulling or disorganization, by making him imaginatively present.

I make order by at once evoking and creating a persona—in this case, fond wife—through which I interpret and organize experience. While this might sound like a disingenuous enterprise, I am only highlighting how the self is rather a vast archive of selves, each one an internalized two-person relationship expressive of a slightly different nuance of psyche and experience. We rarely attempt to make sense of the world alone. Usually we have internal company, though we are often only half aware of it. A friend might say, "Did I tell you about that, or only in my mind?" She means that she has been organizing her experience by calling upon you—as you exist in her mind. And each such conversation evokes a slightly different facet of our sensibility.

If I decide to write to a female friend, I will likely produce a different letter. It might repeat some observations: "The hotel looks out on a piazza with flower boxes filled with cyclamen." "Yesterday, I visited a country church where a one-eared black tomcat slept peacefully on the altar." But then it might take off in a completely different direction. Knowing that the friend loves food, I might describe a dinner of pasta with octopus. "Even though the spaghetti had a black, dirty appearance, the taste was wonderful, intense, and unfamiliar, yet also fishlike. Different from squid." This description is private—in the sense that I have written it for a specific friend—even if it is not terribly intimate.

Then suppose the letter continues:

> Would you believe it. Just as I was wiping the plate with a particularly tasty crust of bread, of all people, Elaine appeared. As always, ostentatiously dressed, a bright yellow dress and too much jewelry. I can't imagine how she parades along a single cobblestone alley in her heels without marring them irreparably and breaking her ankle. If she comes back to work on crutches, don't believe her alibis: Whatever she says, the bottom line is that her vanity doesn't vacation. Fortunately, she didn't see me. I skipped coffee, paid quickly, and fled back to the hotel. I so wish you'd been here. We would have laughed for hours, and dissected the moment with even more catty glee than I managed on my own.

This letter is private and intimate. It has the playfulness and frank, mean ease of a communication to a close friend, for the friend's eyes only. It displays a characteristic psychological mix. It addresses the reader while revealing debates with the self that "I" use the friend to help me resolve: Am I justified in not greeting Elaine, or am I just rude? What is this hostility? Can I manage my envy?

Writing to my friend, I enjoy a female camaraderie. That persona already exists in the relationship with the friend, and is a mutual source of pleasure. The letter is an arena in which it is further invented and savored. On a deeper level, I use the letter to summon the memory of the friend's fondness and loyalty to soothe my slight discomfort.

One way we work out an argument with the boss, a sad moment with a child, a confusing encounter with an acquaintance, is by describing it to someone in our mind. We imagine talking it over. Sometimes the imaginary listener agrees and comforts us. Other times he or she is skeptical or outright critical. Often, she is blessedly neutral, and in her presence we try to make sense of our experience. Letters—even though they are much more formal, ordered, self-conscious, and calculated to appeal to their actual audience—share that private process with another person.

The mere fact that there are people whom we do not want to have read our private letters does not mean that we are hiding secrets. We are often simply enjoying intimacy. As long as no biographer pursued Juliana Bordereau, and she could reveal events as she chose, her history was private. Once a journalist aggressively pursued her, and she actively had to hide her papers, circumstances forced her to become secretive.

Of course, it is possible to be secretive without the *actual* threat of intrusion; one can simply decide that something is a "secret." For instance, I could decide to keep my age secret. Or I could experience it as a private matter: something I choose to reveal in some circumstances and not others. If, at the end of my letter to my friend, I had added the final sentences—"Whatever you do, do not share this with anyone at work. In fact, I would be happiest if you tore it up as soon as you read it."—I would have been attempting to secure the privacy within a shell of secrecy. Often, such admonitions come from shame, which seeks respite in secrecy. They also often backfire, heightening a friend's sense that the letter is special and not to be casually tossed out.

Assuming I did not seek secrecy, I would still consider the letter private, and not wish it displayed. Because the psyche is uncivilized—because it yearns in many directions, includes unacceptably intense or meager feelings of all sorts, contradicts itself incessantly, holds mysterious loyalties and violates obvious ones—many of its dimensions can best be expressed in small private moments when friendship and love create a tolerant space where the particular aliveness of the publicly unwelcome self can be displayed, where both sides in the inevitable and interminable war between individual desire and social restriction can briefly put down their weapons and bathe in the same stream.

Denied such privacy, the self suffers. Forced into secrecy, it may become ill. Neurosis is sometimes the sickness manifesting a conflict between the urgent thwarting of equally urgent psychic expression. This is what Breuer and "Anna O." learned. It is well illustrated by a story I once heard the psychoanalyst Erik Erikson recount: It was the thirties. He had recently arrived in America, and spoke little English. But unlike most American psychoanalysts, he saw children, and so, when a perplexing case arose, a boy— probably eight or nine years old—was sent to him. No one could figure out why the child had suddenly started defecating in his clothes. Erikson had the boy come into his consulting room, and since his English was minimal and talking at any length impossible, he gave his patient some modeling clay and suggested that he play. After hesitating a moment, the boy took a bit of green clay, rolled it into a ball and announced, "This is the mother nut." He then took three more smaller bits of green clay, rolled them into balls, and called them girl or boy "nuts." Clearly, they represented himself and his siblings. He paused, looked anxious, took some red clay, rolled it into a ball, and announced, "This is the Uncle nut." He ran from the room and soiled his pants.

The next day Erikson arranged a meeting with the boy's

mother, and speaking through an interpreter, asked the woman, "Are you having an affair?" She was, and furthermore, she felt so ashamed and guilty, and so afraid of her violent husband's rage, that she had warned her son she would be killed if he told his father about the man who visited the house. By demanding secrecy of the boy, and forbidding him freedom to express his feelings— basically on penalty of death—the mother (together with the violence threatened by the father) put him into an unbearable loyalty conflict. Since his own predicament could be neither expressed nor acknowledged without, he feared, harming one of his parents, it became a symptom.

Once Erikson's suspicion was confirmed, he counseled the mother on ways to help her son out of his difficult bind: She could stop the affair, she could move it away from the house, she could leave her husband. I can no longer remember exactly what he said to her, or what she said to her son, but Erikson avowed that the boy quickly improved.

Though inhibited by lack of English, Erikson managed to create a private space where the woman could answer his question without fear of the consequences the same question would engender if asked and answered in a more public setting. Erikson did not judge the mother; he merely outlined her son's dilemma. Maybe the therapy changed her behavior, but if it didn't, the boy had been allowed to express himself, and in the process discovered someone who understood his position. Not only had the mother's injunction of secrecy intimated real peril, but it had likely created for the boy a mental landscape devoid of companionship: There was no one he could safely imagine telling. After meeting with Erikson, he would have a new companion, someone to whom he could—in his mind—describe his point of view; someone to whom, in the right circumstances, he might write a private letter. Forced into secrecy, he is defined by compliance or defiance. Allowed privacy, though the options for familial action may remain unchanged, he gains the opportunity to experience and articulate an autonomous point of view.

The privacy Erikson helped the boy create is like the private space of letters—a place where you can speak as you choose about matters profound or inconsequential. The adolescent Henry James, living briefly in Germany, wrote his friend Thomas Sergeant Perry, "Shall I tell you what I had for dinner? I took particular note on purpose. Primo, some tepid cabbage soup, its tepidity being the result of Fraulein Stamm's having poured it out almost a half an hour before we were called to dinner. . . . Secundo—some boiled beef in rags and some excellent and greasy potatoes; tertio some Westphalia smoked ham and some black beans. Lastly some stewed cherries and tarts. Voila."[15]

While this bit of a letter is not intimate, James felt all letters were private. But why did he care? Why do any of us? In part, the question puzzles because it is so basic. Why do I care if you pick up a letter that sits on my desk and read it? Because it's "none of your business." Because you're "being nosy." Because my autonomy and well-being are based on choosing what I do and do not show you. My whole capacity to assert a self rests on not having your definition of events continually impede or drown out mine. But also because the gratification of writing, of self-expression generally, is—psychologically—about nothing so much as control.

One explanation of why people seek a sense of control—which seems to be such a fundamental part of the wish for privacy—can be found in a famous story from Freud: The mother of a little boy goes out and leaves him. He does not cry. Instead he plays with a pull-toy on a string. He throws it. He pulls it back.

Freud speculates that the child repetitively throws and retrieves the toy because it gives him symbolic control over his abandonment by his mother. He cannot make her come back, but he can make the toy return. By exerting the little control he has, he creates in fantasy and play a solution for his helplessness.[16] Feeling an absence of control often makes people feel ashamed, and play and fantasy often work to relieve shame and restore a sense of well-being.

On a more sophisticated level, James, writing letters—or stories—does something similar. The writer's father, Henry James Sr., was a restless man. He uprooted and moved his family endlessly, and Henry Jr. never knew where or when he'd move next. What better response than to write letters? Not only would they allow him continuity in disrupted relationships, but they would allow the only available control, the only means of moving from passive to active: He could impose order on his chaotic experience by describing it to someone else.

And for such purposes, writing fiction works well. Even though the process of creating may be painful for the writer as he seeks to describe difficult events, it is often liberating. To the psyche, writing fiction carries a thrill equivalent to driving a car along a crowded road and finding—just when you feel most trapped—that it has grown wings, and you are lifting up over the endless stalled cars, the suffocating exhaust, the unbearable heat. Real memory, real experience, and real facts give way in fiction to the psyche's urge to redress itself by reconstructing experience. Part of what writers like James seek to protect with reticence and burnt letters is the integrity of this transformation and, with it, their power and the power of their art.

If the story ended here, artists, like heroes in old cartoons, would sweep away their tracks and escape. But even as good fiction satisfies, it often creates hunger to know more about the teller of the tale. Although the writer has done what we all seek to do—metaphorically, to master our helplessness by controlling a pull-toy—he has done it with a grace we rarely manage, and he has moved us in the process. When James has the narrator of *The Aspern Papers* rifle Juliana's drawers, he makes us hold our breath; when he is caught, our hearts pound. The writer's skill astounds. We become curious to know about him. We want more. And biographers, especially those writing since Freud and influenced by psychology, are inclined to give us more.

Though Leon Edel describes James's feelings about privacy and biography, he does not consider honoring the writer's wishes. Instead, he portrays James's elusiveness as a battle to be joined. James felt that if a writer could destroy his own trail, readers would be forced to confront his art without distraction. And to a degree, he succeeded; even though James left many letters, Edel has observed that the writer was so private that perhaps "the really important letters of his life—the intimate letters—were never written and that all others were perhaps a necessary, but carefully-worded residue."[17] James left a long track, but one overgrown and obscured by his reticence, and when the path gets lost in undergrowth, taking permission from Freud's enormous impact on how we think about people, how we might connect their creative production with their unconscious, Edel goes to the art to find the man.

Writing about *The Aspern Papers,* Edel suggests that the story may reflect some guilt on James's part for his friendship with Constance Fenimore Woolson. (Edel focuses on guilt more than shame for James, which does not seem quite accurate.) Had he toyed with her affection? Had he, like the narrator of the story, "allowed his own needs for friendship, companionship, understanding, to blind him to what he might stand for in his relationship with Fenimore, and what he might be doing to her affections?" Perhaps, Edel conjectures, James is writing about burning letters because he is worried about how people would judge him for the ones he wrote to her.[18]

Edel locates James's fiction in his life, and extensively and intimately connects the themes of the writer's personal struggles—with women, his brother, his parents, numerous friends—into his work. James may have feared the camera and the telegraph, but the transformation that would most challenge his cherished privacy—at least, after his death—was the psychological one his novels were helping to establish. In his 1908 essay "Writers and Day-dreaming," Freud observed, "I believe that most people construct phantasies at times in their lives. This is a fact which has long been overlooked and whose importance has therefore not been sufficiently appreciated."[19]

Freud makes a point of telling us that most people sometimes fantasize? Apparently his audience did not assume it. He goes on to describe how the writer's fantasies reflect his daydreams—and thus his soul. The storyteller's psyche can be found in his characters. Freud writes, "The psychological novel in general no doubt owes its special nature to the inclination of the modern writer to split up his ego, by self-observation, into many part-egos, and, in consequence, to personify the conflicting currents of his own mental life in several heroes."[20]

When we read these ideas today, we almost can't believe that someone bothers to say them. We have so integrated this perspective, we forget that it is recent. The intrusion James and so many of his contemporaries feared (Emerson and the "reporter under the confessional") from technology and media had a more immediate source. It was inevitable that when the culture turned more attention to the individual, the artist would become a subject. And if one writer more than any other of the era steered the novel toward the introspective and the psychological, it was James. No wonder he worried about privacy.

Were he able to return and comment, I imagine James—who wanted very much for his art to survive—could not help but feel amazed by Edel's effort. Five volumes are a lot by anyone's measure. At the same time, I think he would feel astonished and discomforted by having Edel read his fiction as material that would illuminate his character. He would writhe and squirm. He would blush to hear how his art manifested his unconscious, or opened a window into his psyche: to see how his closely guarded feelings had really been more transparent, more completely revealed through his characters than he realized.

And, of course, about such intimate matters, only he could know (and, Freud suggests, even he couldn't be sure) where Edel went wrong—sometimes, no doubt, badly wrong; where the writer's careful observations of others were actually mislabeled as revelations of his self. I imagine James would have been flustered, enraged, frustrated in his passion to make the fiction prevail. Yet, at the same time, a man who was so successfully elusive might also have felt relieved to discover that someone could know him completely and still admire him fully. Juliana Bordereau is partly withered by her own reclusive secrecy, by the work of keeping the world at bay. No doubt James's evasiveness sometimes exhausted him.

Furthermore, if we join Freud in speculating about the fragmented parts of the self that show up in fiction, *The Aspern Papers'* narrator's harsh characterization of Tina Bordereau as a "ridiculous pathetic provincial old woman" whom he wouldn't marry for "a bundle of tattered papers" makes an interesting psychological point. According to the story, he who wants the letters must wed the person—must earn his right to the intimacy by making a commitment to the human being. Perhaps James is partly describing how, separate from his writing, he unconsciously felt ridiculous and pathetic—unwanted and unbearable to others and himself apart from his talent with words. If this is true, then the story's ending speaks an even more complicated psychic truth. James may have been angry at intrusive journalists and guilty about not leveling with Woolson about his sexual preference, but he seems also to have been struggling with how to bear himself.

Edel's defiance of James's explicit request to be left alone feels a little strange. Yet if a case is to be made for not honoring someone's wishes for posthumous privacy, Edel has made it. But James had been dead for almost forty years before Edel published his first volume, and nearly sixty when Edel finished the last. Edel's effort suggests that a certain passing of time, a respectfulness on the part of the biographer, are vital elements. It may also be that James's own vigorous efforts to secure his privacy in fact contributed to Edel's accomplishment; easy material had been destroyed, and there was much that couldn't be exposed.

It is because an artist or public figure stirs and speaks to our own most private feelings that we wish to know about him. The more private our lives become, the more self-conscious, the more we attempt to define ourselves apart from tradition or communal expectations, the more we turn to memoir, biography, or celebrity tabloid to offer possibility. When we read biographies, we search for a friend, a mentor, a kindred spirit, and ultimately for ourselves. What can we learn from his experience that will confirm, challenge, or enhance our own?

Psychologically, our wishes are complex. Writing about the psychological appeal of drama, Freud described the role of the spectator in terms that apply equally to that of the reader (and perhaps the writer) of biographies:

> The spectator is a person who experiences too little, who feels that he is a "poor wretch to whom nothing of importance can happen," who has long been obliged to damp down, or rather displace his ambition to stand in his own person at the hub of world affairs; he longs to feel and to act and to arrange things according to his desires—in short to be a hero. And the playwright and actor enable him to do this by allowing him *to identify himself with* a hero. They spare him something, too. For the spectator knows quite well that actual heroic conduct such as this would be impossible for him without pains and suffering and acute fears, which would cancel out the enjoyment.[21]

Spectators are the star crop of contemporary life. However active we are in our real lives, celebrity culture creates a faraway fantasy public world of television or *People* magazine from which we are excluded, for which we are spectators. When we pick up Edel's story of James's life, we do so with a host of conscious and unconscious wishes. As Freud suggests, we want to burnish our more mundane, earthbound lives by participating in his. Like kids jumping in elevators just as they come to a stop, we want to use biographies to outwit gravity, to lift us suddenly, briefly, into the air and defy the constant pull of our real lives. We leave our desk jobs and spend spring hiking in Italy; forsaking frozen pizza with our children, we dine with Turgenev, Flaubert, or Edith Wharton. We wander around Paris and Rome, and *Scribner's* pays us generously for our commentary. By placing ourselves beside James, we share the rewards of his labors. Moreover, we want intimacy with him. So we lack his achievement? So that keeps us off his dinner list? Biographies welcome us to the table without demanding that we earn our place. Once there, we examine him closely, and compare him to ourselves and our friends. We scrutinize the magician—sometimes on stage, sometimes off and out of costume—hoping better to understand how he knots the scarves.

And like much admiration, ours is often tinged with envy and ambivalence. If, as we learn about him, his virtues are too many, his talents too large, even as we are awed, we become oppressed. We want him to have pain and suffering not only, as Freud suggests, to remind us that we are lucky not to have lived his life, but also so that he will not leave us feeling too small. We are both disappointed and reassured to learn that Henry James was remote, that he seemed unable until he was almost sixty to make relationships that were deeply intimate or even a little sexual.

Freud casts light on what we want from biography. He sanctions a new depth of exploration, but he also contributes to changing the rules and offering justification for intrusions into privacy heretofore inconceivable. For example, scholars speculated for years about an injury Henry James received as a young man. James was so vague about his "obscure hurt" that inevitably people thought it a specific sexual wound. The story is that there was a fire in Newport. James was helping to mobilize an old engine with which to fight it. Somehow, he got hurt but could not say where. Leon Edel lists a generation of eminent critics—F.O. Matthiessen, Lionel Trilling, R.P. Blackmur, Stephen Spender—who wondered if James had been castrated. Edel believes that in fact the writer injured his back in 1862, and that he may have portrayed it in dramatic and mysterious terms to justify his wish not to fight in the Civil War.[22]

When we stand outside of a person's wish for privacy, we are often suspicious. We feel closed out, so we question his motives. Quickly, unconsciously, we often project our own worries and desire for secrecy onto him. We blur important distinctions, and jump to the conclusion that whatever he wishes to keep private must be what we would keep secret. If James has an "obscure hurt" that he does not name, what would be a mortifying wound that I (in this case, as a male literary critic) might wish to keep secret? Castration.

No doubt James's critics, influenced by Freud, recognized that threat of castration is a central unconscious fear in the psychological development of boys and in the lives of men. So it is simplistic to suggest they were *only* projecting their fears upon him. And a sense of being castrated may have been an unconscious feeling of James. On one level, he may have dramatized an injury to justify not enlisting in the war. On another, he may have struggled unconsciously with a sense of shame that his reluctance to fight was "unmanly." He may have found his view of his own virility diminished by his choice not to follow the "swashbuckling" route of two brothers and countless peers. (That his father, whom the young James viewed as somewhat weak and unfocused, had a badly burned leg amputated after a childhood accident adds psychological complexity.) Furthermore, James may have been aware of homoerotic feelings, and experienced them as a flaw in his manliness. The obscure injury may have been his lack of bearable language to express his own sexuality.

There is no doubt that in the unconscious, matters of privacy are often underpinned by the psyche's fast currents of shame, sexuality, rage. But to move too quickly toward them, to assert that they represent an overarching truth, rather than a resonant and augmenting one, is to indulge in an all too common distortion that fuels the tabloid and disrespects the delicacy of the private. The tabloid—like the unconscious—is elemental. It pulls for its own clarity, but at the expense of subtlety—and truth. No matter what distinctions critics made between James's feelings about his experience and the reality of his injury, inevitably the rumor emerges that James had a mysterious accident that left him a eunuch . . . sort of.

As audience, we seem to hunger almost insatiably for such disclosures. The more intimate the account, the better it sells. We want a view unobstructed by curtains. If we've been too well brought up to press our own faces against the glass, let someone else stand there for us and recount in detail the goings on. We keep ourselves separate from his crass intrusiveness, or so we think.

But is it possible to stand only on one side of the window? If we have learned anything from Freud, we have learned that we can disown nothing in our fantasies: Our identifications are bifurcated. We are always—ultimately—the hunter and the hunted, the performer and the audience, the biographer and the subject, the exposer and the exposed. We gratify half the ambivalence at the expense of the other. Our voyeurism backfires by reinforcing the most repressive dimensions of our own inhibition. The only safety from our own prying eyes is to attempt less and hide more.

It is this capacity to represent both sides—the ambivalence of identification—that makes *The Aspern Papers* a great novella. Even as James leaves his narrator defeated, shamed by seeing his greed held up before him, the reader's emotions are successfully aroused because James understood intimately the biographer's impulse to plunder. Consciously, his sympathies are with the rabbit, but unconsciously—like all of us—he also bays with the hounds. Edel demonstrates beyond any doubt that James wrote continually about his own most piercing and intimate observations of everyone he knew, but he transformed them into fiction. For James, the process of making art redeemed his own aggressive intrusiveness. Because he transformed what he saw, because he gave it beauty and universality, he freed it and himself from any—conscious—culpability.

Janet Malcolm has written, "The concept of privacy is a sort of screen to hide the fact that almost none is possible in a social universe."[23] What she neglects to tell us is that although feeble and flimsy, tottering and imperfect, that screen is critical to our well-being—and ultimately to our dignity. Visiting an acquaintance in the hospital, I avert my eyes when an awkward, pain-filled movement briefly causes his face to lose composure. We are not that close. I know he does not want me to see.

This fragile screen wobbles through the fierce contemporary debates on biography and privacy. Describing its purpose and dimensions is no small task, protecting it is harder still. There are no simple rules. It is not just a question of whether to be frank, to tell the truth, or to disclose particular facts. The screen is ultimately an impression or an essence, or an atmosphere. Upon reading the collected letters of a recently deceased writer, a friend remarked, "They should not have published those letters. At least not at this time, not all together. They leave her too naked." I'm not sure that there's a better way to say it.

It is because Diane Middlebrook's biography of Anne Sexton leaves her too naked that I object to it, and think of it as representing some of the pitfalls of contemporary biography. I first read *Anne Sexton* in the midst of a hurricane in a house filled with people. The book hooked me to a degree Edel never managed. I ignored my guests and the storm and kept reading even when the electricity went out. With fifty pages left, I commandeered a kerosene lantern, and held it up with one hand as I turned pages with the other. I do not think it would be possible for a biography to expose anyone more completely. Middlebrook told everything about Sexton's bad marriage, drinking, suicide attempts, prescription drug abuse, bad mothering, endless affairs, and unethical therapists. I read it avidly—even as I disliked it. And I cried when Sexton finally killed herself.

I learned many intimate things about Sexton, but we were not intimates. It was awkward. I knew more about her than I know about some of my closest friends. I knew about her the way I might know about a patient I had treated for many years. But unlike with the patient or the friend, the book put me under no obligation to hold what I learned in trust. When you know that much about a person, it is better if it comes with love and with some sense of obligation.

During her lifetime, any therapist Sexton saw was required to preserve her confidentiality—unless she spoke about immediate suicidal or homicidal intentions, or unless she asked the therapist to testify in a court case. When, some twenty years after Sexton's death, psychiatrist Martin Orne allowed Middlebrook to use tapes he had made of Sexton's sessions, he stirred up a storm, even though he acted with the family's permission. The controversy made it to the front page of the *New York Times*.[24] The prominence of the story suggests that what transpired was unusual; that the question of confidentiality was newsworthy. If the fight goes back to Curll and Pope, it took a new turn with the availability of such private tapes. Tape recorder technology combined with the self-disclosures of psychotherapy made it possible to massively broadcast the *most* private material verbatim.

Dr. Orne, Ms. Middlebrook, and some of Sexton's friends and family argued that Sexton would have approved having the tapes published. She liked revealing herself, wanted to help others by showing her struggles, and sought exposure. Maybe they are right. But one problem with the argument—aside from how fundamental control seems to be for artists in the matter of self-revelation—is that speaking for the dead is at best an iffy undertaking. It's so hard to untangle one's own motives and wishes, much less a dead person's. Unlike James, Sexton apparently gave little thought to frustrating the "post mortem exploiter." Maybe she welcomed her, understanding better than James the biographer's usefulness to posthumous sales and reputation. Perhaps her experience of childhood privacy had been so miserable, exposure was a matter of indifference. Yet when Sexton committed suicide in 1974, biography was less exposing.

Removing the screen so completely damages the biography. Sexton is left too naked. Biography gets subverted when it is drawn into the odd public ritual of nakedness and sacrifice. Mass culture creates huge celebrity images: Elvis, the Beatles, Frank Sinatra, Lady Diana, Michael Jackson—on a smaller scale, artists like Picasso and Sylvia Plath. Then it attacks them by describing their decadence or pathology. We allow them a triumphant march onto the altar, then we unmask them. It is a primitive ritual. Just when the oppression of the celebrity's perfection becomes too much, we are freed and allowed to ogle his mess.

Voyeuristic ogling provides feelings akin to those of the Romans watching lions eat gladiators: "Tough luck for him, glad it wasn't me." We know that feeling. But one expects better from revelation in the context of intimacy. There we seek relief, assistance, honest criticism. We seek to be known, but in the context of being loved. Remarkably, whatever our inclination to ridicule and deride, we often check it. When people are revealed cynically or gratuitously to satisfy the maw of mass culture, the result is often to create an image of the subject that most resembles the gladiators after their encounters with the lions. But *them* is also *us,* and we are subtly terrorized.

I wish Diane Middlebrook hadn't used the psychotherapy

tapes. Yes, Sexton is dead, but too recently to sanction such expo-sure. If anyone deserves exposure, it is the psychotherapists who treated Sexton. One carried on an affair with her; others appear to have ignored the significant indications that she had been sexually abused, the seriousness of her alcoholism and drug problem, and the evidence that her husband was hitting her. Yet Frederick Duhl, the psychiatrist alleged to have had an affair with her, goes un-named. And Martin Orne writes a self-serving preface where he dismisses her recollections of sexual abuse as fantasies. Was he there? How can he know?

The biography disturbs because, under the guise of "we're just doing what she would have wanted," Sexton is offered up like a drunk girl to a bachelor's party. The people around her—several of whom had some responsibility for the way her life evolved—are protected, their privacy is relatively intact. If Sexton's own asser-tions are accurate—if she was sexually abused as a child—then her privacy was violated early. The releasing of the tapes, the extent of the disclosures in the biography, seem like more violation with ra-tionalization. If Martin Orne had destroyed the tapes, that would have been okay. Or if he'd given them to an archive for use in the future, that would have been fine too. At the least, if the tapes were released only after his death, he and Sexton could have been exam-ined equally.

Think for a moment of the brilliant last scene in *Streetcar Named Desire*. Recall that Blanche is completely crazy. The warden is ready to wrestle her into a straitjacket. But the doctor offers Blanche his arm, suggesting they walk together. If Blanche is the all too human subject, then Middlebrook is the biographer as warden, and Edel the rare observer who can see and know but not humili-ate. In this vein, Leon Edel contends that living in Europe, James gradually "abandoned his American innocence." Although he had once seen European civilization as a facade that hid corruption, he came to understand it as offering "a veil of public decency, codes and standards of judgments, with which to protect 'the private life.' To have a private life was to have freedom; and a loss of freedom, he said, was 'the greatest form of suffering.'"

This discovery changed the "moral substance" of James's work. Evil, to James, was no longer sin or human weakness—it was standing aloof. Edel writes, "The evil in 'The Aspern Papers' lay not in Juliana's ancient indiscretions or Jeffrey Aspern's 'love-life.' It lay in the invasion of privacy, *the failure to enter into human feeling*" (italics added).[25] It seems that in that sentence Edel may have offered us not just a fresh perspective on privacy, but a useful standard. When a biography is written in a way that allows us to disown our own feelings and failings as we examine them in someone else, it invades privacy.

8

Clinton's Nap and
Presidential Privacy

I nvasions of privacy and questions of disclosure take on new
meaning when the privacy under discussion is the president's.
People who run for high office (and their kin) *appear* to sign away
their privacy, or at least to endanger their secrets, though their actual experiences are more unpredictable. If you examine the history
of presidential privacy, you find that much that has been disclosed
is untrue or unimportant, and that some of what has been successfully guarded might have been usefully disseminated. And sometimes news that looks benign can stir considerable worry.

For instance, President Clinton likes to take daily naps. Some
people do, some don't. As a fellow napper, I agree with the president that it is one of life's pleasures; refreshing, quick, it lets you escape without travel. Napping's only real drawback—besides the
inevitable soupçon of guilt—is that it's not presidential. When in
1993 the *Wall Street Journal* reported that President Clinton took
naps, members of the White House staff panicked. They apparently feared that the image of the commander in chief dozing
would plunge his polls. So, according to Ronald Kessler, author of
Inside the White House,[1] they called the naps "occasional," and

claimed they increased when Clinton attacked the huge problem of health care. Only under harrowing circumstances were daily siestas manly.

However clumsy the approach, the White House image makers have a point. Think of Emanuel Leutze's famous painting of George Washington crossing the Delaware River. It is frigid winter, the wind howls over an open boat, there is ice everywhere, and the general is standing tall on the prow. He's not napping. According to the sensors in our psyches that read such images, that one is presidential. In truth, Washington could have undertaken a protracted hibernation, and his public would likely not have known or minded. Times were different: While president, Washington was once out of touch with his own government for two months while he toured the South.[2] Who's to say if his lids fluttered as his coach traversed the dusty roads? And why do we now care if a president naps?

As Kessler sees it, the Clinton staff's nap fib is one more example of the administration's perfidy. This may be true, but President Clinton's nap dilemma is also a quintessential illustration of the double bind of democracy, particularly of the presidency. Many have observed how presidents are hybrids of king and commoner. Mythic, half-human and half-beast creatures, where privacy is concerned they leave the public vacillating, looking for the beast in the human and vice versa. We have not decided what parts of their private life we need to know about, or when or why. No doubt in this case, Clinton's handlers thought that already lacking a military record, the president could not afford the additional weakling image of "daily napper."

Private information about presidents has been of interest since George Washington's day. Looking at the stories across time, one sees a pattern where what is "revealed" often has little to do with real questions of ability, and everything to do with contemporary social fears. Furthermore, only in this century have newspapers decided that printed disclosures should be based in fact.

If we wish to understand how deeply embedded are the privacy issues surrounding the American presidency, Washington's life is a place to start. The first president was remarkable. Very tall for his time (6'2"), with reddish-brown hair, he was a lively, self-educated frontiersman, an ambitious man with a courage that in his youth verged on recklessness. Washington's father died when George was eleven, and he worked surveying the wilderness and fighting. Though in his early soldiering days—"protecting" Virginia from the French and Indians—he made awful mistakes, he was quickly recognized as a leader. A head taller than everyone else, he won admiration by riding through the worst of battles, losing horses out from under him, impervious to the bullets and arrows felling all around him.[3]

Soldiers during the American Revolution found him by turns harsh and humane. To establish discipline amid rowdy men, he punished military infractions seemingly without compassion, yet he was devoted to his troops' well-being and was often kind. Washington was also known for helping his Virginia neighbors, once instructing "that no suppliant should ever be turned away from Mount Vernon 'lest the deserving suffer.'"[4] He owned slaves, but lost enthusiasm for the practice, and on his death freed them all, the only Virginia founding father to do so.

George Washington loved a good time. He drank, danced, gambled, and hunted foxes. He liked wearing fancy uniforms that conveyed high rank. And he enjoyed women. The great romance of his life was with Sally Fairfax, a married woman a few years his senior. He fell in love with her while still in his teens, and even wrote her a love letter on the eve of his marriage to Martha Custis.

Throughout his life, Washington had female admirers and correspondents, but without contemporary scandal.

Washington's marriage made him wealthy, and he scrambled to acquire the manners of his new rank. He may not have felt terribly passionate about his wife, but he considered himself happily married. Martha burned their correspondence after his death[5]—an indication both that it chronicled a private exchange (perhaps one that contradicted his public image) and that the practice of publishing other people's private letters was taking firm hold in the new nation. Yet their relationship would today be viewed by many as distant. They were frequently separated for long periods of time, and when together, were rarely alone. Shortly before he died, Washington invited a friend to dinner, noting that if the guest couldn't make it, he and Martha might dine alone together for the *first time in twenty years.*[6]

The first president was idealized and admired during his life to a degree we can hardly imagine today. The only recent American leaders who compare—John and Robert Kennedy, Martin Luther King, Malcolm X—were martyred. In addition to genuinely appreciating him, Americans needed to feel that their revolution was virtuous, and Washington became the symbol of that wish. People saw in him their new nation in its best light.

Washington also prospered because his understanding of public opinion and its place in democracy was sensitive and prescient. He appreciated that self-government was an untried concept; a president had to be delicate about power, different from a king. So, when he spoke widely about his desire to return to private life after the war rather than become president, it was both because the wish was genuine (today we might say it was one side of his ambivalence) and because he understood that a person reluctant to trade private life for public power was what the historical moment demanded. Psychologically keen, he knew how to present himself, how to use the private man in a way that allowed the leader to balance the conflicting desires of a testy and nascent country. As president, Washington often rode a horse—like any other farmer—but his had a gold-trimmed saddle over a leopard skin to mark the dignity of his office.[7] Citizens loved the juxtaposition.

Washington's nature was reserved; he guarded his privacy. The rare occasions he revealed himself carried weight. One famous moment occurred at the end of the war. Angry about salaries long owed, army officers planned a march on the government to take their pay. Realizing such violence would end the fragile experiment of self-government, Washington met with the men. After appealing unsuccessfully, he decided to read them a letter from a congressman, hoping it would sway them:

> He pulled the letter from his pocket, and then something seemed to go wrong. The General seemed confused; he stared at the paper helplessly. The officers leaned forward, their hearts contracting with anxiety. Washington pulled from his pocket something only his intimates had seen him wear: a pair of eyeglasses. "Gentlemen," he said, "you will permit me to put on my spectacles, for I have not only grown gray but almost blind in the service of my country."[8]

The soldiers wept, and rallied behind him. But why were they so moved? Partly, Washington's reference to sacrifice adeptly reminded them they had made an honorable choice. They, too, had sacrificed; they had not merely been used. Remembering their purpose diffused their anger. But more, Washington's willingness to show himself aged and vulnerable, reluctantly to let the private matter of his failing eyesight become publicly known, confirmed that he was sincere, and evoked compassion. Politically brilliant, it was also genuine. A less intimate moment, one filmed and shown outside of context, could easily have rendered him pathetic, like the image of President Carter exhausted after a race, or insincere.

Washington understood the rules of his age. He controlled impulses that would have drawn criticism, and cultivated virtues his countrymen admired. (In his private letters, he felt free to complain about colleagues, direct how to have a slave recaptured, and flirt.[9]) Nevertheless, early in his first term a furor erupted that his bows were too stiff and formal—the bows of a would-be king, not a patriot![10]

Though newspapers criticized him continually, only toward the end of his tenure was his privacy violated. Aged and weary, perhaps too used to being idolized, Washington lost his touch and, in the polarized political atmosphere of his second term, made enemies. One, his old friend Edmund Randolph, published a pamphlet asserting that the president's mental powers had declined. Apparently they had—though only slightly. Washington felt betrayed and stung, ashamed to have his occasional confusion and forgetfulness publicly trumpeted.[11] (One thinks of Nancy Reagan prompting her husband.) Around the same time, Gilbert Stuart, the portraitist, decided that the first president was haughty, and made a point of painting his face to highlight the bad fit of his false teeth.[12]

Overall, Washington fared well in public opinion. His qualities and the resulting adulation suggest that—on one level—requirements for the presidency are primitive. We seek the human equivalent of the alpha ape: a vigorous man, tall, healthy, brave—one in whom we can feel public pride—who has enough testosterone to thump his chest and keep the tribe in line. By this criterion, Washington both embodied and created the standard of how a president should appear. Possessing the virtues of his time with their emphasis on public demeanor, he behaved with propriety, manifest honesty, fidelity, faith, and courage. One need only remember how John F. Kennedy's campaign played up his PT-109 bravery, minimized his back pain, hid his Addison's disease, and covered over many unheroic personal habits, to realize the template stands.

Beneath a thin rational veneer, our brains react powerfully to ill-defined, unarticulated, simian cues. In the contemporary presidency, this provokes an almost endless struggle between the image makers and consultants, trying to create heroic features for candidates, and the opposition party and press, trying to uncover hidden flaws. Though magnified exponentially by television, the struggle is not new.

Randolph—fueled by rancor—felt entitled to publicize Washington's mild deterioration, though it offered little danger to his countrymen. Whereas in colonial days a printer could be punished for publishing pamphlets critical of the crown, the Revolution mostly ended that practice. (Some loud presidential critics were jailed during John Adams's presidency under the Alien and Sedition Acts.) The very fact of popular government quickly guaranteed that private "information" about politicians would be used to influence public opinion. Fiercely wishing to defeat opponents, people realized that personal attacks and revelations in print of private weakness could work as well as—and often better than—debating issues.

Contemporary criticisms of Washington suggest that each president is scrutinized according to his era's anxieties. While few citizens minded if the first president was served by slaves (and unfortunately many were reassured by it), people did worry that he secretly wanted to become king. So they examined him. Thus the concern about stiff bows. So too, if for a week or so Washington used his carriage more than his horse, it was considered evidence of dangerous growth in his monarchical tendencies.

Washington liked government without monarchy, and appreciated that to sustain it, the public needed information. He read newspapers continually himself, and mostly supported freedom of the press. At the same time, he worried that vicious editorials— often devoid of fact—would undermine government, and he felt pained (and self-righteously insulted) by criticism aimed at him. (Thomas Jefferson describes Washington during a fit of pique in a cabinet meeting, "in one of those passions when he cannot command himself," shouting that "he had rather be on his farm than to be *emperor of the world* and yet they were charging him with wanting to be king."[13])

Writing to Edmund Randolph several years before their falling out, Washington worried about "News-paper abuse" making it impossible "for any man living to manage the helm, or keep the machine together."[14] And many presidents since have felt badly pummeled by the press. Read diaries and letters, and you'll find them, almost to a man, cursing and writhing under the endless attacks. They feel enraged and baffled, ushered in with pomp and ceremony, then endlessly knocked against the ropes. In *The Agenda* Bob Woodward portrays a punch-drunk Clinton, so befuddled by press blows that he rants and bellows. But he is by no means alone. As James Pollard tells it in *The Presidents and the Press,* all have felt stung and bruised—some to the verge of paranoia—by the constant, contradictory, critical attacks.

Whether you are a president, a protestor, an employee, or a prisoner of war, hostile surveillance has a large psychological effect. Little wonder that presidents become touchy and secretive. To

Washington's credit—in the last months of his life—he wrote in favor of openness, at least "with respect to public measures." "*Concealment* is a species of mis-information; and misrepresentation and false alarms found the ground work of opposition."[15] That he was simultaneously sympathetic with the Alien and Sedition Acts testifies to his struggle to distinguish freedom of the press from what he experienced as licentious personal harassment.

Take popular government, add the press, and the result is not only useful checks and balances, but endless oscillation between unreconcilable psychological forces that fuel unstable political forces. Much of the basis of people's feelings is irrational and unconscious. The idealization that empowers a president is inherently unstable. Washington knew this, and worried at the time he became president that his public would "turn the extravagant (and I may say undue) praises which they are heaping upon me at this moment, into equally extravagant (and I will fondly hope unmerited) censures."[16]

Such instability is inherent in the very idea of equality, as Alexis de Tocqueville observed. The admirable desire for social equality has another side: "There exists also in the human heart a depraved taste for equality, which impels the weak to attempt to lower the powerful to their own level and reduces men to prefer equality in slavery to inequality with freedom."[17]

It is no coincidence that school children who know almost nothing about George Washington know he had false teeth. They repeat that fact because they enjoy the awkward juxtaposition between status and vulnerability, because the revelation of his private imperfection liberates their sense of equality. Real social equality is elusive; America often substitutes freedom to comment on the inequities. One feels for Washington, embarrassed by the public flaunting of his grotesque prosthesis, and gloats with Gilbert Stuart at liberty to paint without fear of incarceration.

Scrutiny of private life grew with the country, and the presidents who followed Washington had a tough time. There was Thomas Jefferson's affair with his slave, Sally Hemmings. Ironically, James T. Callender, the ill-tempered man who published the probably false story in 1802, had only the year before been freed *by Jefferson* from jail, where he was imprisoned for defaming President Adams.[18] Jefferson knew Callender, having winked at his earlier—largely inaccurate and ugly—newspaper attacks on George Washington. (Jefferson was an adamant Republican, Washington a Federalist.) Often drunk, easily enraged, Callender quickly found reason to feel slighted by President Jefferson and soon attacked *him* in the Richmond *Recorder*. Recounting the episode, Virginius Dabney writes:

> With no libel laws in that era worthy of the name, Callender could give his imagination free rein, and his allegations concerning "Dusky Sally" and "Black Sal" were broadcast to the world. Jefferson was depicted as capering with "the black wench and her mulato litter," and his long vacations at Monticello while president were, of course, due to his insatiable lust for the "mahogany colored charmer."[19]

Had the widowed Jefferson deeply loved Sally Hemmings, it would have doubtless enhanced his life and—one hopes—mitigated the suffering in hers, though the power disparities may have been insurmountable. Portrayed as insatiable lust, the story seems to have more to do with Callender's wish to humiliate Jefferson and with anxieties about slave/owner sexuality. Many Jefferson experts doubt a Hemmings/Jefferson union, but the rumor has frequently resurfaced.[20] While the truth is unknown, the story speaks to the commonplace but unspoken sexual practices of many slave owners and the accompanying cultural voyeurism about tabooed predation and romance.

Stories about mixed-race sex continued to be used to attack candidates after Jefferson. In 1828, pamphlets reprinted in rival party newspapers claimed that Andrew Jackson's mother was a "prostitute who intermarried with a Negro" and that Jackson had an "eldest brother sold as a slave in Carolina."[21] Stories were also spread that Jackson had premarital relations with his second wife. Jackson became so enraged and sure that his rival, John Quincy Adams, was behind the attacks, that he refused to pay the customary preinaugural White House visit to the outgoing Adams. Meanwhile Adams, smarting from false rumors that *his* wife was really English, and thus an enemy of Americans, waited longingly for release into private life.[22]

In 1836 Martin Van Buren's running mate was Richard Johnson, a popular frontiersman, famous in part because he claimed to have killed the great Shawnee chief Tecumseh in one-on-one combat. Johnson had an African-American mistress, Julia Chinn to whom he was devoted, and with whom he had two daughters. Johnson was open about his love for Chinn, who died in 1833, two years before he ran for office.[23] At least one newspaper expressed outrage over the union—not naming Johnson, but printing a diatribe about "execrable amalgamation" in black/white couples, but the ticket won.[24]

In July 1836, during the campaign, the *Herald* had reported Johnson's visit to New York, and filled a long column tweaking the candidate and his African-American followers:

> On Saturday, Col. Richard M. Johnson, the gallant killer of Tecumseh and Vice President that is to be, received company. . . . A num-

ber of distinguished members of the democratic party paid their respects. . . . In the Park and round about the railings, several groups of white people were holding their noses as several bevies of very pretty black and mulatto girls attended by elegantly dressed boot blacks and steamboat waiters, dressed gaily for the occasion, promenaded the Park.

The story then describes Mr. Johnson's visit to a theater, where "in the dress circle about a dozen and a half pale white women were present, the beauty and fashion being, for the night by particular desire, of a different color."[25]

Herald publisher James Gordon Bennett offers his audience crude "entertainment." But clearly, he also is declaring private lives of politicians fair game for the popular press. Though the then new "penny press" newspapers like the *Herald* declared no party affiliation, they represented themselves as standard-bearers and commentators on all matters. If, in Washington's day, public anxiety focused on tyranny, race relations quickly took the fore.

When Abraham Lincoln ran for Congress in 1846, the accusation about his private life was of religious infidelity: He was charged with scoffing at Christianity, since he did not attend church.[26] After winning the race, Lincoln wrote to the *Illinois Gazette* and acknowledged that he was not a church member, but denied that he scoffed. The issue disappeared.

When, in 1862, the Lincolns' beloved twelve-year-old son, Willie, died, both parents mourned. The heartbroken Lincoln set Thursdays aside to grieve. He seems to have stopped the practice only after a minister told him private grief was sinful because it denied that Willie was alive in heaven. "To mourn the departed as lost belonged to heathenism—not Christianity," the minister admonished.[27] Mary Todd Lincoln, also bereft, became reclusive, not leaving her room for long periods. According to Lincoln biographer Benjamin Thomas, she was criticized in the press for neglecting her public duties.[28] Had the country not been engaged in the mass slaughter of its sons, had so many mothers and fathers not been tempted to withdraw into grief at the expense of their duties, both the minister and the public might have shown more patience with the Lincolns' sorrow. Ironically, Lincoln's private losses were precisely what allowed him to comprehend so profoundly the anguishing war.

Abe Lincoln, not widely known when nominated for president, published a campaign autobiography, a document radically different from the carefully scripted television profiles of contemporary campaigns. Within its eight pages, the candidate offers a self-effacing, sometimes tongue-in-cheek, sometimes serious account of his growing up, schooling (or lack thereof), soldiering, work, and family life. Writing in the third person, Lincoln establishes "A." as a strong, not always successful frontiersman, hardworking and opposed to the westward expansion of slavery. Describing his experience laboring on a flatboat for a man named Denton Offutt, Lincoln tells a funny yet grotesque tall tale that presidential candidates nowadays would be unlikely to imitate:

> It was in connection with this boat that occurred the ludicrous incident of sewing up the hogs eyes. Offutt bought thirty odd large fat live hogs, but found difficulty in driving them from where he purchased them to the boat, and thereupon conceived the whim that he could sew up their eyes and drive them where he pleased. No sooner thought of than decided, he put his hands, including A. at the job, which they completed—all but the driving. In their blind condition they could not be driven out of the lot or field they were in. This expedient failing, they were tied and hauled on carts to the boat.[29]

Why would a presidential candidate tell such stuff on himself? The story was typical of the wild tall tales frontier humor favored in an era when few worried about cruelty to animals. Lincoln also makes fun of campaign literature, and tweaks himself. (Some hundred years later the press photographed Lyndon Johnson lifting pet beagles by the ears, an image that sparked nationwide protest.)

When President-elect Lincoln traveled east in 1861 to take office, his frontier manners dogged him. Benjamin Thomas writes:

> His frontier pronunciation and fund of homely anecdotes created the impression of a man of provincial outlook and shallow mind. New York sophisticates snickered when he appeared at the opera in black kid gloves, his huge hands hanging over the railing of his box. Playing up his every trifling social error, the hostile press dubbed him a "gorilla" and "baboon."[30]

While the attacks on Lincoln were personal, they did not reveal what went on behind closed doors. No one, for instance, attempted to interview him or Mrs. Lincoln about their family life. Wild invective was standard; direct personal questions were still considered invasions of privacy. Yet as the Civil War turned the nation's attention more toward Washington, and as the press expanded to cover the war, papers printed more about the Lincolns' private life.

In August 1861, the *New York Herald* assigned a reporter to write about Mrs. Lincoln's New Jersey beach vacation—a journalistic first. His stories focused on observation: the dresses Mrs. Lincoln wore, the guests she entertained, her carriage route during an afternoon outing. Since Mrs. Lincoln mostly stayed in her room, the reporter wrote filler and complained—with unusual candor— about privacy versus his need to do a job:

> The plain record of a day here can be told in ten words, as far as Mrs. Lincoln is concerned. Then why don't I tell it thus briefly? Simply because all the public wants to know more than ten words about Mrs. Lincoln, and if . . . there is nothing to tell, I must relate something about somebody or other connected with her.[31]

He also observed how much Mrs. Lincoln disliked the attention: "When she does appear she is quite annoyed at the too apparent and inconsiderate curiosity of the people here."

Unlike his wife, President Lincoln often patiently tolerated hostile and personal attacks from the press. Once, when he wanted privacy while visiting his beloved stepmother for what he sensed to be the last time, he simply asked reporters to leave him alone.[32] But even Lincoln had limits. One Sunday, two years into the presidency, he read a critical clipping from Henry Ward Beecher's *Independent*. Overwhelmed by frustration, he appealed to God about Beecher's attack, "Is thy servant a *dog*, that he should do this thing?"[33]

Not until after the Civil War did anything akin to twentieth-century press coverage come into being. Though indifferent to truth, early papers were small, circulation local. Improved technologies (like the telegraph and faster printing presses), denser populations, more professional reporters, and a new interest in mass circulation made newspaper sales skyrocket during the 1880s and 90s. It is no coincidence that Warren and Brandeis's "The Right to Privacy" appeared in 1890.

Grover Cleveland, whose two separate terms bracketed the treatise on privacy, suffered mightily from attention this new fortified press paid to his private life. "Ma, ma, where's Pa? Gone to the White House Ha! Ha! Ha!," doggerel about Grover Cleveland's illegitimate child, was widely recited during the presidential campaign of 1884. The unmarried Cleveland had been one of several men paying court to a young widow who became pregnant. She believed him to be the father, and he took financial responsibility for the child in spite of doubts about his paternity. The story first surfaced in a Buffalo newspaper, the *Evening Telegraph* in July 1884.[34] The larger press corps, with telegraph access, spread the news nationwide within hours. The public apparently came to feel that Cleveland had acted honorably enough (no one interviewed the widow), and gradually the matter settled. (Not surprisingly, Henry Ward Beecher championed Cleveland.[35]) From the simian point of view, rumors that the unmarried Cleveland was in fact sexually potent may have helped his candidacy.

Paternity was not the only scrutinized bit of Cleveland's private behavior. Rival Democrats published rumors that Cleveland was a "dissolute drunkard"[36]—probably an exaggeration, though he had a large thirst. After his marriage, he was accused of wife beating, a charge Mrs. Cleveland denied. Cleveland also drew criticism for buying his way out of the Civil War. When drafted in 1863, he paid $150 to another man to take his place. The practice of purchasing the services of a substitute was customary and legal, but became politically touchy in the aftermath of a brutal war. Cleveland biographer Allan Nevins observes, "During Cleveland's presidency sensational newspaper stories were printed detailing the wounds and hardships his substitute had suffered, but his actual history was uneventful."[37]

It was neither scandal nor false rumor, but Cleveland's wedding, that drew the greatest press attention, though he did not reveal the engagement until four days before the event. A bachelor for forty-nine years, Cleveland married his much younger ward—the twenty-two-year-old Frances Folsom—during his first term, and the newspapers went wild. Though the couple sought privacy, reporters spotted them leaving the White House by a side gate and pursued mercilessly. Tailing the pair to a rented cottage in Deer Park, Maryland, a dozen newsmen spent the six-day honeymoon watching the newlyweds' every move. Railroad detectives kept the journalists back 150 yards; otherwise it was open season. Front-page stories described clothes the Clevelands wore, when *they* napped, how much the president put in the church collection plate, and what they ate.[38]

No detail was too small. On the morning of the wedding the *Herald* reported the president's breakfast habits: "It has been re-marked that he is fond of corn cakes, but he wants them browned and served without oleomargarine."[39] The news story describing his honeymoon residence began, "The cottage in which Mr. Cleve-land is entangled in the silken meshes of love is a two story and a half structure . . ."[40] Try as he might to appear at ease, Cleveland was stunned and infuriated by the surveillance, and many peo-ple—even some members of the press—felt that the coverage was an invasion of privacy. Its most immediate effect appears to have been to make Cleveland more secretive, a response that almost killed him several years later.

In 1893, at the beginning of his second term, doctors discov-ered a malignant growth in Cleveland's mouth. Fearful that public perception of a weak, ill president would panic an already sinking economy (and angry and upset by previous press attention), Cleve-land decided to keep his operation secret.

A group of eminent surgeons, telling no one of their mission, gathered on a yacht in New York's East River. The president, hav-ing quietly left Washington, sneaked aboard *The Oneida* on the evening of June 30, 1893. The next morning, as the boat puttered up the East River, the team of surgeons tipped Cleveland back in a chair, anesthetized him, and operated. The doctors, no doubt quaking from their great responsibility and unlikely operating theater, removed many teeth and much of the roof of Cleveland's mouth as the boat rocked about. Five days later, the yacht, having steamed up the East Coast, dropped the woozy patient at his house in Buzzards Bay. Cleveland spent the early weeks of his summer-long stay weakened and depressed. His first comment to one close friend was a despairing, "They almost killed me." Yet, even visiting cabinet members were not told what really happened. In August, the Philadelphia *Press* printed an account of the operation, but no one believed it. Not until twenty-five years later did the story emerge.[41]

Cleveland's behavior became the model for years of secrecy about presidential illness. The extent—if not the actual fact—of Woodrow Wilson's stroke, Franklin Roosevelt's heart disease, and Kennedy's Addison's disease was hidden. Only in recent years, with Betty Ford's alcoholism, Nancy Reagan's breast cancer, and Ronald Reagan's colon polyps, has there been a recognition that abandoning secrecy is useful for both quelling rumors and promoting public health. Still, the gain is partial. Reagan's diagnosis of Alzheimer's disease may have been suppressed while he was in office. And Paul Tsongas hid his cancer recurrence when he ran for president in 1992.

In 1901 when he took office, Theodore Roosevelt, recognizing newsmen as a powerful social force, gave reporters a small room in the White House, protecting them from inclement weather, and symbolically inviting them in. Roosevelt spoke with newsmen openly, and in return insisted that they shield him by not printing all they learned. Those who resisted became his enemies and were shut out. This style helped create a new role for the press, as insiders who knew secrets they did not tell—a stance not challenged until Watergate.[42]

Roosevelt's other new strategy was litigation. He sued Pulitzer for a story he didn't like, and lost. But he won a suit against a Michigan newspaper that had—during the 1912 campaign—accused him of drunkenness.[43] The successful suit made the press more cautious printing rumors about public figures.

It wasn't that presidents who followed Roosevelt didn't have privacy troubles. Woodrow Wilson almost punched a reporter who photographed his daughter on vacation. And Warren Harding's campaign was rife with rumors that he had "Negro blood," an allegation that newspapers by and large refused to print, though many pamphlets circulated.

While battling to prove Harding's "lily-white" blood, the Republican party also paid hush money to his mistresses. Carrie Phillips, a woman with whom Harding pursued a fifteen-year affair, was given $20,000 plus travel money, and sent off to Japan with her husband, to study silk worms.[44] Nan Britton, a young Ohio admirer with whom Harding fathered a child, steadily received envelopes of money from the president—some delivered by Secret Service agents.[45] That Harding had spent his early adulthood in and out of Kellogg's Sanitarium in Battle Creek, for "nerves," seemed to have been of no interest.

Harding's administration was scandal ridden and mediocre. While his private life offered telltales of his public incompetence, the public record itself was clear from early on, had anyone chosen to examine it. He took few positions, sponsored no important legislation, and hated hard work.

Harding's experience also shows how, during the twentieth century, political parties increasingly borrowed campaign techniques from the new field of advertising. Furthermore, as the

Secret Service and the FBI became more powerful, the agencies sheltered presidents and offered them means of fighting back—sometimes extralegal. Herbert Hoover, enraged when newsmen followed him on fishing trips, used the Secret Service to try to stop them.[46] When the Russian KGB photographed the journalist Joseph Alsop in bed with a man, FBI director J. Edgar Hoover let Alsop know he had been given copies of the picture, a move that must have disinclined Alsop to attack any president too vociferously.[47] One wonders how many other journalists received such calling cards from Hoover.

Public access to the president disappeared during the twentieth century, and the once open White House gradually became a walled fortress. George Washington had held frequent public levees, welcoming all who owned suitable clothes. Even at the height of the Civil War, Lincoln held open levees several times a week. He believed protection was for emperors—not presidents—and made himself accessible. In fact, Lincoln was continually approached by people wanting help—mothers whose sons were about to be shot as deserters, rebels who wished to repent—and he heard each person out.

A woman whose soldier husband had been killed sought help from Lincoln, asking to take her oldest son home from the war. The sympathetic Lincoln wrote a letter ordering the boy's release, but by the time the woman traveled to him, he too had been killed. Brokenhearted, she returned to Lincoln, this time hoping that he would release her second son. Observe the physical and emotional intimacy of the encounter, as witnessed by the portrait artist F.B. Carpenter,

> While [Lincoln] was writing the order the poor woman stood by his side, the tears running down her cheeks, and passed her hand softly

over his head stroking the rough hair as I have seen a fond mother caress a son. By the time he had finished writing, his own heart and eyes were full. She took the paper, and again reverently placing her hand upon his head, said, "The Lord Bless You. May you live a thousand years, and always be head of this great nation."[48]

As recently as the twenties, Warren Harding still held daily public levees, and the White House grounds were open. Mrs. Harding complained that curious citizens continually peered into the windows. Today, a citizen does not expect to visit the president. Even invited guests must undergo extensive security checks. These safety measures appear to have turned the residence into an isolated, almost surreal, mini world.

Ironically, the secrecy may have created some privacy in the face of vastly increased, worldwide interest in the president and his family. On many days the first family's activities are not widely known. Nor are private feelings plumbed. Though rumors surface, the public knows little about the current state of the Clintons' marriage. Each Clinton lost a parent during the first two years in office, and their close friend, Vincent Foster, committed suicide. While for many people such losses demand months of grieving, little was revealed, aside from the news stories of the first few days, about the Clintons' real experience of their current lives. But the price of privacy and sanctuary is imprisonment. No president can even walk freely around Washington.

In 1993 and 1994, when the Clintons vacationed on Martha's Vineyard, newspapers and television offered hour-by-hour accounts of their activities, reminiscent of Mary Lincoln's beach sojourn or Cleveland's honeymoon—but filmed. It is exhausting to imagine taking such a public vacation, and illustrates what happens when the first family ventures from seclusion. One can only wonder at the state of embarrassed overexposure, secrecy, and heightened self-importance the experience creates. We know from other situations—hospitals, prisons, totalitarian surveillance—that stripping privacy confuses people's sense of identity, interferes with their well-being, and quickly makes them hypervigilant, even paranoid. One wonders how any politician relaxes under such conditions.

Yet when the Clintons visited Martha's Vineyard, I eagerly read the daily account. I wanted to know what flavor ice cream the president bought. Why do I remember it was mango?[49] Why did it disappoint me that the president liked a sweet fruit flavor? During the Vietnam War, why did my animosity toward President Nixon find particular satisfaction in the rumor that he ate cottage cheese with ketchup? The tiny details of a president's habits become a way of making contact with and measuring him. It is a primitive approach: Is he like me or not?

Whereas a king has only the obligation to be kingly—an object of idealization at a distance—a president cannot take that course without complaints that he has abandoned the common man. Witness George Bush crunching pork rinds. On the other hand, if we learn too much about the president's private life, he disappoints our wish to idealize.

Idealization is a peculiar phenomenon—and one closely related to shame. When one person idealizes another, he sees virtues writ large and faults diminished—a common example being romantic love. Idealization can be pleasant because it frees you from the normal scrapes of real relationships, but it tends to be unsteady and temporary. One of its prime psychic functions is to keep shame at bay, not always an easy task. Someone consumed by idealization cannot bear an intimate's normal failings and, overwhelmed by a chronic sense of disappointment, endlessly interrupts relationships to search for a perfect union.

Missed in this account is its enormous usefulness for creativity, learning, and survival. Idealization—also a basic component of transference in psychotherapy—can be a route into the new. Read memoirs of musicians, artists, ballet dancers, and all have idealized, even fallen in love with significant mentors. While the process has dangers—especially since mentors are inclined to exploit their prodigy's vulnerabilities and to get touchy about the younger person's eventual need to move on—its great virtue is enabling the intimate knowledge of craft to be passed down. When the young ballerina adores her teacher, she opens herself to the older woman's hard-won experience and knowledge. Because she is protected by feelings of admiration, she feels less harshly the normal shame of not knowing and learning. She is emboldened to risk trying something new.

Similarly, idealization works within countries to allow people to accept a leader, participate as followers, even sometimes change their ways. When colonists idealized George Washington, it allowed them to imagine themselves as a nation, and helped them risk the enormous psychological leap away from Europe. Seeing their own best traits embodied in Washington made them more plausible to themselves, and encouraged them to proceed with inventing a new form of government. Obviously, this is a gross simplification; nevertheless, the psychological process is significant. Nelson Mandela appears to have served the same purpose to South Africans.

George Washington was successfully idealized for many years because he possessed real virtues and because the historical moment so badly needed him. Furthermore, he did not reveal a lot of things about himself that disappointed and most members of the public rarely encountered him. But the psychological dilemma of the presidency is how the urge to idealize a leader must coexist

self, and in this sense, is undignified. The dignity Clinton does have comes from sheer doggedness; he will not quit.

Throughout her public life, Jacqueline Onassis radiated dignity. But was it because she was worthy or honorable? We can say she usually managed to keep unworthy and dishonorable parts of herself out of public view. Mostly, people appeared to love in her what the dictionary, defining dignity, calls "fit stateliness": the way she walked beside her husband's coffin with a black veil and straight posture, the way she dressed well and never talked.

Dignity is related to privacy because it often thrives on reserve. But as such it is complex, as I discovered at a dinner when a fellow guest remarked that she had seen Allen Ginsberg reading poems and sitting naked on a stage, and was struck by *his* dignity. The image confounds conventional notions, and delivers the real thing. Here is a poet who has told much about himself—and looked on willingly as others told the rest—describing his homosexuality, drug use, religious beliefs, sex practices, and the intimate details of his relationship with his insane mother. He has dignity.

Ginsberg is the perfect embodiment of post-Freudian man. Stand him beside George Washington, and it's hard to think of a more opposite pairing: one, a bearded, glasses-wearing, gay, confessional Jew; the other a clean-shaven, heterosexual, glasses-hiding, correct WASP. By simple measures Ginsberg should not have dignity. And yet he does—an important reminder that revelation, confession, or physical nakedness is not inherently undignified. Ginsberg's dignity resides ultimately in his insistent fidelity to his own experience—in his frank, unapologetic presentation of his life. Here. This is who I am. Take it or leave it. Such loyalty is not easy when one embodies what convention disavows. We grant Allen Ginsberg dignity because he refuses to disown his life, and as audience we hold the private knowledge of how hard we have sought to make him do so, how we have forced shame upon him. We are relieved that he has resisted.

Unlike Ginsberg, Clinton has invited scrutiny that he cannot bear—something like Gary Hart, but different. Whereas in 1987 during the presidential primary, Hart challenged reporters to catch him with another woman and they did, Clinton spoke about private feelings as a way to win voters, invited the press and the public to look too closely—and to find him on the one hand, less "presidential" than they desire, and on the other, less forthcoming.

Furthermore, if we accept Clinton's apparent designation of himself as representative of the "new man"—post-Freud, post-sixties, "in touch with his feelings"—we are not yet sure what this means, but the attributes it appears to offer our wish to idealize are personal. And since many politicians lack time or disposition to create idealizable personal lives (if such a thing exists after Freud), their predicament is worse than that of their predecessors.

Consider these excerpts from Clinton's acceptance speech at the 1992 Democratic Convention:

> I never met my father. He was killed in a car wreck on a rainy road three months before I was born, driving home from Chicago to Arkansas to see my mother.
> After that my mother had to support us. So we lived with my grandparents while she went away to Louisiana to study nursing.
> I can still see her clearly tonight through the eyes of a 3-year-old: kneeling at the railroad station and weeping as she put me back on the train to Arkansas with my grandmother.

Other personal remarks in the speech include a reference to his mother's breast cancer and words of love addressed to her and his wife. At the end of the talk, Clinton refers to the birth of his daughter, Chelsea. "I was overcome with the thought that God had given me a blessing my own father never knew: the chance to hold my child in my arms."[51]

Equally remarkable, Al Gore devoted paragraphs of his vice presidential acceptance speech to recounting his six-year-old son's near-fatal accident. Gore begins with an almost apologetic, "I don't know what it's like to lose a father," and then continues.

> Three years ago, my son Albert was struck by a car. . . . Tipper and I watched as he was thrown 30 feet through the air and scraped another 20 feet on the pavement after he hit the ground.
> I ran to his side and held him and called his name, but he was limp and still, without breath or pulse.[52]

During their acceptance speeches, behaving more like talk-show guests than traditional candidates, Clinton and Gore described private experiences to millions of viewers. No doubt their media consultants believed that a public display of emotion was a great way to hit the incumbent hard. Since President Bush had the military hero status and the White House experience, the only free territory had to be personal. They attacked the classical presidential image by setting Woodstock Nation against the stodgier past, showcasing themselves as new men who did the feeling thing. Bush was set up to look stiff and old, unfeeling—like an absent, unavailable father, perhaps the one Clinton never had.

But by using private feeling for public gain, Clinton set the stage for further invasions of his own privacy. "Because of its inherent worldlessness, love can only become false and perverted when it is used for political purposes," Hannah Arendt writes in *The Human Condition.*[53] The process of displaying private feelings to achieve public ends distorts them, and corrupts their meaning. The essence of authentic feeling is that it obeys no master; that is the source of its freshness and its basis for making a genuine contribution both to self-knowledge and to intimacy. In Clinton's case, the feelings described become sentimentalized and one-dimensional, without accountability. Real feelings—in all their ambivalence and complexity—cannot reliably *seek* votes. Those Gore described, while moving, seem to exploit his son's tragedy, to diminish the sincere personal discovery ("that experience changed me forever") he made in the process of caring for the boy. Possibly, had he said more about how the experience changed his political outlook, and less about the anguishing details of the event, he would have told something important.

Trying to figure out how the private disclosure of the psychotherapy consulting room evolved into the public pseudoconfession of the political convention is like trying to trace back—from gibberish to coherent sentence—a kid's birthday party game of telephone. The candidate's goal, to make himself loveable and familiar (the guy next door) by detailing the ways he, too, has suffered emotionally, not only has nothing in common with the often halting and painful disclosure of psychotherapy, but it finesses the political issues. Carefully calculated "personal" emotion replaces ideology as media gurus pray that warm fuzzy feelings will gather votes better than controversial ideas.

Furthermore, as Clinton discovered, once played by you, the personal thing is played *on you* ad nauseam. The part of his sixties history Clinton didn't talk about squarely is his experience smoking dope, avoiding the draft, and enjoying many sex partners. It is hard to wear half a mantle. Had he owned his private behavior, he might have fared better—but it is unclear. When Grover Cleveland's advisers asked him what spin to put on the story of his illegitimate child, he answered, "Just tell the truth." Honesty occasionally plays well with the American public—probably, besides its novelty, because it suggests secure self-esteem.

But the problem is not just Clinton's dodging, it's also the nation's. If, for instance, Cleveland had had to admit to having several children with different women, his nineteenth-century constituency might have balked. My hunch is that Clinton's rumored promiscuity comes partly from the large sexual opportunity success affords men, and partly—like Beecher and Rhodes—as a response to early loss and a difficult growing up. But Americans don't want to know the truth of our candidate's private lives as much as we want a comforting, fictive narrative, highlighting hard work, benign commonality and basic decency; a story that doesn't evoke anxiety by signaling real difference and that doesn't fall apart until after election day. Candidate's emotional disclosures and confessions are carefully pitched to prop up these larger myths.

Overall, candidates succeed for complex reasons. Part of what we claim we want is "good character." What do we mean? Not only Cleveland, but Washington and Lincoln have been particularly admired for their honesty, certainly a significant virtue. But it's unclear any of them could withstand contemporary scrutiny. Lincoln had bouts of serious depression. Washington liked to gamble, and may have been unfaithful more than once. Cleveland *did* like a lot of beer.

The question of how to weigh character has been with American politics from early on. Here is how, in April 1836, the Philadelphia *Public Ledger* defined the relationship of private life and public office.

> Not thirty years since, drunkenness, gaming and licentiousness were not disqualifications for public trust. . . . Formerly, when politics presented only two parties, public acts and measures were the only subjects of discussion, and rigid examination of private life was deemed illiberal. . . . Infidelity to all private engagements did not impeach the patriotism or official fidelity of a public servant. Now,

the current and sounder doctrine is that private vice and public virtue are inconsistent, and that the best patriots are to be found in the
most faithful to all the relations which constitute *society* and consequently a *country.*[54]

Should, as the writer suggests, a man whose private life includes gambling, drinking, womanizing, and fraud be disqualified
for office? Though newspaper editorials have frequently suggested
such principles, the public has preferred to decide character on a
case-by-case basis. For example, Clinton appears to lie a lot, but so
far the public has tolerated it, I think for several reasons. First, it's
transparent, and like the lying of a child, leaves people more often
disappointed than deeply betrayed. Second, people feel this flaw
may be adequately balanced by his intelligence and sincere wish to
solve some of the country's problems. Third, the public is struggling to make sense of the media juggernaut and to what degree it
inhibits candid disclosure. Fourth, Clinton's lying makes people
feel more equal to him and simultaneously supports their inclination to feel cynical and distrustful about government. Fifth, the
Republicans ran candidates that the public liked less.

Clinton's lying also demonstrates how candidates frantically
hide what their opponents thrill to uncover. Believing themselves
wrongly victimized and under siege from the opposition and the
press, candidates come to feel entitled to exempt themselves from
everyday rules. Presidential candidates come to believe that—in
the words of a befuddled Frenchman trying to survive the Reign of
Terror in late-eighteenth-century France—"Christian virtues are
good, but they cannot be applied at the present time."[55]

Putting aside the presidency for a moment, think about the
fate of Clinton's appointees. Daniel Ginsburg was disqualified
from the Supreme Court for smoking marijuana. Zoe Baird was
banned from a cabinet post because of issues regarding her employ-

ment of an illegal immigrant as household help. Surgeon General Jocelyn Elders was fired for publicly mentioning masturbation. When grouped together, these stories highlight how behavior deemed relevant to character circles around current anxieties just as it did in Washington's day. In general, today's media privacy invasions probe current issues of social change.

Are these candidates of poor character? Probably they fail no more than politicians in the past, or more than the public they were not allowed to represent. Rather, they represent something slightly nontraditional and thus become prey to the nation's anxiety and conflict about the newness. The public, struggling with large amounts of change, is wondering if there really is a new man or a new woman, a possibility of equality between the sexes, a marriage that thrives as equal partnership. Can sex be just for fun? Can a drug other than alcohol have safe recreational use?

Untraditional private behaviors are more likely to attract scrutiny. Cocktails Franklin Roosevelt must have sipped during Prohibition never hurt him because, traditionally, men drink. Ronald Reagan's poor job as father slips by because, in this century at least, Americans have paid less attention to how men father than to how women mother. Conversely, Ed Muskie's public tears harmed him because, traditionally, a man may shed a tear from grief but not from pressure.

Whether a candidate will make a good or even a great president is unlikely to be divined from whether he, for instance, tried marijuana at age twenty or suffered bouts of depression. What seems more useful is information about candidates that illuminates their public records, their long-term political and social commitments, and their lifelong style of "doing business." Ultimately, success depends a lot on the marriage between the person and the historical moment.

The worrisome reality is that just as the nation is becoming more interested in the idea of the private person, the task of running for president has become so grueling that people who deeply value private life are unlikely anymore to join the race. During Jesse Jackson's presidential campaign, Marshall Frady observed the candidate working twenty-four hours a day. Jackson was never alone, never off the telephone, even in the middle of the night, leading Frady to wonder "if, after so many years of his moving among multitudes and public occasions, there any longer existed for Jackson an inner sense of difference between the personal and the mass moment—if, in fact, he was left with any private personality at all."[56]

Politicians need to have private personalities, but sometimes these personalities will commit embarrassingly human acts. Occasionally politicians will commit harmful acts that legitimately disqualify them for office. The public deserves information about serious personal problems that might impair performance—grave illness, untreated substance abuse, and repeated ethical lapses or criminal behavior. What they almost always get instead is too much news about embarrassing secrets of dubious importance.

9

Harriet Jacobs's Room:
Women and Privacy

Women's experience is at the heart of contemporary struggles about privacy. Throughout history most women have had little privacy. Since autonomy and liberty—as well as certain kinds of creativity and self-expression—are almost impossible without it, establishing its place in a woman's life is a primary task of any bid for equality.

As the discussion of Beecher suggests, the subtext of contemporary celebrity "news" often explores the question of how much power women should have, and examines their status as victim or perpetrator: Anita Hill versus Clarence Thomas, Woody Allen versus Mia Farrow, Bill Clinton versus Paula Jones, and O.J. Simpson versus Nicole Brown Simpson are but a few examples. Each story seeks to figure out which partner, and thus which gender, was "bad" in private, and in what particular ways. But the media attention to these struggles signals a larger issue. Traditional power divisions between the sexes are shifting slightly, and people feel anxious. This anxiety leads the public to examine some stories very closely as it seeks knowledge about what these changes might mean to private life and relationships.

Creating privacy for women means shifting long-existing power arrangements. An odd paradox emerges: Women have inhabited the "private realm" but lacked the benefits of privacy. Historically, women have worked to create private space and leisure for men. As Sophia Ripley wrote anonymously in an 1841 issue of the Transcendentalist journal *The Dial,* "It seems an unknown, or at least an unacknowledged fact, that in the spot where man throws aside his heavy responsibilities, his couch of rest is often prepared by his faithful wife, at the sacrifice of all her quiet contemplation and leisure."[1]

Because communities have long relied upon women to perform domestic tasks, nurture men, raise children, care for the sick and the elderly, visit the poor, and maintain kin ties, when women think about devoting energy to other pursuits—including those that are personal and private—people become anxious, bemoan the death of community, and notice selfishness and excessive individualism with fresh interest.

So, too, women who are ambitious in the public world continue to be viewed—in the words of Lady Macbeth—as "unsexed." White House efforts to remake Hilary Clinton's image speak volumes on this subject. After several years of political surgery, the assertive lawyer resembles a gentle helpmate. As women step into public life, their private behavior is judged in areas where it is not judged for men. Think about the media exploration of Zoe Baird's household help, or Simpson prosecutor Marcia Clark's quality time with her children. How we might balance individual pursuits (public or private) with communal and familial obligations is an urgent question, but most current talk about it is spurious, an effort to use nostalgia for an imaginary past to avoid the real discussions.

Abortion is a preeminent contemporary controversy because

it sits exactly on the fault line between the privacy and liberty of women and men's urgency to ensure their procreative access. The ferocious debate has bared the power issues that underlie questions of privacy, and its outcome has had—and will continue to have—radical social consequences. When Sarah Weddington, the lawyer who argued *Roe v. Wade* before the Supreme Court in 1973, explained the constitutional basis for abortion, she observed that if the concept of liberty is to be meaningful for women, it must include "liberty from being forced to continue the unwanted pregnancy."[2] In other words, she asserted, women could not experience autonomy within their private lives until they possessed more procreative control.

So, too, the Supreme Court justices who decided *Roe v. Wade* recognized that the only way of securing for women an equal possibility of freedom was to make sure that abortion would be—not absolutely, but relatively—a private choice. While the state clearly had an interest in protecting the unborn child, that was not its only interest. The mother's privacy, her wish to make decisions about herself by herself, and her wish to control her body, were also compelling.

The recognition of the mother's separate perspective is an important historical departure, even a revolutionary one. Consequently, the moment during pregnancy when protecting the unborn child should gain ascendancy becomes a serious question; one has to weigh competing goods, and viability has been chosen as the fulcrum point. With regard to privacy, this has come to mean that a woman, finding herself pregnant but not yet carrying a viable fetus—and able to raise the necessary funds—can choose to tell no one, take herself to an abortion clinic, and have an abortion performed. *Roe v. Wade* laid the groundwork for women to make pregnancy (and the sexuality that preceded it) a more private matter—and thus it created, really for the first time, the possibility of social equality for women in private and in public.

What seems particularly remarkable is that the radical accomplishment of this decision, combined with the landmark 1992 confirmation of *Roe* in *Planned Parenthood of Southeastern Pennsylvania v. Casey*, does not rest on any need to make abortion out to be a good thing. For it is its legality, not its virtue, that releases women from the hobbling threat that their autonomy can be taken away by incest, rape, threatened violence, birth control failure, difficulty speaking up in the midst of a sexual encounter, or a moment of careless abandon. And while it is naive not to recognize that life is fraught for everyone, and sexuality now widely endangered by AIDS, without legal abortion there exists a peril for women that is unique simply because of the asymmetrical nature of the woman's burden during gestation. In the words of the *Casey* majority, "the liberty of the woman is at stake in a sense unique to the human condition and so unique to the law. The mother who carries a child to full term is subject to anxieties, to physical constraints, to pain that only she must bear. . . . The destiny of the woman must be shaped to a large extent on her own conception of her spiritual imperatives and her place in society."[3]

I would prefer that no woman ever had to have another abortion. Yet you do not have to be an enthusiast for the procedure to recognize that privacy, freedom, and the possibility of social equality for women are not possible without legal access. In fact, from the point of view of gender equality and women's privacy, *Roe v. Wade* is arguably the single most important court decision in the history of this country.

Sincere people oppose abortion because they are profoundly disturbed by destroying life. But the anti-abortion movement includes many people who have more complex motives. Were protecting children their primary goal, they could find causes to champion not so dependent upon female submission. For too many "pro-life" advocates, rights for the unborn are a Trojan horse whose real intent is ensuring the prerogative of sperm.

In December 1994, I was driving to a store when word came over the radio that a man had murdered two women at nearby abortion clinics. I parked the car and listened in horror. My grief was visceral, unconsidered, unintended. I felt traumatized. Other women, I learned later, all over the city felt similarly. Terrorism uses violence against one person to inspire fear in all who feel kinship with the victim. The gunman shot particular people, but his gun was aimed at any woman who had ever counted too many days since her last period. It didn't matter if you had never visited a clinic.

Subsequent stories portrayed the killer as a troubled man acting alone. This assessment was literally true, but emotionally speaking, he was acting on behalf of others. Growing up in rural Vermont, I used to ice skate with friends and play crack-the-whip in winter on a local pond. I was enthralled and terrified by how the kid at the end of the line would hurl out over the ice with fierce speed, while the other skaters, once they'd set the game in motion, stood still. Societies have much in common with a line of wobbly kids playing crack-the-whip. Whenever issues get heated, extremists tend to shoot out wildly, carried by the group's intention beyond its common range. Bystanders, watching only a lone child speeding along, might think she had propelled herself. So too with John Salvi, the murderer. Until you appreciate the context that propels him, he resembles a man acting alone.

Amid all the struggle, it is difficult to hold onto the real dilemma of abortion—that it is a sobering choice. In clinical work, one sees women coming for therapy filled with sadness even as they are relieved by an abortion, or men who feel awful about the termination of a wife's or girlfriend's pregnancy. Years later people may note the missing child, or sometimes revisit the decision. But lest this be weighed disproportionately, therapists hear equally about the awful grief of trying to live without adequate income because one has had a child too soon, or the daily shame of having to raise a child one feels unable to raise, or the anxiety of worrying about a child who has been adopted away. These sorrows, too, tend to be abiding.

Once, during a meeting of a mother's group in the housing project, a group member spontaneously spoke about how much she missed a child who, twenty years earlier, she had given up for adoption. Several other women, all of whom as teenagers had given babies up for adoption, wept and echoed her. They thought often of these children, secretly marked their birthdays, and worried about their safety. One woman described vigilantly scanning public places in search of her lost daughter whose neonate features she had imagined and reimagined throughout childhood into adulthood, an experience the others shyly acknowledged sharing. Yet they also hoped their children were better off, and several wished that as children someone had adopted them.

If birth control improves, or men become more willing to use it, abortions may gradually become rare. Until then, the law that protects them also protects a critical domain of privacy and private choice for women. Sometimes—perhaps often—this means that one bears a difficult but chosen grief instead of one forced from the outside. Ironically, chosen grief may be one of the defining features of freedom. So, too, the capacity to notice and experience one's own grief may be one of the ways to safeguard liberty against either tyranny or license.

Much has been written about the private versus the public realm. Theoretically they are separate. Historically, or so the common wisdom goes, the public (government, institutions, commerce) has belonged to men, while the private (home and children, relationships, and the busy weaving of the communal web) to women. Mary Kelley, writing about women in antebellum America, observes, "Schooled in virtue, the Christian helpmate was to meet her responsibility to the republic by being the exemplar and teacher of virtue to husband and sons."[4] She adds, "The male's role would be public and his choice of occupation multiple, while the female's would be private and her occupation singularly domestic."[5] Writings of early-nineteenth-century women—when they did write— are sprinkled with phrases like "Submission is my duty"[6] and one must "learn the pleasure of contentment—and obedience."[7] Many writers have pointed out the process by which women were confined to a narrow domain, then at least ambivalently complicit in glorifying its moral superiority. The proffered ideal was a genteel variation of the proverbial "mafia marriage," where the husband made money in unscrupulous ways and the "innocent" wife transformed the ill-gotten gains into respectability.

You can admire devoted mothering, homemaking, social volunteering, nursing the sick, being a good neighbor or friend, and many other traditionally female practices, but recognize that defining them as belonging exclusively to women or as constituting a "private sphere" is absurd. As the abortion dilemma quickly reveals, such a division is impossible.

Still, it is ironic that women have lived in a place called privacy but hardly tasted its fruit. The important benefit of privacy— its capacity to serve as a wellspring for real freedom, autonomy, intimacy, intellectual endeavor and creative expression—has yet to belong fully to any but the most privileged women. In the simplest terms, if you are not protected and valued—granted full citizenship by the public world—you are not safe in private. All that attacks the fragile and infinitely corruptible, infinitely valuable state of privacy harms first its more vulnerable members. The autobiography of a slave woman offers incontrovertible testimony. (It also illustrates the fallacy of easy nostalgia about lost communal life.)

In June 1857, Harriet Jacobs finished writing *Incidents in the Life of a Slave Girl,* a masterful and deeply moving account of her experience in slavery. Struggling with her own feelings about what she had revealed and whether she could stand to have people know such intimate details about her life, Jacobs wrote to her friend Amy Post, an abolitionist:

> I have My dear friend—Striven faithfully to give a true and just account of my own life in Slavery. . . . Woman can whisper—her cruel wrongs into the ear of a very dear friend—much easier than she can record them for the world to read—I have left nothing out but what I thought—the world might believe that a Slave Woman was too willing to pour out—that she might gain their sympathies.[8]

Published in 1861—without the author's name on the cover—Jacobs's book sold several thousand copies before drifting out of print. Subsequently viewed as a fraud, it was only reprinted in the late 1960s and has since been authenticated, particularly by the careful scholarship of Jean Fagin Yellin. Like accounts by prison camp survivors, or testimonies from Amnesty International, it illustrates the process of human degradation imposed by the abuse of power, particularly, in this case, as it plays out in the privacy of a master's home.

It is miraculous that Jacobs's book came into the world at all, for its author overcame daunting obstacles to write it. Harriet Jacobs, born around 1813 in North Carolina, begins her story thus: "I was born a slave; but I never knew it till six years of happy childhood had passed away."[9] It's an amazing sentence: startling because it insists on a *child* who became a slave, immediately avowing its narrator's force and agency. For a few years Harriet's resourceful family managed to protect her from the cruelest and most demeaning aspects of slavery. "I was so fondly shielded that I never dreamed I was a piece of merchandise, trusted to them for safe keeping."[10]

Love fortifies the child to withstand much future suffering. When her mother dies, the six-year-old slave moves in with her owner, a woman who appears also to have loved her, though *love* is an uneasy word to describe a relationship between a person and her property. This mistress dies when Harriet is twelve, and bequeaths her to a niece, an event that marks the beginning of her torment.

Being owned by a three-year-old girl means that the adolescent slave is actually controlled by the child's father, James Norcom (called "Dr. Flint" in the book), a medical doctor and wealthy town citizen. Freed from his first wife in a sensational divorce and remarried, Norcom apparently remains unsated, for he seeks with singular sadistic intent to force Jacobs's psychological and sexual submission. Much of Jacobs's memoir recounts her efforts to outwit him, forestall his abuse, survive, and, finally, to protect her own children from the psychological insanity and endless suffering of living as property.

However cleverly he schemes to corner her, Jacobs dodges Norcom, and her success goads him, apparently heating both his desire and his wrath. She manages to protect herself for a while because she understands her master's ironic predicament: how he is shackled by hypocrisy. Though Norcom feels entitled to molest and impregnate his slave, he prefers seduction to rape because it fits better with his view of himself as an upstanding citizen and decent man. Furthermore, as Jacobs points out, the small North Carolina town does not sanction complete license; the doctor's wife and neighbors watch him warily. As time passes, Norcom is increasingly caught between an almost haunted need to win Jacobs's romantic compliance and a humiliated rage that the slave resists his charm.

The volatile mix ignites when the sixteen-year-old Harriet asks her master for permission to marry. Outraged, Flint punches her, threatens to jail or kill her, and then, apparently unable to give up his wish to seduce her, lectures on why he *ought* to send her to jail:

> It would take some of your high notions out of you. But I am not ready to send you there yet, not withstanding your ingratitude for all my kindness and forbearance. You have been the plague of my life. I have wanted to make you happy, and I have been repaid with the basest ingratitude.[11]

If she disobeys him or speaks of marriage again, Flint warns, she will be beaten, punished like "the meanest slave on my plantation." If her boyfriend reappears, Flint will shoot him, "as soon as I would a dog."

Elsewhere in the book, Jacobs refers to Flint's ongoing harassment as "the old threadbare discourse."[12] How true. His speech is a classic statement—almost a set piece—of private tyranny. It captures fully the self-righteous, self-pitying feelings of a person who has fallen hard for his own story. He is faultless; she must make amends. The tyrant's gambit is eternal: You will submit to me, or I will terrorize you. Submission commonly includes the psychological twist of coercing the victim to assume the perpetrator's distorted claim: "I am doing this for you."[13]

The violation of safety within private life through abusive domination is widespread, but not terribly imaginative. Though the details vary, the basic form stays predictable. Jacobs described it exactly as I have encountered it—one hundred plus years later—treating, or supervising, the psychotherapies of contemporary women (and men) who as children experienced with adults, or as spouses with abusive partners, the same extreme coercion Jacobs describes.

Whoever wishes to destroy freedom and undermine sanctuary simply uses superior force—or its threat—to transform private space into a secret prison. The more powerful person's cause, often at its deepest level some wish not to feel shame or experience loss, is enforced—in language as well as actions—at the expense of the less powerful person. Harriet Jacobs is heroic because against enormous odds and at great personal cost, she resists Flint, safeguards her children, frees herself, and recounts her story, hoping to help other slaves. To convey her experience, she defies not only her enslavement, but his language, and the public language allowed to women.

After their confrontation, Jacobs's plight intensifies. The doctor seeks to corner her by building a cabin outside of town and forcing her to live there—hidden from his wife's and her grandmother's watchful eyes. Trapped, she eludes Flint by becoming sexually involved with another powerful white man, and bearing two children. The humiliated Flint delivers her to his son's plantation with plans to "break" her by selling her children.

Flint's attempts at revenge are relentless, and Jacobs, knowing that he will eventually destroy her, has no recourse but to hide. For seven years, she lies imprisoned in an attic crawl space in her grandmother's house. It is crushing; she cannot even stand up straight. She glimpses her son and daughter through a tiny hole in a wall, but she cannot speak to them. They must long for her in ignorance. She much watch them without hinting that she is near. The strain and sorrow render her half mad. "Season after season, year after year, I peeped at my children's faces, and heard their sweet voices, with a heart yearning all the while to say, 'Your mother is here.'"[14]

Finally escaping north, befriending abolitionists, and continually dodging capture, Jacobs decides to tell her story. As she gradually writes it—secretly at night, since she lacks a private room or daytime leisure—she struggles with whether she can bear to publish her intimate tale. Jacobs knows firsthand the terrorizing core of slavery, and wants to expose its corruption. Yet she feels shamed by having conceived her children out of wedlock. Must she open herself to public scorn and pious judgment? Hasn't she suffered enough? Jacobs decides to disclose her experience. Though she calls herself "Linda" and leaves her name off the book cover, she realizes that everyone she knows will recognize her. She can find no way to communicate without giving up privacy.

> And now, reader, I come to a period in my unhappy life, which I would gladly forget if I could. The remembrance fills me with sorrow and shame. It pains me to tell you of it; but I have promised to tell you the truth, and I will do it honestly, let it cost me what it may. I will not try to screen myself behind the plea of compulsion from a master; for it was not so. . . . I knew what I did and I did it with deliberate calculation.
>
> But, O, ye happy women, whose purity has been sheltered from childhood, who have been free to choose the objects of your affection, whose homes are protected by law, do not judge the poor desolate slave girl too severely![15]

As she writes, Jacobs trembles with so many contradictory feelings the paragraph wants to burst. Beneath the careful surface, the orphaned child piteously tells her dead mother the subsequent course of her life. The loving granddaughter, cousin, and friend pleads on behalf of her subjugated kin. The ex-slave shakes with rage recalling her violation, and with barely suppressed impatience, the long-suffering woman illuminates moral complexity for an audience she considers naive. Jacobs's words both establish her agency and simultaneously insist that the reader recognize the dire context within which she has acted. Gathering her many unconscious and conscious motives, Jacobs weaves a considered statement, forsaking privacy for a cause.

Jacobs speaks at once boldly and cautiously. Caught in the dual pincers of racism and sexism, publishing a book about sexual exploitation at a time when few women considered public expression much less open self-disclosure, she chooses her words to establish her virtue. She assumes from her audience a thread of sympathy so frail, so based on proving her submission to domestic virtue, it constrains her voice. Hinting that she, for instance, enjoyed conceiving her children, or sometimes hated white people, or found occasional happiness in her enforced solitude, might cost her everything—might overburden and snap the filament that holds her above the abyss of her public powerlessness.

By comparison, consider the easy emotional expression and large success of Harriet Beecher Stowe's slavery novel. *Uncle Tom's Cabin,* published in 1852, sold 300,000 copies in the United States and 150,000 in England the first year it was in print—numbers that, in its time, were phenomenal. Not only did the book sell, the theater version became so successful that "at one time as many as four companies were performing it simultaneously in New York, sometimes giving three shows a day, so great were the crowds."[16] It remained America's most popular play for the next eighty years.

Today, *Uncle Tom's Cabin* makes us nervous. Uncle Tom is too good to be true. The book's Christian righteousness is embarrassing, as is the paper-doll female virtue. The overt, patronizing racism bears witness to what actually has changed in race relations during the past century—and what has not. Yet *Uncle Tom's Cabin* made an enormous contribution to ending slavery. As Langston Hughes observed,

> The truth of the matter is that *Uncle Tom's Cabin* in 1852 was not merely a book. It was a flash, as Frederick Douglass put it, to "light a million camp fires in front of the embattled hosts of slavery." . . . During the Civil War, when Abraham Lincoln met Harriet Beecher Stowe at the White House he said, "So this is the little lady who started this big war." . . . Lincoln knew that thousands of men who had voted for him had read *Uncle Tom's Cabin*, and many a Union soldier must have remembered it as he marched, for the book was a moral battle cry.[17]

Ironically but predictably, Stowe's novel had a larger effect on popular thinking about slavery than Jacobs's true story. There are many reasons: Stowe was familiar to her reading public. Slaves, who might have favored Jacobs's narrative, often were forbidden to read, much less buy books. Some white people wouldn't buy a book written by a slave. Furthermore, Stowe's book appeared in the heat of the protest against the 1850 Fugitive Slave Act, whereas, Yellin observes, Jacobs's sales may have been inhibited by its later publication; "as the nation moved toward civil war, yet another slave narrative seemed of minor importance."[18]

But there is an additional reason. Jacobs, writing autobiography, struggles to balance her wish to shield her experience with her desire to reveal herself for the political end of fighting slavery. Forced to answer personally for whatever she says, Jacobs writes with caution and restraint. Her revelation of sexual predation is taboo and unpleasant for her audience to confront. Stowe suffers no such hindrance. Personally uninvolved with the institution, unencumbered by direct racism, and veiled by fiction, Stowe can write with more unconstrained emotion than Jacobs, whose newfound place within the white world is a wobbling ice floe on a mean river.

Ironically, the punch of *Uncle Tom's Cabin,* the blast of feeling that creates so much social impact, occurs in part because Stowe in fact delivered to the subject of slavery the sorrow, painful loss, and conflict within her own private life. One source of Stowe's identification with her enslaved characters is her powerlessness and servitude as a woman in mid-nineteenth-century America. The second, according to biographer Joan Hedrick, is Stowe's love for her son, Charley, who died of cholera when eighteen months old.[19] Deeply attached to this infant, it was most likely her grief from his loss that made Stowe consider the experience of women in slavery and realize that their situation was hers writ large.

That many women in the reading public at mid-century shared these two conditions—possessed unconscious identifications with the enslaved, and felt powerless in their marriages and bereft by the loss of young children—doubtless contributed to the book's success. As Hedrick has also pointed out, they were psychologically ripe to have their consciousness awakened, especially in an indirect way that allowed them to express anger without violating the strictures of their own femininity and domesticity.

For the northern white women who read *Uncle Tom's Cabin* —women who couldn't vote, couldn't control pregnancy, were likely to die in childbirth, couldn't control property, couldn't earn money except as teachers, servants, or prostitutes (Stowe was among the first female writers to earn a living from their work), for women who were virtually barred from participating in the "public" world—slavery was not only a moral issue and a confrontation with Christian belief, but a ready displacement for their own unnamed malaise. Many construed this despair as a failure in their true femaleness. Yet, the suppressed rage and grief both fed Stowe's writing and fueled her audience's appreciation of what she wrote.

Unlike Jacobs, Stowe was not sadistically terrorized (except perhaps in her childhood by her father's representations of a Calvinist god). Luckier than many of her peers, she was neither owned nor indentured. She was educated and could afford servants. Yet overall, Stowe's relative prosperity, social class, and race did little to protect her from the immense difficulties of nineteenth-century female existence. Marriage meant pregnancy; pregnancy meant illness and frequent death. Bearing children meant losing children. Domestic work was unending. Stowe wrote when she could, though the distractions of maintaining a household plagued her: "Nothing but deadly determination enables me ever to write—it is rowing against wind and tide."[20]

Long before Virginia Woolf pleaded for a room of her own, Stowe expressed the wish. "If I am to write, I must have a room to myself, which shall be *my* room."[21] Privacy has long been recognized as necessary for intellectual and academic endeavors. And it has long been reserved for wealthy men. In their essay "The Use of Private Space," Dominique Barthelemy and Philippe Contamine point out that as early as 1380, privileged young men attending Dainville College in Paris were given private rooms so that they could better pursue their studies (but they were ordered to keep their doors open so they could be occasionally observed.)[22] Even as women were relegated to the private realm, they were denied private space. Certainly, Harriet Jacobs's account of her shattering imprisonment in a crawl space offers a grotesque parody of this truth and of Virginia Woolf's plea. Jacobs had a room in which she could think and maybe read; she just couldn't live or move or love or freely leave.

Even when women like Stowe overcame their impeding context, they paid a high price. Their public voices generally sought harmony with female convention. Predictably, the tune was sentimental. As Ann Douglas has described in *The Feminization of American Culture,* the concept of women dominating the private realm while excluded from the public one could not be anything but sentimental:

> Sentimentalism is a complex phenomenon. It asserts that the values a society's activity denies are precisely the ones it cherishes; it attempts to deal with the phenomenon of cultural bifurcation by the manipulation of nostalgia. Sentimentalism protests a power to which one has already in part capitulated.[23]

In other words, in a psychological sense, we sentimentalize—often from unconscious guilt—as a way of offering compensatory tribute to a deity we know we are in fact ignoring. In this case, nineteenth-century America, moving ever faster toward unleashed, often ruthless materialism, sentimentalized the self-sacrificing pious woman. Harriet Beecher Stowe captures this truth and exposes it early on in *Uncle Tom's Cabin.* Describing how a husband gives his wife "unlimited scope in all her benevolent efforts" for slaves and servants, Stowe observes,

> He really seemed somehow or other to fancy that his wife had piety and benevolence enough for two—to indulge a shadowy expectation of getting into heaven through her superabundance of qualities to which he made no particular pretension.[24]

With the private and the public realm separated by gender, it was possible to freely idealize the supposed domestic virtues and moral influences of women—high-mindedness, big-heartedness, gentility—because they were safely away from the action. Wives received care and freedom from responsibility by agreeing to abdicate public power to husbands. Since no woman could make a single stock market trade, call soldiers to war, or write legislation, she was said to remain pure and to influence men through her virtue. Faced with her husband's having secretly sold a beloved slave child, Mrs. Shelby is bereft, and recognizes her complicity with the preposterous arrangement she helped to sustain. "I was a fool to think I could make anything good out of such a deadly evil."[25]

The real achievement of *Uncle Tom's Cabin* is Stowe's exposure of the bad arguments for slavery, and the resulting moral degradation. She argues compellingly for compassion based on recognition of common feelings: that parents of all races love their children, that no race holds the corner on decent or indecent behavior. Her ideas are brave in an era when many denied that Negroes were fully human beings, and slavery was rationalized through that denial. Stowe offered sentimental characters to her contemporaries, who used them the way citizens used their idealization of George Washington, to help create a sea change.

But there was a price. To win her allegiance her fictional slaves must sacrifice ambiguity, aggression, and sexuality. They become saints and victims. "Uncle Tom's Cabin," writes James Baldwin, "is a very bad novel." And Stowe, he further observes, "was not so much a novelist as an impassioned pamphleteer; her book was not intended to do anything more than prove that slavery was wrong; was, in fact, perfectly horrible."[26]

Baldwin's point, though uncharitable, is important. Two competing truths—his and hers—lay claim. Political tracts often make bad novels (at least in the twentieth-century view of the novel), but the dilemma is deeper. For stories to move people toward political change, they must often, as Stowe did (and Clinton and Gore attempted in their acceptance speeches), create saints and victims. But the cost of this strategy is that social gains based in sentimental portrayals leave unchallenged an insidious, one-dimensional view of human beings. Metaphorically, it is as Paul Fussell observed about photographs of World War II: All the real mess of guts and body parts tends to get left out. Accurate photographs might document how, in war, soldiers usually die blown to pieces, but they would not inspire the home front. Yet the censorship that allows the urgently needed patriotism leaves its audience either naive or bitter: the naive being those who believe the altered pictures; the bitter those whose personal witness is never mirrored in the public text. Stowe accepted the unspoken societal requirement that less powerful groups, whether female or black, must base their claim for equality on demonstrating a kind of gelded virtue.

The narrow ideal of womanhood remains alive today. Its survival is elegantly illustrated by comparing the length of prison sentences given to women who kill husbands versus husbands who kill wives. Women tend to get sentenced to fourteen to twenty years' prison time for the same crime for which men receive two to six years.[27] And it probably isn't the same crime, as women tend to murder men who have beaten them, while men tend to murder women who are fleeing from their control. The sentencing discrepancy suggests that people remain terrified (perhaps mainly unconsciously) by the specter of a woman bursting from her sentimental confinement.

Though the past twenty years has seen much more public expression by women, this small beginning has barely loosened the hold of sentimental perception. Consider Susan Smith. She killed both her children—probably out of profound despair about her own very difficult life, but possibly because she thought it would be easier to keep a man without them. Then she lied about the crime and tried to pin it on an imaginary black man. Had the ensuing public outcry really been about her exploiting racist terror of black men (which has worked for presidential candidates), it would have been newsworthy. But, rather, people were enraged—and probably on a deeper level frightened—that *a woman* killed her children and lied about it. Stories about Smith dominated the news, and politicians called for the electric chair. (News articles discussed an abortion she had once had. Was the implication that a woman who seeks an abortion and one who murders are close kin?)

The idea of a woman killing her own child is absolutely taboo. And while it should be, that is not the point. Men kill their children or stepchildren with appalling frequency, often when the children are in the way of men's rage at wives or ex-wives. These stories rarely make the front page. In the July 24, 1995, *Boston Globe,* the question of whether Susan Smith should get the death penalty was spread across parts of four columns and included two photographs. On the next page was a two-inch story about a father hacking off his son's head. Several days later, the conviction of murder against a divorced father for killing twin fourteen-month-old daughters received an inch and a half of newspaper coverage; apparently he was enraged at having to pay child support.[28]

Both sexes are harmed by this disparity in public reaction. Men, because they have been so alienated from their own tenderness that, too ashamed to speak, they witness its further debasement without comment. Women, because it is so difficult to let go of conditioning that confuses femininity with sainthood. Sophia Ripley described the problem in 1841:

The poet's lovely vision of an ethereal being, . . . his idealized Eve or Ophelia, is an exquisite picture for the eye; the sweet verse in which he tells us of her, most witching music to the ear; but she is not woman, she is only the spiritualized image of that tender class of women he loves the best,—one whom no true woman could or would become.[29]

This fantasy notion of woman continues to stand between us and Smith, and interferes with society's capacity to see her accurately or compassionately. Underlying and distorting the real horror at the real crime is an enraged popular feeling that because Smith has defied this ideal, she should die. Everyone who has ever wished for exquisite gentleness from a mother recoils from Smith. Most identify with her helpless and vulnerable children and disown feelings that might put them in even slight sympathy with her. (Though anyone who has tended an infant knows that the occasional wish to murder is one disconcerting part of the experience.)

Where is it that we can stand to know the real range of a person's experience, her feelings, her sensibility? Sometimes in fiction, theater, poetry, dreams, or memoirs. Sometimes in psychotherapy. Sometimes in letters or conversations between intimates and close friends. So much depends on a safe place, a wish to tell honestly, and a listener who can bear to hear. And honesty about one's own harmfulness is particularly difficult. In private (as opposed to on the street, where bravado rules) people tend to speak last about ways that they hurt because it creates the greatest vulnerability. However shameful it feels to have been the victim of indecent acts—the stepson (like Rhodes) of a cruel woman, the slave (like Jacobs) of a sadistic man—to have committed the acts that destroyed oneself and others may be harder still to accurately describe. When we speak about harm we have committed, we are certain other people will shudder and recoil. We put them on notice about our potential to hurt them. We approach an unbearable clarity.

What did Susan Smith say during the fifteen hours she spoke with a psychologist? Newspapers reported that she expressed much remorse. *Time* magazine stated that she told about her own sexual abuse by her stepfather and her confused sexual encounters the week before she murdered, including one with her stepfather, one with her ex-husband, one with her lover at the time, and one with this man's father—her employer.[30] One wonders if she spoke honestly, or lied.

How should we understand Smith? The defense lawyer has suggested she is mentally ill. The prosecution portrays her as cunning, calculating, and evil. Certainly she is a desperate woman unable to glimpse any possibility beyond an impinging context. Did she want to spare her children her own fate? Attention focuses on her not just because of the real events of her life, but because she is caught in the treacherous confluence of two merging, competing, and difficult to reconcile ideas: one advocating female submission for the sake of society, another suggesting female liberty. The unstated, unconscious question: Will women not held in check by patriarchy become loveless demons who know no loyalty and kill their young? This same fear underlies the abortion battle. American society unconsciously fears that if women are allowed liberty they will become uncontrolled monsters, Dr. Jekyll and *Mrs.* Hyde.

But what about the men who surround Susan Smith? It seems unrealistic to separate her behavior from theirs. Her father committed suicide and abandoned her when she was a child. Could he have sought help and tried to stay in the world for her sake? Perhaps her stepfather could have loved her without sexually molesting her. Maybe her boyfriend should have thought before courting a woman for whose children he wanted no responsibility. Or her boss might have hesitated before having sex with an employee. It takes a village, or so the adage goes, to raise a child. If Smith is telling the truth, we have to ask what, besides their penises, the men in Union, South Carolina, contributed to her effort?

I am not suggesting that boys are bad and girls good, or that Smith be treated like a "victim" or not held "responsible" for her actions—terms we toss with terrifying ease and little sense. It is fashionable at the moment to attack and silence people with important grievances by suggesting they are crying "victim." How we acknowledge both context and individual action is complex—and insists on a tragic perspective. Smith killed her children. If through some unlikely twist, society saw her only as a pawn and failed to punish her, everyone would suffer. Such a stance would undermine all notions of individual control and restraint—the ability to chose not to act. But it is also likely Smith would create ways to punish herself, if not commit suicide.

So, too, the vehement call for her death is in part a projection of our own unconscious feelings that if we had done as she did, we could not bear to live. The internal aftermath is all but unimaginable. Yet it is only by recognizing this truth that we can encounter the tragic awfulness of her act and feel that in the quest for justice, after everything else is passed, one becomes like the ghost of the child (murdered by its mother to save it from slavery) in Toni Morrison's *Beloved*, "just sad."[31]

Smith's situation is complicated further because she so hatefully lied and exploited people's goodwill, especially at the expense of black men. Like Harriet Beecher Stowe, she invented a dehumanized black man. As James Baldwin points out, Stowe could not imagine how to make a black man sympathetic unless she made him a saint. All that Stowe repressed by forcing Uncle Tom to become a christ-figure, Smith summoned. Smith's fantasy of Uncle Tom inverted is as unreal as Stowe's, but this time armed and acting ugly. She exploited the hateful myth of the murderous, loveless black man to preserve another: the ideal of a sweet, loving motherliness, an acceptable womanhood. And this exactly is the price of sentimentalizing. What is disowned by one person inevitably returns to dehumanize someone else. As Baldwin observed almost fifty years ago, "The ways in which the Negro has affected the American psychology are betrayed in our popular culture and in our morality; in our estrangement from him is the depth of our estrangement from ourselves."[32]

While Susan Smith was quickly found guilty, her trial became more interesting during the sentencing hearing. Witnesses intentionally and unintentionally spoke to years of previously unnamed harm. Smith's ex-husband, eager for her to get the death penalty, claimed he didn't "throw her down or anything."[33] Her stepfather, publicly admitting the sexual abuse, tearfully allowed to Smith, "All you needed from me was the right kind of love. . . . I want you to know that you don't have all the guilt for this tragedy."[34]

A thought-provoking comment came from Smith's aunt, Tomi Vaughan, who, according to a newspaper account, "talked about the humiliation of watching the family's deepest, unthinkable secrets spread out for the world to witness." She said, "We're just an ordinary family who have had everything hung out for the whole world to examine."[35] Hearing such a pronouncement, one is tempted to respond, "Ordinary family!" But somehow, grimly, the remark rings true. There is something very ordinary—at least ordinary looking—about Smith's family.

As long as the lawn is mowed and the anguish inaudible, much goes unchallenged within family life. It is private. But to whom does this privacy belong, and what is its purpose? In the "privacy of the home"—and here again we are talking about privacy soured into secrecy—men and women may harm or tyrannize their families or feel entitled to something approaching absolute control over the people who live with them. Too many people have never known safety. As Susan Smith intuited, the public focuses on violence from strangers, but the more frightening truth, the one that though oft repeated remains very difficult to face, is that in many homes, the threat is internal. When Warren and Brandeis wrote "The Right to Privacy," it was this problem, particularly as it affected people with less power, that they left unconsidered.

Some people argue that the contemporary world is ever more violent toward women. Read history and that notion doesn't hold up terribly well. Instead, I suspect that sanctioned violence against women (death for adultery, castration punishment for insubordination, legal dominion) is lessening in some countries, and the ensuing struggle provokes more chaotic violence. In nineteenth-century America, women had so few rights that it was extraordinarily difficult for them to leave violent, brutal marriages. Beating one's "disobedient" wife was legal. (As it continues to be in much of the world today. Harvard professor Arthur Kleinman has compelling statistical evidence to show that wife beating is a major contemporary public health issue worldwide.[36]) When the society effectively controlled women, individual men did not have to violate the law to maintain control. If, in this circumstance, fewer men killed their wives, it was not a terribly meaningful indicator of female safety.

Now, by comparison, a battered woman is most likely to be murdered by her husband when she leaves a marriage, according to Sarah Buel, an expert on domestic violence. (Even the comparatively staid Supreme Court justices writing the decision in *Casey* quote statistics suggesting that in America "one-fifth to one-third of all women will be physically assaulted by a partner or ex-partner during their lifetime.")[37] Since the society no longer legally prevents women from leaving men nor openly sanctions male control, the large occupying army of male hegemony that, by its very mass, maintained social order through threat of violence (and sanctioned "discipline"), has been driven slightly back. In its place are more messy uprisings and skirmishes. Though some laws and social practices have changed, many men (and women) are more ambivalent. And the man who batters or kills his wife represents one extreme. Somehow, he lacks faith that love freely given is bearable and substitutes a desperate, sadistic, individual control. A man intent on dominance can no longer count on society to control his partner for him or to openly help him.

But such harshness is not just man's domain. Years ago in a Laundromat in Ohio I witnessed an unforgettable scene of female cruelty. It was a hot summer Saturday, my not-yet-husband and I were in the midst of a long hike. Finding ourselves in a town with a Laundromat, we had dumped the dirty clothing from our backpacks into a washing machine, and were waiting. A woman in her twenties arrived lugging several bags of laundry, accompanied by her fiftyish mother and her toddler son, who was maybe one-and-a-half. The three played out a ghastly tableau. It began when the baby, placed on top of the washing machine with nothing to amuse him, grew restless and wiggled. His mother slapped him in the face, telling him he was bad for not sitting still. He might fall. He might get dirty. She had just cleaned him.

Predictably, the child started to cry. His grandmother put her face near his, and yelled at him to stop. He was behaving like a baby or a girl; boys don't cry. She cuffed him. Completely terrorized, the child mustered control that he was not old enough to have, snuffed his sobs, and tried to sit very still. The women did not speak to him or play with him. Instead, they watched, like foxes tracking a mouse. And a few minutes later, with the inevitable physiology of a young child, he started to wiggle. His mother struck him again and the cycle repeated. What were those women doing? What had been done to them? Certainly, they were helping to create a man likely to harbor large amounts of rage.

Control—often sadistic—is the default position of human relationships that lack adequate love, respect, or protection. And while some degree of sadism and efforts to control for its own sake are present in all relationships, they are often held in check by love, identification, and empathy. Whether the sexes turn out to be equal in their tendency to cruelly abuse and overcontrol intimates with less power remains to be seen. But the more immediate point for a discussion of privacy is that behavior in private is often so difficult to determine, much less fairly adjudicate, that it tends to get publicly articulated in favor of those with social power. Historically, this arrangement has favored men—particularly white men. As the common law long recognized, a man's home was to be "his castle."

We are far from knowing whether extreme exploitation can be checked in families and in societies. In many ways, this is a new question, reframed thanks to new information about people's emotional development. One outcome of the psychological revolution since Freud has been dramatically increased awareness of the consequences of specific human behaviors, particularly their implications for the psychological development of children. What has been less articulated is the way in which the private/public barrier is a permeable membrane. It is very difficult for people who are badly treated—shamed and exploited—by the larger world to absorb that treatment without inflicting it upon intimates and *vice versa*. As Theodore Zeldin observes in *An Intimate History of Humanity,* "We are all of us descended from slaves, or almost slaves. All our autobiographies, if they went back far enough, would begin by explaining how our ancestors came to be more or less enslaved, and to what degree we have become free of their inheritance." Furthermore, Zeldin adds, historically, "unquestioning obedience was also imposed on the majority of humanity in most parts of the world, whether officially slave or not."[38]

How much have we emerged from that condition? How much can we emerge? As Harriet Jacobs's story so readily demonstrates, "unquestioning obedience" in the public world and cruelty in the private are closely related. The prerogative to impose such obedience tends to sanction force. Faced with inevitable resistance, this force often becomes excessive and tyrannical. Much of the contemporary debate about privacy includes an effort to push society toward a more sophisticated awareness of the interconnectedness of private and public behavior, and the dilemmas of abuse and undue force.

The idea that the society should work to protect women's privacy, and thus her liberty and safety in private, is very new. Consider Margaret Sanger. In 1916, she opened the *first* birth-control clinic in America.[39] It managed to offer sex education and advice—perhaps an occasional contraceptive—to poor immigrant women for about ten days before it was shut down by the police, and Sanger arrested. As recently as 1917—eighty years ago—Sanger spent a month in jail for simply telling women about their physiology—that they had a vagina, a clitoris, two ovaries, cycles of fertility and infertility—and advising them on ways to avoid pregnancy.

Furthermore, remarkably, not until 1965 did the Supreme Court decide in *Griswold v. Connecticut* that Connecticut's 1879 anticontraception statute was unconstitutional. In this famous court ruling, Justice William O. Douglas suggested the controversial idea that "the First Amendment has a penumbra where privacy is protected from governmental intrusion."[40] What Douglas and other members of the 7–2 majority sought to confirm within the society, and to extend to women, was an idea of privacy as personal liberty—the right to make for oneself decisions concerning one's body and intimate well-being.

While Justice Douglas's assertion of a "penumbra of privacy" has remained controversial among constitutional scholars, his contributions to *Griswold, Roe,* and many other decisions helped give validity to the idea that privacy deserves protection *particularly* as it refers to individual autonomy within an intimate realm, and particularly as it refers to women. Douglas asserted that liberty is not just freedom from unlawful government restraint, but "must include privacy as well, if it is to be a repository of freedom. The right to be let alone is indeed the beginning of all freedom."[41]

The expression "the right to be let alone" was coined by Thomas Cooley in 1879[42] and has since been oft repeated as a battle cry among privacy advocates. Cooley uses "let alone" to define a state in which one is allowed to remain unbothered. People have long thought that Cooley did not refer explicitly to privacy because no "right" to privacy had yet been articulated. But, in fact, it had been. Recall how in her 1872 newspaper discussion of Henry Ward Beecher, Victoria Woodhull twice refers to a "right of privacy" within a single paragraph: "I believe in the law of peace, *in the right of privacy,* in the sanctity of individual relations." What Mr. Beecher and Mrs. Tilton did together, according to Woodhull, was "nobody's business" and "between themselves," a lesson, she declared, that the world needed to be taught. "I am the champion of that very right of privacy and of individual sovereignty."[43]

In 1873, only months after Woodhull published her opinion, *Bradwell v. State* "reaffirmed the common-law principle that 'a woman had no legal existence separate from her husband, who was regarded as her head and representative in the social state.'"[44] What Victoria Woodhull recognized well ahead of her time, and what the Supreme Court would in 1973 proclaim (and in 1992 confirm) as the law of the land, was that real freedom demanded privacy, including the right for an individual to freely make intimate and personal choices *for herself.* The fierceness of the abortion battles has been proportionate to the momentous meaning of the outcome. We witness a beginning.

Conclusion

I have long been awed by how far detail can be elaborated in a particular moment or place, the way very sophisticated knowledge is often local and ephemeral. You might travel to a town where many people work gold exquisitely, carve ivory into concentric spheres, or cut stone to resemble living things, and as a witness, you feel the extremity of their mastery: how completely they have developed a skill. A Maine lobsterman told me that at any moment he remembers exactly where, over miles of ocean, he has set more than nine hundred traps, though he moves some of them each day, and most of them many times a season. Out on the boat, I watch him casually perform a prodigious feat of memory.

So, too, a worldwide audience enthusiastically views the Olympics not just for the suspense of competition, but because in athletic prowess we see people push against physiological limits. Just how fast can a man run without tearing his hamstring muscles? How many midair flips can a young gymnast perform without breaking her back? The edge between exquisite performance and disaster from overreaching rivets us. We want to know the boundaries of our human instrument.

Exploring privacy leads us to ask analogous questions about it, and about the psyche, even if both phenomena are less immediately visible. Throughout this book I have suggested that the amount of privacy and private choice now possible for most people is, historically speaking, new. Close a door and shut everyone out, seek an abortion, marry across race, change religious affiliation, walk unrecognized on a city street, read a book undisturbed, talk for hours with a friend, speak frankly to a therapist, sit alone in your apartment listening to CDs. Most Americans enjoy an unprecedented amount of privacy, for they not only control access to much information about themselves, but they are freed from many impinging forms of surveillance and communal restriction. Yet the question arises whether America's interest in privacy is local and ephemeral or larger and more lasting. And which aspects of privacy push our emotional limits, which ones fit easily with our biology?

For instance, a current ideal of marriage—that it originate in private (i.e., arranged by the participants based on their desire) and that it also be equal, monogamous, loving, and long lasting—may represent a plausible evolution of an institution, or it may push the boundaries of what is humanly possible as far as any Olympic athlete pushes his body. So, too, the ideal of a relatively benign, egalitarian, and rich private life within families might make us wonder how successfully people can learn to suppress tendencies toward excessive domination, submission or exploitation.

The human attributes that privacy sanctions and encourages are on one edge of what instinct allows culture to elaborate. When we use privacy to make temporary space for the individual (or couple) apart from the group, we make possible a place for various exquisite aspects of humanness. Throughout much of history, this margin, like the larger world in which it is imbedded, has been mostly ruled by urgencies of survival and varieties of domination and enslavement. Now, potentially freer than in the past, we are offered opportunity to explore privacy's possibilities. But the efforts are delicate, based in a vulnerability that is easily compromised and exploited. If our communal and biological instincts are an ocean, how far—tide shifting water—can the moon of individual desire pull us? What moves, and what doesn't?

Just as an artist sometimes wonders whether she can add one more detail to an intricate carving, exploring privacy leads us to wonder how far we can expand people's capacity to engage its opportunities—the pleasure, emotional sustenance, and deep gratification of intimacy, sexuality, conversation, intellectual endeavor, the space in which to create art or master craft, to plan one's public life, the chance to construct a life one recognizes as one's own. We may discover that the care and restraint needed to make large amounts of privacy safe and bountiful is as unusual as the lobsterman's memory or the ivory carver's prowess. Or it may be that, like reading, it is an adaption and skill that, given opportunity, most will master.

The deeper question these analogies outline is whether we can protect privacy and realize the possibilities within it without succumbing to a sentimental view of human nature. The answer in turn depends on organizing society to support reasonable safety and freedom both in public and in private. Too often, the two are described as separate and competing realms when, in fact, they are interdependent chambers of the same heart. Abuses of power in one chamber create diseases that spread into the other. Social oppression, poverty, and injustice diminish access to resources; they undermine self-worth and thus the confidence to take advantage of privacy's assets. As our understanding of the psyche becomes more sophisticated, can we better integrate into our public world the knowledge of how people are made and broken?

At the same time, the amount of freedom available within contemporary America makes many people anxious. Read the gossip columns or the serious pundits, and the same debates emerge. People are wondering when privacy becomes corrupted into harmful secrecy; when it spins itself into solipsistic stagnation; when it creates unsupportable chaos or unchecked exploitation; when it allows people to be too alone.

These are good questions. But often, instead of struggling with them, people market commodities that play upon and exploit anxiety while they harm privacy. Tabloid television is one example of these phenomena, but they are everywhere. I open a magazine and find an ad for "Nanny Watch"—covert video surveillance systems, some apparently hidden in stuffed animals—designed to allow parents to spy on baby-sitters and nannies. Do such devices really make private life better? I doubt it. While the ad implies that the video camera increases safety, I would imagine that in most cases it actually decreases it by undermining trust and by letting the employers disown their own harmfulness. How do you build a genuine relationship with another person while you are secretly videotaping him or her? The potential for misuse of the equipment is staggering.

Furthermore, the whole trend toward casual spying is dehumanizing. The nanny's employers can film her wrongly slapping a child, fire her, and never be even slightly tempted to confront the possibility that her nasty humor comes from working fourteen-hour days for bad pay. Meanwhile, the nanny has no secret camera with which to document her point of view. Still, if her employers are famous, she might be able to sell a story about their private mischief. And how insane the results if they did and she did.

What is clear is that the personal surveillance and information gathering now facilitated by computers, videotapes, voice recorders, and other sophisticated technologies, combined with the anxiety of contemporary life and the ingenuity of a commodity culture, make it possible to completely end privacy—and thus the personal life—as we have lately known it, without necessarily advancing real safety or social justice. Unless we are willing to think much more carefully about protecting privacy, its present abundance is going to be lost, remembered as a brief time when a historically remarkable number of people were allowed large freedom.

Ironically, part of protecting privacy is recognizing the ways surveillance usefully contributes to safety. A paradoxical question emerges: How much and what kinds of surveillance *are* necessary to prevent the real abuses of privacy? Self-knowledge, honor systems, and love may contain us only so far. How much do all of us need to be watched communally to hold in check our violence, greed, lying, destructive entitlement, anger, or lust? When Oprah invites abused women to talk on her show, she is—in part—using television to provide a social surveillance that increases awareness about secret abuses of power. Harriet Jacobs knew that no matter how unsafe she was in town, she would be more endangered if her master could isolate her in a cabin away from the witnessing community. Freedom (as opposed to license) may thrive best not when we avoid all surveillance, but when we have a say in who watches us and when and how.

For instance, contemporary daily life can sometimes be made safer by placing a video camera in an isolated parking lot. (But only if laws carefully restrict the uses of that film.) Drugstores that keep computer records of people's prescriptions might protect them from being mismedicated or poisoned by drug interactions. (But not if the drugstore sells that record to a health insurance company that then discontinues coverage.) When the Registry of Auto Vehicles lets the police trace addresses from license plates to locate stolen cars, it provides a helpful service. (But not if computer-competent detectives can access the same data to check license plates and find out who among a company's workers attended a union meeting over the weekend.)

Sometimes, as well, the biography is more valuable than the subject's wish not to be written about, and the magazine article about a candidate's private business deals is valid muckraking. Sometimes telling all about someone is healing rather than harmful. And sometimes we are better off forced to grapple with people from whom we have attempted to sequester ourselves. Yet all these diverse forms of surveillance—social, personal, technological, professional—need to be very carefully monitored so that they respect privacy and support efforts to create a good life, rather than heightening shame and totalitarian kinds of social control and eroding individual worth and dignity.

Unfortunately, the temptation to misuse private data appears to be almost irresistible. Newspapers run frequent stories of confidential databanks—tax returns, HIV status lists, criminal records—illegitimately invaded, and information wrongly and harmfully disseminated. Tabloid media and some biographers and journalists daily do the equivalent to public figures. If we decide to better protect privacy, we will have to examine the sale or exposure of all kinds of personal information more carefully than we have of late; we will have to write laws and reinforce them.

Instead, we witness a mushrooming of spastic and inadequately regulated attempts on the one hand to exploit the profitability of private information, and on the other to heighten repressive social control through work surveillance, DNA checks, proposals for national identity cards, or video traffic monitors.

The bottom line is clear. If we continually, gratuitously, reveal other people's privacies, we harm them and ourselves, we undermine the richness of the personal life, and we fuel a social atmosphere of mutual exploitation. Let me put it another way: Little in life is as precious as the freedom to say and do things with people you love that you would not say or do if someone else were present.[1] And few experiences are as fundamental to liberty and autonomy as maintaining control over when, how, to whom, and where you disclose personal material.

Henry James went to Europe in part to seek such freedoms. One function of psychotherapy is to create them for people who wish to stay closer to home. In a sense, psychotherapy not only elaborates and focuses knowledge about ways to improve both intimacy and psychic privacy, it attempts to untangle important relationships so that they feel less oppressive and to create a self-surveillance that is neither cruel or indulgent.

The individual that psychology describes elaborates a particular dimension of humanness—the idea of a self loved well enough to bear a certain true autonomy. Over the past century or so, we have created a secularized idea that optimal psychic development rests on children being given loving and attentive care so that they can develop both a steady connection to others and a truer independence.

The psychoanalyst D.W. Winnicott has postulated that another paradox of love helps create the capacity to be alone and thus to experience a private self. "Although many types of experience go to the establishment of the capacity to be alone, there is one that is basic. . . . This experience is that of being alone, as an infant and small child, in the presence of the mother."[2] (Elsewhere he uses "mother-substitute.") His point is that when a child can have the experience of being safely alone with a loved adult, proximate but not intruded upon or disturbed, he is freed to relax and attend to his inner world. "In the course of time there arrives a sensation or an impulse. In this setting the sensation or impulse will feel real and be truly a personal experience."[3]

Winnicott is speaking more metaphorically than concretely. He is suggesting that when a child has the experience of being with a loving adult who allows him privacy (i.e., does not overwhelmingly impose upon the child the adult's own emotional urgencies), the child is able to attend to the images and feelings that bubble up within him. They are his private self, one large source of his vitality and originality. When the poet Gerard Manley Hopkins suggests that "there lives the dearest freshness deep down things," he refers directly to nature and God, but indirectly to this same psychic phenomenon whereby experience is continually made fresh by its contact with authentic sources within the self (and others).

I'm not sure, ultimately, that you can separate the value of privacy from the value of a loved person. One experience that Robert Louis Stevenson, Henry James, and Harriet Jacobs share is that they were all apparently cherished early in their lives. And it seems that when children are carefully loved early on, it sets within them a kind of gyroscope of volition and self-worth that resists changing its alignment in situations with less love. Access to privacy becomes one way of brokering the distance between what one has known and what one now encounters. At the same time, privacy becomes a place away from love's own intrusions, a way of being with the other but alone.

When Stevenson went to France, England, America, and Samoa, when James similarly expatriated himself, when Jacobs fled the South and then, once north, stayed up late at night to write, each of them created a space from which he or she could articulate a separate perspective. And while writers are only a small part of our contemporary world, one of their purposes in this story has been to help make visible processes that rightly belong to everyone, whereby the self is allowed to develop and express its own point of view.

Such a perspective is not separate in a simple way—it does not come from isolating oneself—but in a paradoxical way. It comes from how through love we endlessly tie ourselves to others, borrow from them for better and worse, lose them continually in everyday or more permanent circumstances, and then struggle—often using the diverse resources of privacy—to sort through each love's legacy and grapple with our residual allegiances.

And in this sense, of course, this book has been about my father and about love and separateness. It has explored his need for privacy, and helped me understand mine. In the ten years since he died I have recognized that one among many reasons for wishing to fend off his biographers was a wish to protect him from my own desire to write and thus invade his privacy. Wouldn't you know that even as I rightly felt worried about having family privacy violated, I was also hiding from myself as potential violator.

Glimpsing my unconscious, I am reminded—yet again—how complicated and paradoxical are most truths, especially the ones in which we have to live our lives, and how painstaking the process by which we untangle hard questions. Whether we speak about ourselves, about the media, or about laws and court decisions, we must be extraordinarily careful in determining when to protect privacy and how. In our willingness to look closely, and in our *care*, is our best safeguarding of a precious *part* of life.

References

Prologue

1. Janna Malamud Smith, "Where Does a Writer's Family Draw the Line?" *New York Times Book Review,* Nov. 5, 1989, p. 1.
2. "Leniency on Defied Order," *Boston Globe,* Apr. 17, 1996, p. 16.
3. Jane Austen, *Pride and Prejudice,* p. 189.
4. Alain Corbin, "The Secret of the Individual," in Michelle Perrot, ed., and Arthur Goldhammer, trans., *From the Fires of Revolution to the Great War,* p. 460.
5. "Essayist Irving Howe Dies," Segment 5, *All Things Considered,* National Public Radio, May 5, 1993.

1
My Daughter, My Sister

1. "Family Inter-breeding," *The Oprah Winfrey Show,* Feb. 19, 1988, transcript W375, New York: Journal Graphics, p. 2.
2. "I Had My Stepfather's Baby," *Sally Jesse Raphael,* Sept. 16, 1992, transcript 1053, Denver: Journal Graphics, p. 2.
3. "Pregnancy from Incest," *Donahue,* Jan. 6, 1989, transcript 010689, Cincinnati: Multimedia Entertainment, p. 1.
4. "Family Inter-breeding," p. 15.
5. Quoted from *The Oprah Winfrey Show,* Channel 5, Boston, Mar. 18, 1993.
6. "Family Inter-breeding," p. 12.

7. "Pregnancy from Incest," p. 5.

8. Quoted from *48 Hours: Everybody's Talking,* Channel 7, Boston, June 2, 1993.

9. Sigmund Freud, "The Future of an Illusion," p. 36.

10. Gary Miranda, "Magician," in *Grace Period,* p. 12.

2
Privacy and Private States

1. Primo Levi, *If This Is a Man: Remembering Auschwitz,* p. 329.

2. Ibid., p. 15.

3. Ibid., p. 67.

4. Bernard Bailyn, review of *The American Revolution in Indian Country* by Colin B. Calloway, *New York Review of Books,* 42-15, Oct. 5, 1995, p. 16.

5. Stephen Kinzer, "East Germans Face Their Accusers," *New York Times Magazine,* Apr. 12, 1992, p. 24.

6. Nadezhda Mandelstam, *Hope against Hope,* p. 88.

7. Curt Gentry, *J. Edgar Hoover: The Man and the Secrets,* p. 388.

8. Ibid., p. 572.

9. Alan F. Westin, *Privacy and Freedom,* p. 31.

10. John Bowlby, quoted in Barrington Moore, Jr., *Privacy: Studies in Social and Cultural History,* p. 59.

11. Marie Cardinal, *The Words to Say It,* p. 17.

12. John Updike, *Self-consciousness,* p. 43.

13. Henry David Thoreau, *Walden,* pp. 65, 66.

14. Julie Hatfield, "For Cuban, Yoga Was a Lifesaver," *Boston Globe,* Nov. 16, 1992, p. 30.

15. Anthony Storr, *Solitude: A Return to the Self,* p. 140.

16. Ralph Waldo Emerson, "Culture," p. 155.

17. Ralph Waldo Emerson, "Society and Solitude," p. 7.

18. Robert D. Richardson, *Emerson: The Mind on Fire,* p. 21.

19. Susan Brison, "Survival Course," *New York Times Magazine,* Mar. 21, 1993, p. 20.

20. Ernest Hemingway, *A Moveable Feast,* p. 6.

21. Ellen Chesler, *Woman of Valor: Margaret Sanger and the Birth Control Movement in America,* p. 224.

22. Moore, *Privacy,* p. 11.

23. Edith Wharton, *The Age of Innocence,* p. 282.

24. Kazuo Ishiguro, *The Remains of the Day,* p. 104.

25. Leston Havens, Cambridge Hospital Forum, Nov. 13, 1991.

26. Grace Paley and Vera B. Williams, "Midrash on Happiness," in *Long Walks and Intimate Talks,* unpaged.

27. William Shakespeare, *Othello,* Act 2, Scene III, p. 29.

28. Leo Tolstoy, *War and Peace,* p. 1292.

3

Stevenson at the Inn

1. Robert Louis Stevenson, *Travels with a Donkey in the Cevennes,* pp. 70–71, 74–75.

2. Ian Bell, *Dreams of Exile—Robert Louis Stevenson: A Biography,* p. 217.

3. David Daiches, *Robert Louis Stevenson and His World,* p. 24.

4. Sidney Colvin, ed., *The Letters of Robert Louis Stevenson to His Family and Friends,* vol. 1, p. 441.

5. Philippe Aries, *Centuries of Childhood,* p. 398.

6. Bell, *Dreams of Exile,* p. 22.

7. Sissela Bok, *Secrets: On the Ethics of Concealment and Revelation,* pp. 10–11.

8. David Freeman Hawke, *Everyday Life in Early America,* p. 168; and Stephanie Coontz, *The Social Origins of Private Life,* p. 270.

9. David H. Flaherty, *Privacy in Colonial New England,* pp. 43, 76, 175.

10. Antoine Prost and Gerard Vincent, eds., and Arthur Goldhammer, trans. *Riddles of Identity in Modern Times,* p. 106.

11. Laurie Lee, *Cider with Rosie,* p. 98; and Henry Louis Gates, *Colored People,* 1994.

12. Nathaniel Hawthorne, *The Scarlet Letter,* p. 192.

13. Emilie Carles, *Une Soupe aux Herbes Sauvages.*

14. *Historical Statistics of the United States: Colonial Times to 1970,* Part 1 (Washington, D.C.: U.S. Department of Commerce, Bureau of the Census, 1975), p. 11; *Statistical Abstract of the United States* (Washington, D.C.: Bureau of the Census, 1991), p. 27; and *1991 World Almanac* (New York: Press Pub., 1990), pp. 794–96.

15. Anne Cronin, "This Is Your Life, Generally Speaking: A Statistical Portrait of the 'Typical' American," p. 5.

16. David F. Linowes, *Privacy in America: Is Your Private Life in the Public Eye?*, pp. 21, 171; George F. Will, "A Feast for Washington's Parasite Class," *Boston Globe*, Dec. 21, 1992, p. 19; and Jeffrey Rothfeder, *Privacy for Sale*, p. 172.

17. James Rule, et al., *The Politics of Privacy: Planning for Personal Data Systems as Powerful Technologies*, pp. 31, 34, 41.

18. Linowes, *Privacy in America*, p. 81.

19. William Miller, "Charles, Mum Over Tape, Is Said to Bet on Forgiveness," *Boston Globe*, Jan. 16, 1993, p. 2.

4
Reverend Beecher and the Press

1. "The Ice Bridge, Temporary Union of New York and Brooklyn," *New York Herald*, Jan. 24, 1875, p. 5.

2. Quoted in Robert Shaplen, *Free Love and Heavenly Sinners*, p. 163. Shaplen wrote this account of the trial for the *New Yorker*. He remains the best secondary source for the story.

3. Ibid., p. 199.

4. Paul Lancaster, *Gentleman of the Press: The Life and Times of an Early Reporter, Julian Ralph of the Sun*, p. 4.

5. Shaplen, *Free Love and Heavenly Sinners*, p. 203.

6. "Tilton vs. Beecher," *New York Herald*, Jan. 12, 1875, p. 8.

7. Ibid.

8. Altina L. Waller, *Reverend Beecher and Mrs. Tilton: Sex and Class in Victorian America*, p. 31.

9. Ibid.

10. Edna Dean Proctor, *Life Thoughts, Gathered from the Extemporaneous Discourse of Henry Ward Beecher, By One of His Congregation*, p. 134.

11. "Bessie Turner a Witness. Mr. Tilton's Remarkable 'Moods' at Home," *New York Daily Tribune*, Mar. 20, 1875, p. 3.

12. Waller, *Reverend Beecher and Mrs. Tilton*, p. 57.

13. *Woodhull and Claflin's Weekly*, Nov. 2, 1872, p. 11.

14. Ibid.

15. Ibid., p. 12.

16. Lois Beachy Underhill, *The Woman Who Ran for President: The Many Lives of Victoria Woodhull*, p. 199.

17. Theodore Zeldin, *An Intimate History of Humanity*, p. 37.

18. Joan Von Mehren, *Minerva and the Muse: A Life of Margaret Fuller,* p. 111.

19. Ralph Waldo Emerson, *Journals of Ralph Waldo Emerson* (1820–1870), vol. 8 (1849–1855), p. 117.

20. Thomas C. Leonard, *The Power of the Press: The Birth of American Political Reporting,* p. 53.

21. Lois Ames, personal communication.

22. Francis P. Williamson, *Beecher and His Accusers,* pp. 91–92.

23. "The Tilton-Beecher Trial," *New York Daily Tribune,* Mar. 26, 1875, p. 3.

24. Lancaster, *Gentleman of the Press,* p. 13.

25. David H. Flaherty, *Privacy in Colonial New England,* p. 106.

26. George Juergens, *Joseph Pulitzer and the New York World,* pp. 109–10.

27. Samuel D. Warren and Louis D. Brandeis, "The Right to Privacy," p. 195.

28. Edward J. Bloustein, "Privacy as an Aspect of Human Dignity: An Answer to Dean Prosser," p. 971.

29. Warren and Brandeis, "The Right to Privacy," p. 196.

30. Bloustein, "Privacy as an Aspect of Human Dignity," p. 984.

31. Quoted in David J. Seipp, *The Right to Privacy in American History,* p. 99.

5

Dr. Jekyll and Mr. Freud

1. Quoted in George Juergens, *Joseph Pulitzer and the New York World,* p. 72.

2. Richard Aldington, *Portrait of a Rebel: The Life and Work of Robert Louis Stevenson,* p. 165.

3. Robert Louis Stevenson, *The Strange Case of Dr. Jekyll and Mr. Hyde,* p. 105.

4. Quoted in Ian Bell, *Dreams of Exile—Robert Louis Stevenson: A Biography,* p. 174.

5. Stevenson, *Jekyll and Hyde,* p. 16.

6. Sigmund Freud, "A Case of Hysteria," pp. 7–8.

7. Josef Breuer, "Fraulein Anna O.," p. 34.

8. Stephen Greenblatt, *Marvelous Possessions: The Wonder of the New World,* p. 104.

9. David Daiches, *Robert Louis Stevenson and His World,* p. 26.

10. Stevenson, *Jekyll and Hyde,* p. 35.

11. Lucy Freeman, "The Immortal Anna O.," p. 30; H. F. Ellenberger, "The Story of 'Anna O': A Critical Review with New Data," pp. 267–79; and Peter Gay, *Freud: A Life for Our Time,* pp. 63–69.

12. Robert Kegan, *In Over Our Heads: The Mental Demands of Modern Life,* p. 236.
13. Philip Rieff, *The Triumph of the Therapeutic,* p. 55.
14. Ibid. Also, Harold Bloom, "Freud: A Shakespearean Reading," pp. 345–66.
15. Arthur Conan Doyle, *Famous Tales of Sherlock Holmes,* pp. 5, 14.
16. Sigmund Freud, "Fragment of an Analysis of a Case of Hysteria," pp. 8–9.
17. Ann Douglas, *Terrible Honesty: Mongrel Manhattan in the 1920s,* p. 127.
18. Jonathan Lear, "The Shrink Is In," *New Republic,* Dec. 25, 1995, pp. 18–25.
19. Sidney Colvin, ed., *The Letters of Robert Louis Stevenson to His Family and Friends,* vol. 2, p. 23.

6
Shame, Sex, and Privacy

1. Richard Rhodes, *Making Love: An Erotic Odyssey.*
2. Erik Erikson, *Childhood and Society,* p, 253.
3. Rhodes, *Making Love,* p. 101.
4. Martin Amis, review of *Making Love: An Erotic Odyssey,* by Richard Rhodes, *New York Times Book Review,* Aug. 30, 1992, p. 1.
5. Ibid., p. 21.
6. Rhodes, *Making Love,* p. 13.
7. Amis review, p. 1.
8. Charles Darwin, quoted in Carl D. Schneider, *Shame, Exposure and Privacy,* p. 3.
9. Ibid., p. 4.
10. Helen Block Lewis, "Shame and the Narcissistic Personality," in Donald L. Nathanson, ed., *The Many Faces of Shame,* p. 95.
11. Helen Block Lewis, quoted in Donald L. Nathanson, "A Timetable for Shame," in Nathanson, ed., *The Many Faces of Shame,* p. 9.
12. Leon Wurmser, *The Mask of Shame,* p. 69.
13. Philip Shenon, "U.S. Teen-ager Resigned to Singapore Caning," *New York Times,* Apr. 20, 1994, p. 45.
14. Schneider, *Shame, Exposure and Privacy,* p. 35.
15. Leon Wurmser, "Shame: The Veiled Companion of Narcissism," in Nathanson, ed., *The Many Faces of Shame,* p. 76.
16. Havelock Ellis, "The Evolution of Modesty," p. 44.

17. Helen Merrell Lynd, *On Shame and the Search for Identity*, p. 42.

18. Wurmser, *The Mask of Shame*, pp. 27–28.

19. Lynd, *On Shame and the Search for Identity*, p. 38. He says to Goneril, "I am asham'd that thou hast power to shake my manhood thus, that these hot tears, which break from me perforce, should make thee worth them" (Act 1, Scene IV, p. 301).

20. Barrington Moore, Jr., *Privacy: Studies in Social and Cultural History*, p. 59—but he mentions John Bowlby's *Attachment* as one source.

21. D.H. Lawrence, *Studies in Classic American Literature*, pp. 93–94. (With thanks to Myron Sharaf.)

22. Leston Havens, *Learning to Be Human*, pp. 60–61.

23. Helen Block Lewis, *Sex and the Superego: Psychic War in Men and Women*, p. 195.

24. *Webster's Seventh New Collegiate Dictionary*, 1967.

25. Lewis, *Sex and the Superego*, pp. 195–96.

26. Richard Rhodes, *A Hole in the World*, p. 105.

27. Rhodes, *Making Love*, p. 14.

28. Ibid., pp. 15–16.

29. Ibid., p. 102.

30. Ibid., p. 105.

7

Burnt Letters, Biography, and Privacy

1. Henry James, "The Aspern Papers," p. 142.

2. Ibid., p. 48.

3. Ibid., p. 125.

4. Ibid., p. 138.

5. Ian Hamilton, *Keepers of the Flame*: Dickens, p. 156; Eliot, p. 145; Auden, p. 292.

6. Leon Edel, ed., *Henry James Letters*, Vol. 4, p. 541.

7. Quoted in Leon Edel, *Henry James—The Master: 1901–1916*, p. 142.

8. The stories include "The Reverberator," "The Real Right Thing," "The Abasement of the Northmores," "The Birthplace," "The Private Life," "Sir Dominick Ferrand," "John Delaney," and "The Aspern Papers."

9. Edel, ed., *Henry James Letters*, Vol. 4, pp. 212–13.

10. Leon Edel, ed., *The Selected Letters of Henry James*, p. xiv.

11. Plutarke of Chaeronea, "Romulus," pp. 31–72.

12. Hamilton, *Keepers of the Flame,* p. 50 (quoting Richard Savage in Maynard Mack, *Alexander Pope: A Life* [New Haven, Conn.: Yale University Press, 1985], p. 457).

13. Ibid.

14. Janet Malcolm, *The Journalist and the Murderer,* p. 110.

15. Edel, ed., *The Selected Letters of Henry James,* p. 14.

16. Sigmund Freud, "Beyond the Pleasure Principle," p. 14.

17. Edel, ed., *The Selected Letters of Henry James,* p. xv.

18. Leon Edel, *Henry James—The Middle Years: 1882–1895,* p. 226.

19. Sigmund Freud, "Writers and Daydreaming," p. 145.

20. Ibid., p. 150.

21. Sigmund Freud, "Psychopathic Characters on the Stage," pp. 305–6.

22. Leon Edel, *Henry James—The Untried Years: 1843—1870,* pp. 176–77.

23. Janet Malcolm, *The Silent Woman,* p. 9.

24. Alessandra Stanley, "Poet Told All; Therapist Provides the Record," *New York Times,* July 15, 1991, p. 1.

25. Edel, *Henry James—The Middle Years,* p. 237.

8

Clinton's Nap and Presidential Privacy

1. Ronald Kessler, *Inside the White House,* pp. 233–234.

2. James Thomas Flexner, *Washington: The Indispensable Man,* p. 258.

3. John R. Alden, *George Washington: A Biography,* p. 41.

4. Flexner, *Washington,* p. 54.

5. Ibid., p. 367.

6. Ibid., p. 368.

7. Barry Schwartz, *George Washington: The Making of an American Symbol,* p. 61.

8. Flexner, *Washington,* p. 174.

9. Schwartz, *George Washington,* p. 186.

10. Ibid., p. 59.

11. Flexner, *Washington,* p. 337.

12. Ibid., p. 339.

13. James E. Pollard, *The Presidents and the Press,* p. 15.

14. Ibid., pp. 13–14.

15. Ibid., p. 30.

16. Ibid., p. 6.

17. Alexis de Tocqueville, *Democracy in America*, Vol. 1, p. 56.

18. Virginius Dabney, *The Jefferson Scandals: A Rebuttal*, p. 8.

19. Ibid., p. 11.

20. Ibid., p. 18.

21. Pollard, *The Presidents and the Press*, p. 152 (letter dated Aug. 16, 1828).

22. Ibid., p. 136.

23. John Niven, *Martin Van Buren: The Romantic Age of American Politics*, p. 375.

24. "Miscellaneous," *U.S. Telegraph*, July 11, 1834, p. 1.

25. "On Saturday, Col. Richard M. Johnson," *The Herald*, July 11, 1836, p. 2.

26. Benjamin Thomas, *Abraham Lincoln: A Biography*, p. 106.

27. F.R. Carpenter, *Six Months at the White House with Lincoln*, p. 43.

28. Thomas, *Abraham Lincoln*, p. 480.

29. Roy P. Basler, ed., *Abraham Lincoln: Speeches and Writings, 1859–1865* (New York: Library of America, 1989), pp. 160–67.

30. Thomas, *Abraham Lincoln*, p. 241. See also Henry Clay Whitney, *Life on the Circuit with Lincoln* (Caldwell, Idaho: Caxton Printers, 1940).

31. "Movements of Mrs. Lincoln," *New York Herald*, Aug. 22, 1861, p. 2.

32. Pollard, *The Presidents and the Press*, p. 340.

33. Ibid., p. 349. Pollard is here quoting an earlier edition of Carpenter.

34. Allan Nevins, *Grover Cleveland: A Study in Courage*, p. 162.

35. Ibid., pp. 163–65.

36. Ibid., p. 149.

37. Ibid., p. 52.

38. Paul Lancaster, *Gentleman of the Press: The Life and Times of an Early Reporter, Julian Ralph of the Sun*, p. 120.

39. "Eve of the Nuptials," *New York Herald*, June 2, 1886, p. 3.

40. "The Honeymoon," *New York Herald*, June 4, 1886, p. 2.

41. Nevins, *Grover Cleveland*, pp. 530–33.

42. For one view, see Adam Gopnik, "Read All about It," *New Yorker*, Dec. 12, 1994, p. 84.

43. Pollard, *The Presidents and the Press*, p. 589.

44. Francis Russell, *The Shadow of Blooming Grove: Warren G. Harding in His Time*, p. 402.

45. Ibid., p. 397.

46. Pollard, *The Presidents and the Press*, p. 749.

47. Leslie H. Gelb, "The Ultimate Inside," (review of *Joe Alsop's Cold War* by Edwin M. Yoder, Jr., *New York Times Book Review,* Apr. 2, 1995, p. 9.

48. Carpenter, *Six Months with Lincoln,* p. 81.

49. Jeff McLaughlin and Adam Pertman, "Bill and Chelsea Hit the Trail," *Boston Globe,* Aug. 26, 1993, p. 61.

50. Elizabeth Kolbert, "Frank Talk by Clinton to MTV Generation," *New York Times,* Apr. 20, 1994, p. A14.

51. "Transcript of Speech by Clinton Accepting Democratic Nomination," *New York Times,* July 17, 1992, p. A14.

52. "Excerpts from Speech by Gore at Convention," *New York Times,* July 17, 1992, p. A14.

53. Hannah Arendt, "The Public and the Private Realm," in *The Human Condition,* p. 52.

54. "The Present State of Society," *Public Ledger,* Apr. 28, 1836, p. 1.

55. Quoted in Nicole Castan, "The Public and the Private," in Roger Chartier, ed., and Arthur Goldhammer, trans., *Passions of the Renaissance,* p. 440.

56. Marshall Frady, "Profiles: Jesse Jackson—Part 1," *New Yorker,* Feb. 3, 1992, p. 60.

9
Harriet Jacobs's Room: Women and Privacy

1. Sophia Ripley, "Woman," *The Dial,* 3 (Jan. 1841): p. 363. (Article signed only with initials *W.N.*; author identified by Joan Von Mehren in *Minerva and the Muse,* p. 134.)

2. Quoted in David J. Garrow, *Liberty and Sexuality: The Right of Privacy and the Making of Roe v. Wade,* p. 525.

3. Planned Parenthood of Southeastern Pennsylvania et al. v. Casey, Governor of Pennsylvania, p. 852.

4. Mary Kelley, *Private Woman, Public Stage,* pp. 60–61.

5. Ibid., p. 61.

6. Ibid., p. 54.

7. Ibid., p. 59.

8. Harriet A. Jacobs, *Incidents in the Life of a Slave Girl Written by Herself,* p. 242.

9. Ibid., p. 5.

10. Ibid.

11. Ibid., p. 40.

12. Ibid., p. 76.

13. See Judith Lewis Herman, *Trauma and Recovery.*

14. Jacobs, *Life of a Slave Girl,* p. 148.

15. Ibid., p. 54. Jean Fagan Yellin examines this text in her introduction, which is where it first caught my attention.

16. Harriet Beecher Stowe, *Uncle Tom's Cabin,* "Introduction" by Langston Hughes.

17. Ibid.

18. Jacobs, *Life of a Slave Girl,* p. xxiv.

19. Joan D. Hedrick, *Harriet Beecher Stowe: A Life,* p. 192.

20. Ibid., p. 195.

21. Ibid., p. 139.

22. Dominique Barthelemy and Philippe Contamine, "The Use of Private Space," in Georges Duby, ed., *Revelations of the Medieval World,* p. 488.

23. Ann Douglas, *The Feminization of American Culture,* pp. 11–12.

24. Stowe, *Uncle Tom's Cabin,* p. 10.

25. Ibid., p. 33.

26. James Baldwin, *Notes of a Native Son,* p. 14.

27. Sarah Buel, "What Clinicians Need to Know about Family Violence." Talk given at the Harvard Medical School, Cambridge Hospital, May 5–6, 1995, at the conference, Women: Contemporary Treatment Issues. Buel is quoting the work of lawyer Michael Dowd, head of the Battered Women's Justice Center, Pace University Law Center, White Plains, New York.

28. *Boston Globe,* Aug. 2, 1995, p. 7.

29. Ripley, "Woman," p. 362.

30. Steve Wulf, "Elegy for Lost Boys," *Time,* July 31, 1995, p. 36.

31. Toni Morrison, *Beloved,* p. 8.

32. Baldwin, *Notes of a Native Son,* p. 24.

33. Christopher Sullivan, "Smith's Ex-husband Testifies," *Boston Globe,* July 26, 1995, p. 3.

34. Brian McGrory, "Plea to Spare Smith Made," *Boston Globe,* July 28, 1995, p. 3.

35. Ibid.

36. Arthur Kleinman, "World Mental and Social Health: An Overview," Grand Rounds lecture, Cambridge Hospital Department of Psychiatry, Feb. 21, 1996.

37. Planned Parenthood v. Casey, p. 891.

38. Theodore Zeldin, *An Intimate History of Humanity*, p. 7.
39. Ellen Chesler, *Woman of Valor: Margaret Sanger and the Birth Control Movement in America*, p. 150.
40. Quoted in Garrow, *Liberty and Sexuality*, p. 253. See also Alan F. Weston, *Privacy and Freedom*, p. 355.
41. Garrow, *Liberty and Sexuality*, p. 262.
42. Thomas McIntyre Cooley, *A Treatise on the Law of Torts* (Chicago: Callahan, 1879), p. 29. Microfiche.
43. *Woodhull and Claflin's Weekly*, Nov. 2, 1872, p. 12.
44. Planned Parenthood v. Casey, p. 896–97.

Conclusion

1. Alan Aycborn, *Henceforward*, p. 50, inspired this phrasing.
2. D.W. Winnicott, "The Capacity to Be Alone," p. 30.
3. Ibid., p. 34.

Bibliography

Books

Alden, John R. *George Washington: A Biography.* Baton Rouge: Louisiana State University Press, 1984.

Alderman, Ellen, and Caroline Kennedy. *The Right to Privacy.* New York: Alfred A. Knopf, 1995.

Aldington, Richard. *Portrait of a Rebel: The Life and Work of Robert Louis Stevenson.* London: Evans Brothers, 1957.

Allison, Dorothy. *Bastard out of Carolina.* New York: Plume, 1993.

American Press Institute. *The Public, Privacy and the Press: Have the Media Gone Too Far?* J. Montgomery Curtis Memorial Seminar, Sept. 1992. Reston, Va.: American Press Institute, 1992.

Anonymous. *Primary Colors.* New York: Random House, 1996.

Aries, Philippe. *Centuries of Childhood: A Social History of Family Life.* New York: Vintage Books, 1962.

Austen, Jane. *Pride and Prejudice.* New York: Dodd, Mead, 1945.

Aycborn, Alan. *Henceforward.* Boston: Faber and Faber, 1989.

Baker, Nicholas. *Vox.* New York: Vintage Books, 1992.

Baldwin, James. *Notes of a Native Son.* Boston: Beacon Press, 1984.

Basler, Roy P., ed. *Abraham Lincoln: Speeches and Writings, 1859–1865.* New York: Library of America, 1989.

Bateson, Mary Catherine. *Composing a Life.* New York: Plume, 1990.

Beecher, Henry Ward. *Sermons.* Vol. 1. New York: Harper and Brothers, 1869.

Bell, Ian. *Dreams of Exile—Robert Louis Stevenson: A Biography.* New York: Henry Holt, 1992.

Bellah, Robert N., Richard Madsen, William M. Sullivan, Ann Swidler, and Steven M. Tipton. *Habits of the Heart: Individualism and Commitment in American Life*. New York: Perennial Library, 1986.

Blanchard, Paula. *Sarah Orne Jewett*. Reading, Mass.: Addison-Wesley, 1994.

Bok, Sissela. *Secrets: On the Ethics of Concealment and Revelation*. New York: Pantheon Books, 1982.

Boorstin, Daniel J. *The Image: A Guide to Pseudo-events in America*. New York: Vintage Books, 1992.

Brill, Alita. *Nobody's Business: The Paradoxes of Privacy*. Reading, Mass.: Addison-Wesley, 1990.

Brooks, Paul. *The People of Concord*. Chester, Conn.: Globe Pequot Press, 1990.

Capper, Charles. *Margaret Fuller: An American Romantic Life*. New York: Oxford University Press, 1992.

Cardinal, Marie. *The Words to Say It*. Cambridge, Mass.: VanVactor and Goodheart, 1983.

Carles, Emilie. *Une Soupe aux Herbes Sauvages*. Paris: Jean-Claude Simoen, 1977.

Carpenter, F.R. *Six Months at the White House with Lincoln*. Edited by John Crosby Freman. Watkins Glen, N.Y.: Century House, 1961.

Carroll, Jim. *The Basketball Diaries*. New York: Penguin Books, 1987.

Chartier, Roger, ed. *Passions of the Renaissance*. Translated by Arthur Goldhammer. Vol. 3 of *A History of Private Life*. Edited by Philippe Aries and Georges Duby. Cambridge, Mass.: Belknap Press, 1989.

Chesler, Ellen. *Woman of Valor: Margaret Sanger and the Birth Control Movement in America*. New York: Simon and Schuster, 1992.

Coles, Robert. *The Call of Stories*. Boston: Houghton Mifflin, 1989.

Colvin, Sidney, ed. *The Letters of Robert Louis Stevenson to His Family and Friends*. Vols. 1 and 2. New York: Charles Scribner's Sons, 1899.

Coontz, Stephanie. *The Social Origins of Private Life*. New York: Verso, 1988.

Crouthamel, James L. *Bennett's New York Herald and the Rise of the Popular Press*. Syracuse, N.Y.: Syracuse University Press, 1989.

Cuddihy, John Murray. *The Ordeal of Civility: Freud, Marx, Levi-Strauss, and the Jewish Struggle with Modernity*. New York: Basic Books, 1974.

Dabney, Virginius. *The Jefferson Scandals: A Rebuttal*. New York: Dodd, Mead, 1981.

Daiches, David. *Robert Louis Stevenson and His World*. London: Thames and Hudson, 1973.

Dew, Robb Foreman. *The Family Heart*. Reading, Mass.: Addison-Wesley, 1994.

Douglas, Ann. *The Feminization of American Culture.* New York: Avon Books, 1978.

Douglas, Ann. *Terrible Honesty: Mongrel Manhattan in the 1920s.* New York: Farrar, Straus and Giroux, 1995.

Doyle, Arthur Conan. *Famous Tales of Sherlock Holmes.* New York: Dodd, Mead, 1958.

Duby, Georges, ed. *Revelations of the Medieval World.* Translated by Arthur Goldhammer. Vol. 2 of *A History of Private Life.* Edited by Philippe Aries and Georges Duby. Cambridge, Mass.: Belknap Press, 1988.

Edel, Leon. *Henry James—The Untried Years: 1843–1870.* New York: Avon Books, 1978.

Edel, Leon. *Henry James—The Conquest of London: 1870–1881.* New York: Avon Books, 1978.

Edel, Leon. *Henry James—The Middle Years: 1882–1895.* New York: Avon Books, 1978.

Edel, Leon. *Henry James—The Treacherous Years: 1895–1901.* New York: Avon Books, 1978.

Edel, Leon. *Henry James—The Master: 1901–1916.* New York: Avon Books, 1978.

Edel, Leon, ed. *Henry James Letters.* Vol. 4. Cambridge, Mass.: Belknap Press, 1984.

Edel, Leon, ed. *The Selected Letters of Henry James.* New York: Farrar, Straus and Cudahy, 1955.

Edelman, Hope. *Motherless Daughters: The Legacy of Loss.* Reading, Mass.: Addison-Wesley, 1994.

Ellenberger, Henri. *The Discovery of the Unconscious: The History and Evolution of Dynamic Psychiatry.* New York: Basic Books, 1970.

Emerson, Ralph Waldo. *Journals of Ralph Waldo Emerson, 1820–1870.* Edited by Edward Waldo Emerson and Waldo Emerson Forbes. Vol. 8 (1849–1855). Cambridge, Mass.: Riverside Press, 1912.

Erikson, Erik. *Childhood and Society.* New York: W.W. Norton, 1963.

Ernaux, Annie. *La place.* Paris: Gallimard, 1983.

Ernst, Morris L., and Alan V. Schwartz. *Privacy: The Right to Be Let Alone.* Milestones of Law series. New York: Macmillan, 1962.

Ettinger, Elzbieta. *Hannah Arendt: Martin Heidegger.* New Haven, Conn.: Yale University Press, 1995.

Ettinger, Elzbieta. *Kindergarten.* Boston: G.K. Hall, 1986.

Ettinger, Elzbieta. *Quicksand.* London: Pandora, 1989.

Etzioni, Amitai. *The Spirit of Community.* New York: Crown, 1993.

Faludi, Susan. *Backlash: The Undeclared War against American Women.* New York: Crown, 1991.

Fisher, M.F.K. *Long Ago in France: The Years in Dijon.* New York: Prentice-Hall, 1991.

Fitzgerald, F. Scott. *The Great Gatsby.* New York: Charles Scribner's Sons, 1953.

Flaherty, David H. *Privacy in Colonial New England.* Charlottesville: University Press of Virginia, 1972.

Flexner, James Thomas. *Washington: The Indispensable Man.* Boston: Little, Brown, 1974.

Gabler, Neal. *Winchell: Gossip, Power and the Culture of Celebrity.* New York: Alfred A. Knopf, 1994.

Garrow, David J. *Liberty and Sexuality: The Right of Privacy and the Making of Roe v. Wade.* New York: Macmillan, 1994.

Gates, Henry Louis. *Colored People.* New York: Alfred A. Knopf, 1994.

Gay, Peter. *Freud: A Life for Our Time.* New York: W.W. Norton, 1988.

Gentry, Curt. *J. Edgar Hoover: The Man and the Secrets.* New York: Plume, 1992.

Gilfoyle, Timothy J. *City of Eros: New York City, Prostitution, and the Commercialization of Sex, 1790–1920.* New York: W.W. Norton, 1992.

Goodwin, Doris Kearns. *The Fitzgeralds and the Kennedys: An American Saga.* New York: Simon and Schuster, 1987.

Goodwin, Doris Kearns. *No Ordinary Time.* New York: Simon and Schuster, 1994.

Greenblatt, Stephen. *Marvelous Possessions: The Wonder of the New World.* Chicago: University of Chicago Press, 1991.

Grumbach, Doris. *Fifty Days of Solitude.* Boston: Beacon Press, 1994.

Hale, Nathan G., Jr. *Freud and the Americans: The Beginnings of Psychoanalysis in the United States, 1876–1917.* New York: Oxford University Press, 1971.

Halpern, Sue. *Migrations to Solitude.* New York: Pantheon Books, 1992.

Hamilton, Ian. *Keepers of the Flame.* Boston: Faber and Faber, 1992.

Havens, Leston. *Coming to Life.* Cambridge, Mass.: Harvard University Press, 1993.

Havens, Leston. *Learning to Be Human.* Reading, Mass.: Addison-Wesley, 1994.

Hawke, David Freeman. *Everyday Life in Early America.* Everyday Life in America series. Edited by Richard Balkin. New York: Perennial Library, 1988.

Hawthorne, Nathaniel. *The Scarlet Letter* [1850]. New York: New American Library, 1980.

Hedrick, Joan D. *Harriet Beecher Stowe: A Life.* New York: Oxford University Press, 1994.

Hemingway, Ernest. *A Moveable Feast* [1964]. New York: Bantam Books, 1967.

Herman, Judith Lewis. *Trauma and Recovery.* New York: Basic Books, 1992.

Hixson, Richard F. *Privacy in a Public Society: Human Rights in Conflict.* New York: Oxford University Press, 1987.

Hochschild, Adam. *The Unquiet Ghost: Russians Remember Stalin.* New York: Viking Press, 1994.

Hoffman, Eva. *Lost in Translation: A Life in a New Language.* New York: Penguin Books, 1990.

Holmes, Richard. *Footsteps: Adventures of a Romantic Biographer.* New York: Penguin Books, 1986.

Holmes, Richard. *Dr. Johnson and Mr. Savage.* New York: Pantheon Books, 1993.

hooks, bell. *Talking Back: Thinking Feminist, Thinking Black.* Boston: South End Press, 1989.

Inness, Julie C. *Privacy, Intimacy, and Isolation.* New York: Oxford University Press, 1992.

Ishiguro, Kazuo. *The Remains of the Day.* New York: Vintage Books, 1990.

Jacobs, Harriet A. *Incidents in the Life of a Slave Girl Written by Herself.* Edited by Jean Fagan Yellin. Cambridge, Mass.: Harvard University Press, 1987.

Jacoby, Russell. *The Repression of Psychoanalysis: Otto Fenichel and the Political Freudians.* New York: Basic Books, 1984.

James, William. *Varieties of Religious Experience.* New York: Collier Books, 1961.

Jong, Erica. *The Devil at Large.* New York: Grove Press, 1993.

Jong, Erica. *Fear of Flying.* New York: Signet, 1974.

Juergens, George. *Joseph Pulitzer and the New York World.* Princeton, N.J.: Princeton University Press, 1966.

Kaminer, Wendy. *I'm Dysfunctional, You're Dysfunctional: The Recovery Movement and Other Self-help Fashions.* Reading, Mass.: Addison-Wesley, 1992.

Kaplan, Alice. *French Lessons: A Memoir.* Chicago: University of Chicago Press, 1993.

Karr, Mary. *The Liars' Club.* New York: Penguin Books, 1995.

Kegan, Robert. *In Over Our Heads: The Mental Demands of Modern Life.* Cambridge, Mass.: Harvard University Press, 1994.

Kelley, Mary. *Private Woman, Public Stage.* New York: Oxford University Press, 1984.

Kessler, Ronald. *Inside the White House.* New York: Pocket Books, 1995.

Lancaster, Paul. *Gentleman of the Press: The Life and Times of an Early Reporter, Julian Ralph of the Sun.* Syracuse, N.Y.: Syracuse University Press, 1992.

Lasch, Christopher. *The Culture of Narcissism.* New York: W.W. Norton, 1979.

Lasch, Christopher. *Haven in a Heartless World.* New York: Basic Books, 1977.

Lasch, Christopher. *The Minimal Self: Psychic Survival in Troubled Times.* New York: W.W. Norton, 1984.

Lawrence, D.H. *Lady Chatterley's Lover.* New York: Modern Library, 1959.

Lawrence, D.H. *Studies in Classic American Literature.* New York: Viking Press, 1968.

Lear, Jonathan. *Love and Its Place in Nature.* New York: Farrar, Straus and Giroux, 1990.

Lee, Laurie. *Cider with Rosie.* New York: Penguin Books, 1962.

Leonard, Thomas, C. *The Power of the Press: The Birth of American Political Reporting.* New York: Oxford University Press, 1986.

Levi, Primo. *If This Is a Man: Remembering Auschwitz.* New York: Summit Books, 1985.

Levi, Primo. *The Periodic Table.* New York: Schocken Books, 1984.

Lewis, Helen Block. *Sex and the Superego: Psychic War in Men and Women.* Rev. ed. Hillsdale, N.J.: Lawrence Erlbaum, 1987.

Lewis, R.W.B. *The James: A Family Narrative.* New York: Farrar, Straus and Giroux, 1991.

Linowes, David F. *Privacy in America: Is Your Private Life in the Public Eye?* Chicago: University of Illinois Press, 1989.

Lodge, David. *Changing Places.* New York: Penguin Books, 1978.

Lynd, Helen Merrell. *On Shame and the Search for Identity.* New York: Harvest Books, 1958.

Mairs, Nancy. *Ordinary Time.* Boston: Beacon Press, 1993.

Malcolm, Janet. *In the Freud Archives.* New York: Alfred A. Knopf, 1984.

Malcolm, Janet. *The Journalist and the Murderer.* New York: Alfred A. Knopf, 1990.

Malcolm, Janet. *The Silent Woman.* New York: Alfred A. Knopf, 1994.

Mandelstam, Nadezhda. *Hope against Hope.* Translated from the Russian by Max Hayward. New York: Atheneum, 1970.

Mellen, Joan. *Hellman and Hammett.* New York: HarperCollins, 1996.

Miranda, Gary. *Grace Period.* Princeton, N.J.: Princeton University Press, 1983.

Modell, Arnold M. *The Private Self.* Cambridge, Mass.: Harvard University Press, 1993.

Monette, Paul. *Becoming a Man: Half a Life Story.* New York: Harcourt Brace Jovanovich, 1992.

Moore, Barrington, Jr. *Privacy: Studies in Social and Cultural History.* Armonk, N.Y.: M.E. Sharpe, 1984.

Moore, Susanna. *In the Cut.* New York: Alfred A. Knopf, 1995.

Morrison, Toni. *Beloved.* New York: Alfred A. Knopf, 1987.

Naipaul, V.S. *The Enigma of Arrival.* New York: Vintage Books, 1987.

Nathanson, Donald L., ed. *The Many Faces of Shame.* New York: Guilford Press, 1987.

Nevins, Allan. *Grover Cleveland: A Study in Courage.* New York: Dodd, Mead, 1934.

Niven, John. *Martin Van Buren: The Romantic Age of American Politics.* New York: Oxford University Press, 1983.

Noble, Jane, and William Noble. *The Private Me.* New York: Delacorte Press, 1980.

Paley, Grace, and Vera B. Williams. *Long Walks and Intimate Talks.* Women and Peace series. New York: Feminist Press, 1991.

Penn Warren, Robert. *All the King's Men.* New York: Bantam, 1951.

Perrot, Michelle, ed. *From the Fires of Revolution to the Great War.* Translated by Arthur Goldhammer. Vol. 4 of *A History of Private Life.* Edited by Philippe Aries and Georges Duby. Cambridge, Mass.: Belknap Press, 1990.

Pinsky, Robert. *Sadness and Happiness.* Princeton, N.J.: Princeton University Press, 1975.

Pitt-Kethley, Fiona. *The Literary Companion to Sex.* New York: Random House, 1992.

Polacheck, Hilda Satt. *I Came a Stranger: The Story of a Hull House Girl.* Edited by Dena J. Polacheck Epstein. Urbana: University of Illinois Press, 1991.

Pollard, James E. *The Presidents and the Press.* New York: Macmillan, 1947.

Proctor, Edna Dean. *Life Thoughts, Gathered from the Extemporaneous Discourses of Henry Ward Beecher, By One of His Congregation.* Boston: Phillips, Sampson, 1858.

Prost, Antoine, and Gerard Vincent, eds. *Riddles of Identity in Modern Times.* Translated by Arthur Goldhammer. Vol. 5 of *A History of Private Life.* Edited by Philippe Aries and Georges Duby. Cambridge, Mass.: Belknap Press, 1991.

Raymond, Janice G. *A Passion for Friends.* Boston: Beacon Press, 1986.

Rhodes, Richard. *A Hole in the World.* New York: Simon and Schuster, 1990.

Rhodes, Richard. *Making Love: An Erotic Odyssey.* New York: Simon and Schuster, 1992.

Richardson, Robert D. *Emerson: The Mind on Fire.* Berkeley: University of California Press, 1995.

Ridley, Matt. *The Red Queen.* New York: Macmillan, 1993.

Rieff, Philip. *Freud: The Mind of the Moralist.* New York: Viking Press, 1959.

Rieff, Philip. *The Triumph of the Therapeutic.* New York: Harper and Row, 1966.

Rilke, Rainer Maria. *Letters to a Young Poet.* Translated by Stephen Mitchell. New York: Random House, 1986.

Roazen, Paul. *Meeting Freud's Family.* Amherst: University of Massachusetts Press, 1993.

Roberts, Sam. *Who We Are: A Portrait of America Based on the Latest U.S. Census.* New York: Times Books, 1993.

Roszak, Theodore. *The Cult of Information.* Berkeley: University of California Press, 1994.

Rothfeder, Jeffrey. *Privacy for Sale.* New York: Simon and Schuster, 1992.

Rule, James, Douglas McAdam, Linda Stearns, and David Uglow. *The Politics of Privacy: Planning for Personal Data Systems as Powerful Technologies.* New York: Elsevier, 1980.

Russell, Francis. *The Shadow of Blooming Grove: Warren G. Harding in His Times.* New York: McGraw-Hill, 1968.

Schneider, Carl D. *Shame, Exposure and Privacy.* New York: W.W. Norton, 1977.

Schwartz, Barry. *George Washington: The Making of an American Symbol.* New York: Free Press, 1987.

Seipp, David J. *The Right to Privacy in American History.* Cambridge, Mass.: Harvard University Program on Information Resources Policy, 1981.

Shaplen, Robert. *Free Love and Heavenly Sinners.* New York: Alfred A. Knopf, 1954.

Staples, Brent. *Parallel Time.* New York: Pantheon Books, 1994.

Star, Jonathan, and Shahram Shiva, trans. *A Garden beyond Paradise: The Mystical Poetry of Rumi.* New York: Bantam Books, 1992.

Stevens, John D. *Sensationalism and the New York Press.* New York: Columbia University Press, 1991.

Stevenson, Robert Louis. *The Strange Case of Dr. Jekyll and Mr. Hyde.* Boston: J.H. and A.L. Brigham, n.d.

Stevenson, Robert Louis. *Travels with a Donkey in the Cevennes.* New York: T. Nelson and Sons, n.d.

Stoller, Robert J. *Sexual Excitement.* New York: Touchstone, 1980.

Storr, Anthony. *Solitude: A Return to the Self.* New York: Ballantine Books, 1989.

Stowe, Harriet Beecher. *Uncle Tom's Cabin.* Introduction by Langston Hughes. New York: Dodd, Mead, 1952.

Thomas, Benjamin P. *Abraham Lincoln: A Biography.* New York: Alfred A. Knopf, 1952.

Thoreau, Henry David. *Walden.* New York: Signet Classic, 1960.

Tocqueville, Alexis de. *Democracy in America.* Vol. 1. New York: Vintage Books, 1945.

Tolstoy, Leo. *War and Peace.* New York: Signet Classic, 1968.

Underhill, Lois Beachy. *The Woman Who Ran for President: The Many Lives of Victoria Woodhull.* Bridgehampton, N.Y.: Bridge Works, 1995.

Updike, John. *Self-consciousness.* New York: Alfred A. Knopf, 1989.

Verghese, Abraham. *My Own Country.* New York: Simon and Schuster, 1994.

Von Mehren, Joan. *Minerva and the Muse: A Life of Margaret Fuller.* Amherst: University of Massachusetts Press, 1994.

Waller, Altina L. *Reverend Beecher and Mrs. Tilton: Sex and Class in Victorian America.* Amherst: University of Massachusetts Press, 1982.

Westin, Alan F. *Privacy and Freedom.* New York: Atheneum, 1968.

Wharton, Edith. *The Age of Innocence.* New York: Signet Classic, 1962.

Whitney, Henry Clay. *Life on the Circuit with Lincoln.* Caldwell, Idaho: Caxton Printers, 1940.

Whittemore, Reed. *Pure Lives: The Early Biographers.* Baltimore: Johns Hopkins University Press, 1988.

Whittemore, Reed. *Whole Lives: Shapers of Modern Biography.* Baltimore: Johns Hopkins University Press, 1989.

Williamson, Francis P. *Beecher and His Accusers.* Philadelphia: Flint, 1874.

Woodward, Bob. *The Agenda: Inside the Clinton White House.* New York: Simon and Schuster, 1994.

Wurmser, Leon. *The Mask of Shame.* Baltimore: Johns Hopkins University Press, 1981.

Yerushalmi, Yosef Hayim. *Freud's Moses: Judaism Terminable and Interminable.* New Haven, Conn.: Yale University Press, 1991.

Zeldin, Theodore. *An Intimate History of Humanity.* New York: HarperCollins, 1994.

Zinsser, William, ed. *Inventing the Truth: The Art and Craft of Memoir.* Boston: Houghton Mifflin, 1987.

Articles and Chapters

Allen, Anita L., and Erin Mack. "How Privacy Got Its Gender." *Northern Illinois University Law Review* 10 (1990): 441–78.

Arendt, Hannah. "The Public and the Private Realm." In *The Human Condition,* pp. 22–78. Chicago: University of Chicago Press, 1958.

Bloom, Harold. "Freud: A Shakespearean Reading." In *The Western Canon,* pp. 345–66. New York: Riverhead Books, 1994.

Bloustein, Edward J. "Privacy as an Aspect of Human Dignity: An Answer to Dean Prosser." *New York University Law Review* 39 (Dec. 1964): 962–1007.

Breuer, Josef. "Fraulein Anna O." In Josef Breuer and Sigmund Freud, *Studies on Hysteria,* pp. 21–37. Vol. 2 of *The Standard Edition of the Complete Psychological Works of Sigmund Freud.* Translated and edited by James Strachey with Anna Freud. London: Hogarth Press/Institute of Psycho-analysis, 1978.

Cronin, Anne. "This Is Your Life, Generally Speaking: A Statistical Portrait of the 'Typical' American." *New York Times* (July 26, 1992): 5.

Davison, Peter. "To Edit a Life." *The Atlantic* 270/4 (Oct. 1992): 92–100.

Eigner, Edwin M. "The War in the Members." In *Robert Louis Stevenson and Romantic Tradition,* pp. 143–64. Princeton, N.J.: Princeton University Press, 1966.

Ellenberger, H.F. "The Story of 'Anna O': A Critical Review with New Data." *Journal of the History of the Behavioral Sciences* 8/3 (July 1972): 267–79.

Ellis, Havelock. "The Evolution of Modesty." In *Studies in the Psychology of Sex,* pp. 1–48. Philadelphia: F.V. David, 1901. Microfilm.

Emerson, Ralph Waldo. "Culture." In *Conduct of Life,* pp. 131–66. Vol. 6 of *The Complete Works of Ralph Waldo Emerson.* Cambridge, Mass.: Riverside Press, 1904.

Emerson, Ralph Waldo. "Friendship." In *Essays, First Series,* pp. 189–218. Vol. 7 of *The Complete Works of Ralph Waldo Emerson.* Cambridge, Mass.: Riverside Press, 1903.

Emerson, Ralph Waldo. "Love." In *Essays, First Series,* pp. 167–88. Vol. 7 of *The Complete Works of Ralph Waldo Emerson.* Cambridge, Mass.: Riverside Press, 1903.

Emerson, Ralph Waldo. "Nature." In *Nature Addresses and Lectures,* pp. 3–77. Vol. 1 *The Complete Works of Ralph Waldo Emerson.* Cambridge, Mass.: Riverside Press, 1903.

Emerson, Ralph Waldo. "Society and Solitude." In *Society and Solitude,* pp. 1–16. Vol. 7 of *The Complete Works of Ralph Waldo Emerson.* Cambridge, Mass.: Riverside Press, 1904.

Freeman, Lucy. "The Immortal Anna O." *New York Times* (Nov. 11, 1979): sec. 6, p. 30.

Freud, Sigmund. "Beyond the Pleasure Principle." In *The Standard Edition of the Complete Psychological Works of Sigmund Freud.* Vol. 18, pp. 3–64. Translated and edited by James Strachey with Anna Freud. London: Hogarth Press/Institute of Psycho-analysis, 1978.

Freud, Sigmund. "A Case of Hysteria." In *The Standard Edition of the Complete Psychological Works of Sigmund Freud.* Vol. 7, pp. 3–112. Translated and edited by James Strachey with Anna Freud. London: Hogarth Press/Institute of Psycho-analysis, 1978.

Freud, Sigmund. "Civilization and Its Discontents." In *The Standard Edition of the Complete Psychological Works of Sigmund Freud.* Vol. 21, pp. 59–145. Translated and edited by James Strachey with Anna Freud. London: Hogarth Press/Institute of Psycho-analysis, 1978.

Freud, Sigmund. "Fragment of an Anlaysis of a Case of Hysteria." In *The Standard Edition of the Complete Psychological Works of Sigmund Freud.* Vol. 7, pp. 7–122. Translated and edited by James Strachey with Anna Freud. London: Hogarth Press/Institute of Psycho-analysis, 1978.

Freud, Sigmund. "The Future of an Illusion." In *The Standard Edition of the Complete Psychological Works of Sigmund Freud.* Vol. 21, pp. 3–56. Translated and edited by James Strachey with Anna Freud. London: Hogarth Press/Institute of Psycho-analysis, 1978.

Freud, Sigmund. "Psychopathic Characters on the Stage." In *The Standard Edition of the Complete Psychological Works of Sigmund Freud.* Vol. 7, pp. 305–6. Translated and edited by James Strachey with Anna Freud. London: Hogarth Press/Institute of Psycho-analysis, 1978.

Freud, Sigmund. "'Wild' Psycho-analysis." In *The Standard Edition of the Complete Psychological Works of Sigmund Freud.* Vol. 11, pp. 219–27. Translated and edited by James Strachey with Anna Freud. London: Hogarth Press/Institute of Psycho-analysis, 1978.

Freud, Sigmund. "Writers and Daydreaming." In *The Standard Edition of the Complete Psychological Works of Sigmund Freud.* Vol. 9, pp. 145–53. Translated and edited by James Strachey with Anna Freud. London: Hogarth Press/Institute of Psycho-analysis, 1978.

Goffman, Erving. "On the Characteristics of Total Institutions." In *Asylums,* pp. 1–124. New York: Anchor Books, 1961.

James, Henry. "The Abasement of the Northmores." In *The Complete Tales of Henry James.* Vol. 11, pp. 111–32. London: Rupert Hart-Davis, 1964.

James, Henry. "The Aspern Papers." In *The Aspern Papers and The Turn of the Screw,* pp. 43–142. London: Penguin Books, 1984.

James, Henry. "The Birthplace." In *The Complete Tales of Henry James.* Vol. 11, pp. 403–65. London: Rupert Hart-Davis, 1964.

James, Henry. "The Private Life." In *The Complete Tales of Henry James.* Vol. 8, pp. 189–228. London: Rupert Hart-Davis, 1963.

James, Henry. "The Real Right Thing." In *The Complete Tales of Henry James.* Vol. 10, pp. 471–86. London: Rupert Hart-Davis, 1964.

May, Antoinette. "Victoria Woodhull." In *Different Drummers: They Did What They Wanted,* pp. 7–33. Millbrae, Calif.: Les Femmes, 1976.

Planned Parenthood of Southeastern Pennsylvania et al. v. Casey, Governor of Pennsylvania, et al. 505 U.S. 833, 112 S.Ct. 2791 (1992): pp. 833–901.

Plutarke of Chaeronea. "Romulus." In *The Lives of the Noble Grecians and Romans.* Vol. 1, pp. 31–72. Translated from Greek into French by James Amyot; and from French into English by Thomas North. London: Nonesuch Press, 1929.

Ward, Geoffrey C. "Outing Mrs. Roosevelt." *New York Review of Books* (Sept. 24, 1992): 49–56.

Warren, Samuel D., and Brandeis, Louis D. "The Right to Privacy." *Harvard Law Review* 4/5 (Dec. 1890): 193–219.

Winnicott, D.W. "The Capacity to Be Alone." In *The Maturational Processes and the Facilitating Environment: Studies in Theory of Emotional Development,* pp. 29–36. The International Psycho-Analytical Library. Edited by John D. Sutherland. London: Hogarth Press and Institute of Psycho-Analysis, 1976.

Woodward, Richard B. "The Disturbing Photography of Sally Mann." *New York Times Magazine* (Sept. 27, 1992): 28–36.

Index